LILLIE LANGTRY

A Biography

Noel B. Gerson

SAPERE
BOOKS

LILLIE LANGTRY

Published by Sapere Books.

20 Windermere Drive, Leeds, England, LS17 7UZ,
United Kingdom

saperebooks.com

ISBN: 978-1-80055-179-4.

For Marion G. Cook

Table of Contents

I

"LILLIE LANGTRY," SAID JOHN EVERETT MILLAIS, the distinguished painter and her so-called discoverer, "happens to be, quite simply, the most beautiful woman on earth."

"Lillie's beauty has no meaning," Oscar Wilde declared. "Her charm, her wit and her mind — what a mind! — are far more formidable weapons."

"To look at Lillie," said the American-born James Abbott McNeill Whistler, "is to imagine one is dreaming. She is so extraordinary that not even I can do her justice in a painting."

"I resent Mrs. Langtry," George Bernard Shaw told a group of his friends. "She has no right to be intelligent, daring and independent as well as lovely. It is a frightening combination of attributes."

"I refuse to discuss my daughter with the press, or with anyone else," said the Reverend William Corbet Le Breton, Dean of the Isle of Jersey and Rector of St. Saviour's Church there.

His Royal Highness, Albert Edward, Prince of Wales, Duke of Cornwall, Earl of Chester, Earl of Albany, Knight of the Garter, was even more succinct. Several brash members of the press accosted the future Edward VII regarding his supposed close friendship with Mrs. Langtry, and he replied, "I neither affirm nor deny that I am acquainted with the lady."

"Lillie," said Diamond Jim Brady, "is the greatest there ever was."

"What I find astonishing about Mrs. Langtry," Mark Twain observed, "is that she has a genuine talent on the stage."

"It gives me a feeling of great pride," said William Ewart Gladstone, Prime Minister of Great Britain, "that Lillie Langtry acknowledges me as her friend."

"That woman is a real marvel," said Theodore Roosevelt, President of the United States. "And she's so pretty she takes away a man's breath."

"Sure, we named our town after her," declared the Honorable Roy Bean of Texas, the self-styled hanging judge. "I dare any man alive to tell me a better name for a town than Langtry."

Artist Frank Miles, whose sketches of the fabulous Jersey Lily were partly responsible for her rapid rise to fame, was reluctant to talk about her. "Oscar Wilde usually speaks for Lillie," he said, "and her beauty speaks for itself."

Frederick Gebhard, the millionaire who was the most celebrated of her American lovers, was never bashful. "I don't give a damn if Lil did sleep with the Prince of Wales," he declared. "I love her, and I issue a public appeal to her. Marry me, Lillie!"

Benjamin Disraeli, Earl of Beaconsfield, former British Prime Minister and part-time novelist, said, "I was somewhat surprised to find, at our first meeting, that Mrs. Langtry's thinking is as cogent — and as cogently expressed — as that of any man."

The Jersey Lily's colleague, Sarah Bernhardt, herself hailed as the greatest actress of her time, was lavish in praise of her friend. "Lillie," she said, "is a superb actress."

Ellen Terry, one of the first ladies of the English theatre, was equally generous. "Lillie," she said, "breathes life into a theatre."

But Lillian Russell, whose champions called her the most beautiful woman of the age, took a dimmer view of her rival.

"I am not competent to judge Mrs. Langtry," she declared, "because I have never enjoyed the privilege of seeing her perform. It would be inappropriate for me to comment on her appearance."

Sir Henry Irving, the first member of the acting profession to be knighted by the British Crown, maintained his own standards. "I am no judge of feminine pulchritude, but Mrs. Langtry displays such rare intelligence on stage that I regret our separate schedules have made it impossible for us to play together."

Joaquin Miller, the American poet who wore cowboy attire, was lyrical in his praise. "Mrs. Langtry is herself a poem," he said. "She is complete and perfect, and in no way could be changed for the better."

Walt Whitman, his colleague, echoed his sentiments. "There shines in Lillie Langtry a purity of spirit. Therein lies the essence of human poetry."

Edward Langtry, the lady's first husband, and the man whose name she made famous, for many years refused to speak her name either in public or in private.

II

EMILIE CHARLOTTE LE BRETON LIVED HER ENTIRE life as a contradiction of her era, and perhaps the greatest of incongruities was her background. She was the unlikeliest of trailblazers.

Dean Le Breton, her father, was a pious and conservative Anglican clergyman, and his wife, Emilie Martin Le Breton, was equally modest and self-effacing. Their six sons grew up to be quiet men who took pride in their accomplishments and avoided the limelight. Their only daughter, thanks to a combination of genes, circumstances and the stifling aura of the Victorian age into which she was born, was an iconoclast who willfully smashed traditions and became the most famous — some would say infamous — woman of her time.

The Isle of Jersey, where the girl was born and reared, was partly responsible, and it is impossible to understand Lillie Langtry without knowing something about the homeland that helped shape her astonishingly rugged individualism. Compatriots who have disapproved of her, down to the present day, still explain the phenomenon known as Lillie Langtry by saying, "Well, she did come from Jersey, after all."

The tiny island, like its people, can claim to be unique. Only eleven miles long and five miles wide, Jersey, the largest of the Channel Islands, has an area of less than fifty-five square miles. Its influence, like that of its renowned daughter, is out of proportion to its size.

Although located only a few miles off the coast of Saint-Malo, France, Jersey enjoys a subtropical climate, in part because the Gulf Stream sweeps past her many inlets and bays, in part because the cliffs on her northern shores form a barrier that cuts off Atlantic gales and the winds that sweep down from Scotland. Palm trees flourish in Jersey, as do many tropical flowers, and fruits are grown in profusion there. Nature made Lillie Langtry's home a geographical incongruity.

What nature initiated, the island's inventive natives developed. In Roman times, fishing was the island's only occupation, and it was impossible to coax crops from the soil. Then an unsung genius began to use seaweed as fertilizer; unlimited quantities were on hand, and applications of seaweed down to the present time have transformed the sand of Jersey into one of the richest soils on earth. Crops of tomatoes and potatoes prized by gourmets are alternated, both grown within the same year, and the famous Jersey cattle grow fat and sleek grazing in fields where the grass is extraordinary.

The people, about thirty thousand of them in Lillie Langtry's time, are even more remarkable than their tiny country. Long isolated, Jersey was a part of the realm of the rulers of Normandy, and its modern history began in the eleventh century, when Duke Rufus the Red established his summer home there. His son, William, expanded the dwelling, and the hollow construction blocks he used provided a marvelous form of insulation, keeping the place cool in summer and warm in winter.

William became known for more than his innovations in architecture, however, and when he conquered England in 1066, a surprisingly large number of Jerseymen — at least two hundred of them — were members of his personal regiment. And the results of the Battle of Hastings created an attitude that persists down to the present.

"We are not part of England," the Jerseyman says. "We are England's conquerors. If you want to be technical about it, we *own* England." This spirit of independence is no laughing matter.

Jersey, like the other Channel Islands, acknowledges the sovereignty of the British Crown, but recognizes the king or queen as monarch of the island, not of Great Britain. Similarly, Jersey is self-governing, her Deliberative States, or parliament, being an outgrowth of the old Norman feudal system. She graciously permits the Crown's ministers in London to administer her foreign affairs and to defend her from external foes. In all other matters she is completely self-governing.

Her people are bilingual, and every Jerseyman speaks a Norman patois that is similar to the French spoken on the mainland. The use of English has crept in over the centuries because the sons of the upper and middle classes have attended universities in England, and because the mild climate has made the island one of England's favorite summer resorts. The natives think of themselves as neither English nor French. They are Jerseymen, first and always.

It was on this proud, individualistic island that Emilie Charlotte Le Breton was born on October 13, 1853. The occasion was celebrated by the entire, socially prominent Le Breton clan, as well as by her immediate family: she had five older brothers, and yet another would be born within the next two years.

No one knew how the girl came to be called Lillie. Mrs. Le Breton, reminiscing after her daughter became famous, couldn't remember whether Lillie was a form of Emilie, or whether she had used a nickname because the baby's skin had been such a pure white. One thing was certain: the name was spelled Lillie, and the celebrated Mrs. Langtry reserved her greatest scorn for those who dared to spell it in any other way.

The girl's lily-white skin gave way to a healthy suntan early in childhood, and she remained tanned for many years. Family recollections, including her own, indicate that she was a tomboy from the time she first learned to walk. Her older brothers protected her, to an extent, but demanded that she hold her own in games and exercises. So she climbed cliffs and was an expert swimmer at four, and learned to ride a horse bareback before she was six.

Family discipline was almost nonexistent. Mrs. Le Breton, as the wife of the island's head of the Church of England, as well as the mother of seven, was a busy woman. Dean Le Breton was a harried man, and, in addition, his own nature was so gentle and vague that he rarely inflicted punishment on his children.

The family governess and housekeeper, one Madame Brisson, was largely responsible for Lillie's upbringing during her early years and taught her to read and write. But the antics of the Le Breton boys were too much for Madame, who retired, and thereafter the girl was educated by tutors who worked under the Dean's supervision. There were no schools for girls in Jersey at the time, and Lillie later claimed she received an education only because she had nothing better to occupy her while her brothers attended classes.

At all other times she and they were inseparable. Frank, William and Trevor were so much her senior that they didn't want to be handicapped by a small girl, but admitted her to their races and other sports. She was closer to her immediate seniors, Maurice and Clement, and eventually her younger brother, Reginald, became her best friend. It is small wonder that the glamorous Mrs. Langtry felt at home with males, but was usually shy and withdrawn in the presence of other women. In her formative years she was a stranger to other members of her own sex.

The boys had pets, and so did Lillie. There were dogs, cats, white mice, turtles and goldfish in the rectory, and each of the Le Breton children owned his or her own horse. The Dean earned a very small salary, but the Le Bretons were landowners of prominence, and one didn't need much money to live well in Jersey.

Lillie first achieved a dubious prominence of sorts when she sneaked out of the house one night with Maurice and Clement and helped them tar and feather a statue of Queen Victoria that stood in the center of Saint Helier, Jersey's capital. The deed was discovered the following day, and the culprits were identified immediately by the tar on their hands, faces and clothes. The boys were spanked, but Lillie escaped lightly, and was punished by being confined to her room for twenty-four hours.

Her later pranks, performed with Reggie, made her something of a nuisance. The pair set up a raised trip-wire that neatly knocked off the top hats of visitors who came to attend the Dean's annual tea for the island's Anglicans. Neighbors complained because she and Reggie romped in the graveyard of St. Saviour's Church at midnight, pretending to be ghosts.

One practical joke caused her to be remembered in Saint Helier for years. At the beginning of the Christmas season, when people were paying calls on all their relatives and friends, Lillie and Reggie went out one night and stole door knockers from every house in the neighborhood. No one saw the criminals at work, but the long finger of suspicion inevitably pointed toward the Le Breton children. For the first and only time in Lillie's life, the Dean intervened in person, and found the collection of door knockers in the cellar. He forced his children to return them, and, after affixing them to the appropriate doors, to tender their apologies to their victims. He also decided they would not participate in any of the holiday festivities that year.

"But he relented on Christmas Eve," Lillie wrote in later years. "Papa couldn't help spoiling me, and I always knew it."

By the time the girl was fifteen her physical maturation was astonishing. She stood five feet, eight inches tall, weighed one hundred and thirty pounds and was full-breasted. Her hair, sometimes described as Titian red, sometimes as chestnut, was worn in a bun at the nape of her neck; it had never been cut, but she no longer allowed it to fall freely. Her eyes were her most arresting feature. They were a flawless, deep blue that seemed to change color in candlelight, and Lillie discovered that when she stared hard at a boy, he became flustered.

She enjoyed the experience. Lillie, who had envied and wanted to emulate her brothers, apparently had a need to dominate the male. All she knew, at fifteen, was that boys — and young men — would do her bidding when she smiled at them.

Reggie, to be sure, was disgusted by the change in her personality. When they went riding every afternoon, as they had done since they were small, Lillie now wore a big-brimmed hat and a dress with long sleeves to protect her from the sun. She even smeared cream of some sort on the backs of her hands to shield them. And when he threatened not to go with her, Lillie told him, truthfully, that there would be no lack of escorts to take his place.

Her parents were introducing her into the limited social life of Jersey, and she attended the chaperoned dances and assemblies, went off with other young people on the chaperoned beach picnics, and sometimes took chaperoned walks with boys.

It was at this period that Lillie first made the acquaintance of other young ladies. A half-dozen prominent English nobles owned small country estates in Jersey, and the well-bred daughter of the Anglican Dean was regarded, naturally, as a suitable companion. Most of the girls whom Lillie saw over a two- to three-year period were slightly older, so they weren't jealous of her growing beauty. They could make up in worldliness what she lacked in sophistication, and most of them patronized her, although she didn't realize it until much later in life.

When Lillie was fifteen she also enjoyed her first romance, although it was short-lived. Lieutenant Charles Spencer Longley of the Royal Army, twenty-three years of age, was posted to the Jersey garrison, and, as a son of the Archbishop of Canterbury, he immediately paid his respects to Dean and Mrs. Le Breton. There he met the girl with the Titian hair, blue eyes and mature figure, and promptly fell in love with her.

Lillie was too young and inexperienced to realize what was happening to him until he proposed marriage to her, and then she had to confess her age to him. The lieutenant was stunned, and refused to believe she was only fifteen until he went to her parents and confirmed the fact. He was so shaken that he applied for a transfer.

This experience helped convince Mrs. Le Breton that her daughter needed the broadening, enlightening experience of a trip to London. The following year, at sixteen, Lillie accompanied her there, and the visit became an unexpected nightmare.

At first the girl was ecstatic. She had spent her entire life within the limited confines of the Isle of Jersey, and the world's largest city fascinated her. But she soon realized she couldn't cope with London. The people she met were polished, and spoke a language she scarcely understood. She was totally unprepared for their aristocratic gossip, their talk of Court and society, affairs and scandals. She had never seen an art gallery, never attended a concert or a professional theatrical performance.

The climax of the trip was a dinner party given in Lillie's honor by the daughters of Lord and Lady Suffield, part-time Jersey neighbors, at their London town house. "When I walked into the ballroom," Lillie wrote many years later, "I felt like a clumsy peasant. My one 'party gown,' which had been made for me in St. Helier, made me look like one of the serving maids. I had never waltzed, and could follow the leads of none of my dancing partners. The food was strange, and never having seen so many forks and spoons at one's supper place, I had no idea which to use. I disgraced myself so often I could scarcely wait until the evening came to its abysmal end."

Mrs. Le Breton knew the visit had been a failure, but when she and her daughter returned to Jersey, even she did not realize how traumatic the experience had been. But she soon learned. Lillie not only went riding with Reggie every day, but wore the tomboy clothes of earlier years. No longer caring whether she became sunburned, she no longer bothered to wear protective attire. She climbed rocks, she fished, she sailed.

Above all, she avoided titled visitors from England, and she refused to attend local dances or other social functions. Young men who called at the rectory were turned away. William, the eldest of her brothers, thought she was a boy when, on a return to the island for a visit, he first saw her riding bareback at a breakneck pace down a deserted beach.

Dean and Mrs. Le Breton tried in vain to persuade their daughter to behave like a lady, and the efforts of Lillie's tutors were equally fruitless. She studied hard, for the first time in her life, and she spent most of her evenings reading the plays of Shakespeare and Ben Jonson aloud to her father. "Between the ages of sixteen and twenty," she wrote in later years, "I learned the magic of words, the beauty and excitement of poetic imagery. I learned there was something in life other than horses, the sea and the long Jersey tides."

During the interminable four years of Lillie's emotional maturation, an idea began to form in her mind. All five of her elder brothers had gone off to various parts of the British Empire, and she could understand why they had been anxious to leave Jersey. She saw no real future for herself here, and was determined to follow them. But she had no desire to live in a remote corner of India, or to stultify in the English provinces, which were no more interesting than Jersey. Her one, brief experience in London had taught her that it was the hub of her universe.

She intended to conquer it in her own way, once she was prepared for the renewal of the battle. But she had no training of any sort for a profession, and, in fact, was unsuited for a middle-class life as a housewife. She had been reared as a lady, and couldn't sew, cook or even clean a house. She had been reared to become the wife of a gentleman.

Marriage, she knew, offered her the only escape route, and she intended to use it. There was no one in Jersey who interested her, and she wasn't aristocratic enough for the sons of the nobility who were part-time Jersey residents. So her future husband would be a stranger.

Until he appeared she refused to change her ways, and continued to ride, climb, swim and fish. The exercise changed her figure, which became even more supple, and she created a sensation when she wore one of her wasp-waisted dresses to communion at her father's church.

Then, soon after Lillie's twentieth birthday, a large yacht from England, the *Red Gauntlet*, put into her harbor of Saint Helier during a storm. In later years Lillie was quoted as saying, "One day there came into the harbor a most beautiful yacht. I met the owner and fell in love with the yacht. To become the mistress of the yacht, I married the owner, Edward Langtry."

Lillie's friends regarded the statement as a distortion of the truth, and it may be, as they claimed, that she was too sensitive to have made such a remark. But she did not deny its validity.

Edward Langtry, the owner of the *Red Gauntlet*, was about five years Lillie's senior, a dashing young man with dark hair and black eyes, who wore his handsomely tailored clothes with an air. He was a widower who had been married to a Jersey girl, and was a friend of Lillie's eldest brother, William.

It appeared that Langtry was very wealthy. His yacht was eighty feet long and exceptionally well appointed. In his pay were a captain and a crew of five. And, it developed, he was a sportsman who also owned several other yachts.

Hotel accommodations in Jersey were limited, so Dean Le Breton invited his son's friend to stay at the rectory, where so many bedchambers stood vacant. He accepted, and opportunity knocked at Lillie's door.

She heeded the sound, and overnight mended her ways. Now, as she accompanied the guest on walks, she wore her prettiest dresses, and always carried a parasol to shield her from the sun. She was so demure, in fact, that she even feigned seasickness when she went out for a sail on the *Red Gauntlet*. It was no wonder that her attitude disgusted Reggie.

An unexpected family celebration caused Edward Langtry to prolong his visit in Jersey. William Le Breton returned from India to be married in Jersey, and all of his brothers came home for the great event. Langtry gave a ball for the bridal couple at the Jersey Yacht Club, and spent a small fortune on the event. Lillie was enthralled.

Two days after William's wedding Edward Langtry approached Dean and Mrs. Le Breton. His father was a member of the landed gentry in Ulster, he said, and was prominent in Belfast shipping. He had settled a handsome sum on his son, who owned three yachts in addition to the *Red Gauntlet*, the *Gertrude*, the *Ildegonda* and the *Bluebird*. Edward had taken a degree at Oxford and had also studied law, although he had never taken the bar examinations. He was able to support a wife, he said, and asked for the privilege of proposing to Lillie.

The Le Bretons believed that their daughter was too young, and Mrs. Le Breton wanted the girl to enjoy the benefits of a season as a debutante in London. But Lillie made it clear to them that she was in love, and insisted on the right to be married. She did not reveal to her parents, either then or later, that Edward had already given her a large diamond ring as a betrothal gift, and that she had accepted it. Not until her parents gave their reluctant approval did the ring make its belated public appearance.

Dean Le Breton took charge of his daughter's financial affairs, and displayed unexpected sagacity. His future son-in-law, he discovered through Clement, who had just been admitted to the bar, enjoyed an income of only three thousand pounds per year, which he realized as rent on properties he owned near Belfast. He also owned a cottage there, as well as a fine house near Southampton. But his yachts had consumed virtually all of his capital, and the clergyman insisted that he sell most of them.

The Dean also demanded that a settlement be made on his daughter, and Robert Langtry was pleased to comply. Edward's father was a devout member of the Society of Friends, and although he would have preferred a marriage within the bounds of his own church, he was relieved that his son had chosen the daughter of an Anglican dean. So the sum of ten thousand pounds was put aside for Lillie, on the stipulation that she would receive the principal when her husband died. In the early 1870's that sum was worth approximately seventy-five thousand dollars.

It began to dawn on Lillie that her husband wasn't as wealthy as she had believed, but she wouldn't consider postponing the marriage. Edward still offered her escape, and she saw no other means in view.

The wedding was a small affair, held quietly on the morning of March 9, 1874. Dean Le Breton performed the ceremony in St. Saviour's Church, and Clement was the only one of his sons who attended. Reggie, who disapproved of Edward and was the only member of the family who recognized his sister's motives, had ridden off to the cliffs at dawn. Thanks to a series of unexpected tragedies in the years that followed, Lillie and her favorite brother never met again.

The wedding breakfast was held at the yacht club, and the bridal couple went off on the *Red Gauntlet*. They spent a month at sea, and then went to Belfast for a visit with the Langtry family.

Robert Langtry approved of the shy but straightforward young beauty his son had married, and offered Edward a place of responsibility in his shipping business. But the young man refused, and Lillie was relieved; London was still her goal, and she had no desire to exchange Jersey for Ulster.

Mrs. Langtry, a quiet, passive woman, seemed to appreciate her new daughter-in-law, but they apparently had little in common, and in the years that followed Lillie rarely mentioned her mother-in-law in the presence of others. Edward's young sister, Agnes, was awed by Lillie's beauty, and thereafter corresponded with her regularly, sometimes arriving unannounced for brief visits. In all, Lillie's conquest of the Langtry family was complete.

Edward kept his word to Dean Le Breton, and sold all of his boats except the *Gertrude*, a yawl of eighty tons. He and Lillie spent most of their time on board the vessel during the next eight or nine months, attending yachting regattas in Cowes and Le Havre, and twice putting into Jersey for brief visits with the Le Bretons. On both occasions Reggie left the house when he heard his sister had arrived, and did not reappear until she had gone.

Living as an inconspicuous member of the yachting set gave Lillie an opportunity to observe the wealthy, the renowned and the aristocratic. Many years later she was frank to admit, "I gained an appreciation of the power exerted by the owners of large yachts. One day, I decided, I would become one of them."

If she was truly in love with Edward she admitted it to no one, either then or later. But it was not until long after their marriage had foundered that she confessed he had failed to arouse her sexually. In all justice to Edward, it must be remembered that a wife, in the Victorian era, was not expected to enjoy marital intimacy; it was sufficient if she did her duty and made sure she satisfied her husband.

In the late autumn of 1874 the honeymoon finally came to an end, and the couple went to Southampton. There Lillie became mistress of Cliffe Lodge, a handsome mansion of seventeen rooms, richly furnished, and was expected to supervise the activities of a trained domestic staff consisting of a butler, a cook, a chambermaid and a coachman-gardener. The girl knew literally nothing about housekeeping, and soon found that her efforts merely caused confusion. She was inept and blundering when she tried to order meals, she knew nothing about household budgets, and she discovered that the operation was smooth only if she left everything to the butler.

For Edward's sake, however, and because convention demanded it of her, she went through the motions of behaving like the active mistress of Cliffe Lodge. Now that boating no longer kept them busy, she and Edward soon learned that they enjoyed fewer interests in common than they had assumed. "We had so little to say to one another," Lillie later wrote, "that we began to eat breakfast separately. Edward usually went off to join friends in Southampton at noon, so we rarely spent much time with each other until we dined together in the evening."

Marriage, the young bride was learning, was not the escape she had believed, and London was still a mirage somewhere in the distance. There was no lack of social life, of a sort, in Southampton, however, and the Langtrys were accepted in the town's best circles. But Lillie had very little patience with the ladies who called on each other every afternoon, played cards and filled in their days with idle gossip. Their talk was meaningless and provincial, they accomplished nothing and their interests were confined to their own small circle.

It was maddening, too, that these ladies thought her totally lacking in sophistication. To them Jersey was a provincial nowhere, while Southampton was a glittering metropolis. They neither knew nor cared about life in London. To make matters worse, Lillie's activities were circumscribed. Ladies in Southampton never went out alone for brisk walks, and no one in Edward's circle owned a horse other than the huge beasts used to draw coaches. Riding was an unknown sport.

Lillie corresponded regularly with her mother and occasionally with her father. She also wrote a number of letters to Reggie, but received no replies, which caused her even greater depression. Bored, out of sorts and listless, she began to brood; she lost her appetite, she couldn't sleep, and one morning she woke up with a raging fever.

When Edward discovered his wife was ill he jumped to the wrong conclusion, and announced to his friends that she was pregnant. To his intense chagrin he was forced to retract the assertion, however, and he became alarmed when the physician he had summoned diagnosed Lillie's illness as typhoid fever.

Her basic health was good, and she soon passed the crisis, but her convalescence was as boring as it was long. As the days stretched into weeks Lillie had time to think clearly, and eventually she evolved a new plan of which, she reasoned, Edward would be unable to disapprove. He invariably had rejected her suggestions that they visit London, but he would be in no position to refuse the idea if it came from a physician.

Whether she flirted with the doctor in order to achieve her ends is unknown. Perhaps it was enough that a very attractive young woman held a long, earnest consultation with her physician, and that he had no difficulty in adjusting to her point of view.

The doctor had a long talk with Edward, and said that Mrs. Langtry's mental and physical health required a long sojourn in

London, where the weather would be less severe and there would be enough activities to keep her occupied.

Edward had no choice, and gave in. He sold the house and its furnishings, disposed of his coach and dismissed the staff. Lillie was ready to assault the city that had defeated her at the age of sixteen, and she arrived there with her husband in March, 1875, on the first anniversary of her marriage. Not even she could have imagined what lay ahead for her.

III

LONDON, IN THE MID-1870'S, CONSIDERED HERSELF the hub of the civilized world, and the partisans of no other city could dispute her claim. The capital of the widowed Queen Victoria's still expanding empire, the rapidly growing metropolis of four million persons was a financial, industrial and commercial center without equal, and stood preeminent in the arts. She boasted more theatres and published more books than any other city on earth, and was crowded with artists, composers and sculptors. Her ladies were regarded as the most handsome, the best-dressed, her gentlemen the most powerful and influential.

Paris was still recovering from the disaster of the Franco-Prussian War and the Commune revolt that had followed in its wake; she was alert and alive, but could not regain her former predominant place unless and until the Third Republic became a stable force. The Berlin of Chancellor Otto von Bismarck was still a country town, and only in recent years had her cow pastures given way to solid, stately buildings. Vienna, the capital of Franz Josef's Austro-Hungarian Empire, had her music, her medical research and her gay spirit, but in spite of a patina of sophistication, her outlook was still provincial, almost bucolic. Saint Petersburg, home of the Tsars, remained isolated, a brooding and remote community that exerted little influence on her sister cities. Across the Atlantic stood London's principal challenger, the great funnel of the American melting pot, but New York, brash and brawling, pulsing with life but still crude, could not yet pretend she had become cosmopolitan.

So London shone alone, the most glittering star in the firmament of metropolitan areas, the Mecca of all who sought power, fame and success. At the apex, a step below the inaccessible Queen Victoria, stood her eldest son, the plump, bearded Albert Edward, and his sweet, even-tempered wife, Alexandra of Denmark, the Prince and Princess of Wales. Edward was the social arbiter, the patron of the arts, the titular head of the armed forces, the man who encouraged the continued growth and expansion of the greatest empire in the history of man. Alexandra founded hospitals, worked indefatigably for charitable causes and showed a compassionate understanding of the needs of the poor that was unusual in her time.

London was not perfect, of course, although her slums were no worse than those of any other major city and her working classes, thanks to the recent granting of universal-male suffrage, were more emancipated. Her weather was miserable, as the Romans had discovered two thousand years earlier, and her upper classes, in an inexplicable annual migration, deserted her during the few summer months each year when the sun made living there tolerable.

Her food, as the French — and even the Americans — complained, was execrable. Strangers found the meals in hotels and restaurants inedible, and those visitors fortunate enough to dine in private homes and gentlemen's clubs fared little better. "There is not one gourmet in all of Britain," wrote Victor Hugo, France's greatest living author and culinary expert *extraordinaire*. "Nowhere in the realm of Queen Victoria is it possible for one to sit down to a meal that includes a single palatable dish. But the Almighty has extended His infinite mercy to the English. He has created them without taste buds.

So they live, eat and die, never knowing their food is abominable."

One of the strangest phenomena of the period was the cult of the P.B.'s, or Professional Beauties. Actually, the name was a misnomer: the so-called P.B.'s were, almost without exception, amateurs in virtually every sense. They were high-born ladies, most of them married, who happened to be lovely, and who enhanced their beauty by dressing handsomely and indulging in exceptional grooming. Each inspired an enthusiastic following, much as Jacqueline Kennedy did in a later age.

Behind the furor lay a new art, that of photography. A P.B. was badgered by a professional photographer, who distributed her photos by the thousands as a form of advertisement for his talents, and these pictures were seen in the windows of countless shops, on small billboards all over London, and in the private homes of the poor.

The painters of London, who comprised a large and thriving colony, struck back at the photographers by doing portraits of the P.B.'s in oils and watercolors, and for a time further abetted the craze by making pen and ink sketches of the ladies, which were then reproduced in large numbers. A number of prominent artists had made their reputations by these means.

The fad was as harmless as it was widespread, and various young ladies of no talents achieved considerable renown because they were photogenic and because they had the patience and time to sit for portrait painters. They earned no money as models, they engaged in no work, but they did achieve a higher rating in the social standing of socially conscious London.

Certain unwritten rules were observed. Only ladies of impeccable aristocratic backgrounds were eligible. Under no circumstances were such low persons as actresses, courtesans or professional artists' models allowed to become P.B.'s. The ranks were limited to those who stood to gain nothing but a pleasant measure of fleeting fame.

The lovely ladies and their patient husbands tolerated the nonsense because social competition in London was so fervid. It has been estimated that there were no more than one thousand families of consequence, and there was intense competition for invitations to their town houses and country estates. There was also competition between hostesses; authors and artists had been admitted to the ranks of the socially acceptable, and were in great demand, as were others — barring members of the theatrical profession, self-made men and similar undesirables — who were interesting, attractive or scintillating.

It was into this atmosphere that Lillie and Edward Langtry moved. Not knowing a fashionable district from one that was socially unacceptable, they rented an unpretentious flat in Eaton Place, a borderline district of relatively new housing built on swampland that had been drained about a decade earlier. Edward, who longed for his comfortable house in Southampton, complained bitterly, but Lillie, who had won her campaign, was triumphant.

She was delighted when she discovered that her husband had visited the city only a few times, and was unfamiliar with it, too. For a month or more the Langtrys were tourist sightseers, and each day they set out for a different destination, usually on foot.

Their idyll was interrupted when Lillie received a telegram from her father, informing her that Reggie had been killed in an accident. She returned to Jersey immediately, but arrived too late for the funeral, which the Reverend Le Breton had conducted in Saint Helier, where he was now the Rector.

The circumstances of Reginald Le Breton's death were somewhat mystifying. He had been thrown from his horse while riding on the cliffs, and had fallen more than three hundred feet to the beach below, dying instantly. What made the accident strange was that the young man was an accomplished horseman who had spent countless hours riding on the cliffs.

There was considerable speculation that he had ended his life deliberately, but the rumor could not be verified. Later, after Lillie became renowned and notorious, the story was revived, and it was hinted that her brother had been in love with her. There is no evidence whatever, other than their strained relations from the time of Lillie's marriage, to suggest there might be any truth in the allegation. Reggie was a moody, introverted young man who had made few friends, and who spent much of his time alone after his sister's departure from Jersey. He had become increasingly isolated over a long period, and there were many people in Saint Helier who had regarded him as unstable, an eccentric.

He had opposed Lillie's marriage because he had believed Edward Langtry unworthy of her, a judgment that was justified by later events. But he had paid court to several young ladies in Saint Helier over the years, and there was nothing in his attitude that indicated he had been suffering from an abnormal emotional fixation.

Lillie remained at home for several weeks, and before she left for London her parents tried to cheer her by buying her a new dress. Always indifferent to clothes, Lillie was not interested in the simple black gown made for her by Madame Nicolle, Jersey's only dressmaker of standing. The truth of the matter was that she and Edward led such a circumscribed life that she had no opportunity to wear the dress.

After she returned to London, she and her husband resumed their sightseeing. One day, she wrote her parents, they had caught a glimpse of the Prince of Wales, who had been riding through the park with an entourage. "He is a very large man," she wrote, "but appeared to ride well for one of his bulk."

Life in London was so quiet for the couple, so uneventful that Lillie must have wondered whether their move had been a mistake. Edward yearned for the life of a yachtsman, but he had sold the *Gertrude*, and could not afford to buy a new boat. For better or worse, the couple appeared doomed to remain in the city and to dwell there in anonymity. Since Edward neither was engaged in business nor had any avocational interests, they met literally no one, and spent virtually all of their time together.

In later years Lillie hinted that her husband began to drink to excess during this period. At the time, however, she made no mention of his drinking in her correspondence with her parents. Her letters, which were brief and infrequent, do convey her own growing sense of lethargy. She had grown accustomed to London, and found it almost as dull as Southampton. She grew somewhat thinner, and her maturation removed the last traces of adolescence from her face and figure.

In only two communications to Dean and Mrs. Le Breton did she show signs of enthusiasm. She and Edward had seen Henry Irving in *Hamlet*, and she had been "thrilled beyond my powers to describe my feelings." Several weeks later they saw Ellen Terry in *The Merchant of Venice*, and again she found the performance enthralling.

The seasons changed, and Edward found the bright sunlight of summer in the city almost unbearable. He might have been sailing in the Channel, fishing in deep waters, but he was condemned to the uneventful existence of a metropolitan dweller. Summer gave way to the dampness of autumn, and then the raw cold of a London winter made the young couple miserable. Lillie, like so many who came after her, wrote to her parents that she found the flat so cold she had taken to spending most of her time in bed.

When spring approached the Langtrys had been living in London for a year, and during that time they had met no one, enjoyed no social life of any sort and had drifted into a stultifying existence. Edward had grown so desperate that he was actually considering the possibility of accepting his father's offer and entering the family's shipping business in Ulster.

But Lillie was not yet ready to give up. She apparently had no idea what she wanted or how she might achieve some amorphous goal, but, as she later wrote, "I was possessed by the conviction that my destiny lay in London. I can offer no logical explanation for my feeling, but know only that not even the uneventful tenor of my life could rid me of it."

With nothing better to occupy them, the Langtrys decided to attend the opening of the new Royal Aquarium in Westminster in late April, 1876, an event to which the public was invited. There, at last, fate intervened.

While wandering through the new building, Lillie and Edward came face to face with Lord and Lady Ranelagh, one of the wealthy couples who sometimes visited Jersey. Lady Ranelagh immediately recognized Lillie, and invited the Langtrys to attend their regular Sunday afternoon tea party that week. Lillie, who wouldn't have presumed to get in touch with the Ranelaghs, was delighted by the break in a routine of tedium.

The Ranelagh house was a mansion, the grounds extended downward toward the Thames on one side, and inland for acre after acre on the other. It was astonishing that anyone other than members of the royal family could own this much land in the heart of London. The guests were dressed in the latest fashions, and everyone, laughing and chatting, seemed to know everyone else.

Edward Langtry, red-faced and stiff, stood awkwardly, running a finger inside his stiff collar, occasionally removing his top hat and dabbing ineffectually at the sweat-soaked band. He knew no one, and his expression indicated that, if any of the other guests spoke to him, he might bolt.

"He felt very uncomfortable," Lillie later wrote in a masterly understatement, then added in strict candor, "As for me, I was badly frightened."

But the daughter of the Dean of Jersey looked like a remarkably poised young woman. She had attended too many of her parents' social functions to let anyone see she felt flustered and out of place. Wearing her unadorned black gown, with her hair fixed in a knot at the nape of her neck, she wandered through the grounds with her husband, then retired to a chair at one end of the gardens. She sat there for a long time, a simulated smile at the corners of her mouth, her hands folded demurely in her lap. She thought of herself as a detached observer, and subsequently confessed that she kept her mind busy by trying to record scenes and incidents she would report to her parents in a letter.

Lillie had literally no idea that she was creating a sensation, that guests were questioning the host and hostess about the identity of the very beautiful, seemingly poised young lady who displayed an air of aloof amusement.

Not until the following week did Lillie learn that she and Edward had been noticed. They returned to the Eaton Place flat from a walk, and learned from her maid that a letter had been delivered by a footman riding on the box of an elegant coach-and-four. The contents proved to be an invitation from one Lady Sebright to attend an at-home party at her house that Sunday evening. The hostess, Lillie knew from the newspapers, was a patroness of the arts, and her guest lists always included authors and artists.

A serious marital dispute erupted immediately. Edward, who had been bored by the Ranelagh party, had no desire to suffer a similar experience, and told Lillie to decline. She refused. "I knew," she later wrote, "that good things were happening to me."

Only when she threatened to go alone did Edward agree to escort her.

Although clothes had never meant anything to her, Lillie realized it might be wrong to wear her one appropriate dress again. She was still in mourning for Reggie, however, so she made the best of the situation by lowering the neckline, and she changed her hair style slightly by twisting her long hair into a single braid and arranging it in a figure-eight at the back of her neck. She cut short bangs in the front, hoping to shorten her deep forehead, and had to be satisfied with the result. She owned no rings, bracelets or necklaces of value.

The Sebright town house was a mansion on Lowndes Square, and Edward rented a coach for the occasion. Lord and Lady Sebright greeted them with vague cordiality, then left them strictly to their own devices. Again Lillie sought refuge in a corner chair, and Edward, standing behind her, swore in a low tone that nothing she said or did would persuade him to be humiliated in this neglectful way again.

Then, suddenly, an explosion occurred, and the many accounts of what happened that night are surprisingly similar. In brief, the greatest and most popular artists in London descended on Lillie in a body to admire her beauty and what was called "the artful simplicity" of her attire.

Leading the pack was John Everett Millais, the eminent portrait painter and member of the Royal Academy. A native of Jersey, he was delighted when he learned that Lillie was a fellow countryman, and before the startled girl quite realized what was happening, Millais persuaded her to sit for him.

Her second conquest was considered the most significant at the time, although the reputation of the artist declined somewhat over the ensuing decades. Lord Frederick Leighton was a noted sculptor, but was even more important because he held the post of president of the Royal Academy. He made an appointment for Lillie to visit his studio so he could do a bust of her in marble.

A third artist who crowded around Lillie was the diminutive James Abbott McNeill Whistler, an American-born iconoclast, the only man present wearing informal attire. Homely, sardonic and possessed of a razorlike wit, Whistler was the only member of the company who took the trouble to present himself to Edward Langtry before bowing to Lillie. It was not accidental that Whistler subsequently was the only artist in London of whom Edward approved.

The great Henry Irving was present, and demanded an introduction to the beauty from Jersey. So did William Yardley, a poet and sports enthusiast, who couldn't believe that Lillie not only thoroughly understood the game of cricket, but had played it with her brothers. Abraham Hayward, an industrialist who dabbled in the arts and would be knighted in a few years, brought up a chair and insisted on sitting beside the glamorous creature who had appeared out of nowhere.

But it was Frank Miles, an artist still in his twenties, as brash as Whistler, who stole a march on his colleagues. Miles lacked the distinction of the others, and at this early stage of his career earned his living by drawing pen-and-ink illustrations for newspapers and magazines. Taking a tailor's bill from a pocket, he drew two sketches of Lillie with a pencil, and presented her with one. The other, which was reproduced by the hundreds a few days later, was the first portrait of Lillie to appear in shops and to be made available to the general public for a penny. Although it wasn't a good sketch, as Miles later admitted, it was Lillie's initiation card, and made her a member in good standing of the exclusive circle of Professional Beauties.

Certainly she knew she had scored a triumph of sorts long before the evening ended. A score of men claimed the honor of escorting her to supper, and she finally chose Millais, in part because he was a fellow native of Jersey, in part because she shrewdly recognized the importance of his name as an artist. The unexpected success did not rob her of her ability to think clearly and swiftly.

She was astonished to find her wildest dreams coming true, of course, and reacted as would any young, inexperienced girl. Her face was flushed, her breathing was shallow and her eyes shone, enhancing her beauty and causing even the attractive women present to congratulate her.

No one has ever bothered to note the reaction of the bewildered Edward Langtry. Lillie wrote extensively about her own feelings, but neglected to mention what her husband felt. The various artists, authors and aristocrats seemed to forget his existence, too. No one has ever recorded whether he found another lady to escort to the table, and no one could have blamed him had he decided to stay in the drawing room and take another drink.

He would have been other than normal had he failed to appreciate and perhaps enjoy the furor his wife created. But he must have felt, too, that he had been left out in the cold and forgotten.

Regardless of what Edward may have felt, Lillie was the center of attention at the supper table. But the atmosphere changed when the ladies withdrew so the men could enjoy their port and cigars. She retired to the sitting rooms with the ladies, several of whom went out of their way to treat her curtly. But she was protected by Mrs. Millais, a charming, round-faced woman, who, it developed, had been well acquainted with Dean and Mrs. Le Breton. The hour passed without undue incident, and then the men reappeared to claim Lillie again.

There is no record of the conversation in the rented carriage when the Langtrys returned home that night, or of what may have been said after they reached the Eaton Place flat.

If Lillie thought she was dreaming when she awakened the following morning, the next few hours convinced her that her social triumph was real. A steady succession of coaches drew up before the building, and scores of invitations from dukes and duchesses, earls and countesses, as well as lesser members of the nobility, were delivered. Mr. and Mrs. Edward Langtry were asked to attend dinner and tea parties, luncheons and formal balls, informal at-homes and formal receptions, weekends in the country. Lillie later estimated that in one day they received enough invitations to keep them busy for at least six months.

Perhaps the most significant invitation was that sent by Lord Randolph Churchill and his wife, the American-born Jenny Jerome. Churchill, a son of the Duke of Marlborough, was politically as well as socially prominent, and was known not to bother with people who didn't matter. There were members of the Prince of Wales' inner circle who had never been asked to the Churchill house, and Lord Randolph, as much of an individualist as his son, Winston, would become in later generations, delighted in going his own way. The invitation from the Churchills alone was a guarantee of Lillie's success.

She insisted on going everywhere, and accepted literally every invitation.

Edward cannot be blamed for protesting. They were acquainted with virtually none of their hosts and hostesses, the pace was too swift and they could not afford the wardrobes that such extensive party-going would require.

But Lillie had her answers ready. Aware of the contribution made by her black dress, she would continue to wear it, and needed no new clothes. She had waited all her life for the events of the past twenty-four hours, and although she had no idea what might lie ahead, she intended to find out. She accepted all of the invitations.

Thereafter she took command, and Edward wilted. Lillie made the decisions, and Edward went along. Until this time he had been the ostensible master in his own house, but his wife's new sense of independence jarred him, and he retired permanently into the background. Although he escorted Lillie to scores of parties, flower shows and bazaars, shooting matches and entertainments of every conceivable sort, there were many ladies and gentlemen in London who, in later years, couldn't remember meeting him. He became part of the background, the weak nonentity who was the husband of a celebrity, but who did nothing memorable in his own right.

The Langtrys received so many invitations that Lillie frequently attended three or four parties in a single evening. Within a few weeks of her discovery her presence at a party was mandatory to ensure its success, and her failure to appear spelled ruin for a hostess. The attitude was absurd, of course, and reflected the artificial atmosphere that prevailed. But Lillie Langtry was a very real person living in that era, and cannot be blamed if, at this juncture, she accepted the acclaim.

Millais canceled other appointments so he could finish her portrait quickly, and it was he who presented her to the great William Gladstone, leader of the Liberal party, who had been out of office as Prime Minister for three years and currently was head of the Opposition. Gladstone was one, Lillie was mortified to learn, whose sitting had been postponed so Millais could accommodate her.

An exchange took place in the painter's studio that Gladstone himself delighted in telling. Learning that the lovely young woman with whom he was chatting had come from Jersey, he made conversation by asking, "When was it we conquered Jersey?"

Lillie's reply was swift, patriotic and truthful: "You didn't, sir. We conquered you, and England belongs to us!"

Few people dared to address Gladstone with such spirit, and he became Lillie's devoted friend. When scandal sent scores of aristocrats scurrying in the opposite direction, Prime Minister Gladstone, while in office from 1880 to 1885, and again from 1892 to 1894, went out of his way to be seen with her in public and to let it be known that he was her firm admirer. He became her adviser at a critical time in her life, and Lillie always claimed that her lifelong success was due to the help he gave her. Unlike many of his contemporaries, Gladstone saw the depth of character behind the lovely facade.

It was Millais who first made that facade immortal, and who gave Lillie the name by which she became known. She held her hands awkwardly when sitting, the painter discovered, so he gave her a small flower from their native Jersey, a crimson lily, to hold. Everything concerning her had become news, so it was inevitable, even before the portrait was completed, that she should become known as the Jersey Lily. In fact, before the Millais portrait was done, vendors went through the streets of London selling reproductions of a hastily done portrait by an unknown artist, showing her with a lily in her hand.

Lillie was also posing steadily for Frank Miles, who would have commanded an hour or two of her time each day, had it been possible for her to give him that much. He turned out literally hundreds of pen-and-ink sketches, some of which were reproduced in magazines and newspapers, and many of which found their way onto penny cards. "My sketches of Lillie during her first London season," he wrote twenty years later, "earned far more than I've ever made on the largest commissions for my most expensive paintings."

Miles also painted Lillie's portrait, and tried to race Millais for the honor of being the first to finish. But Lillie herself dissuaded him, telling him he was less accomplished, and therefore needed more time. She was always forthright, even when the truth hurt.

Other painters also clamored for sittings. She could not refuse the request of George Frederic Watts, a member of the Royal Academy, who may have been the most distinguished portrait painter of the century, and she was flattered when he added her to his gallery of noted persons. Edward John

Poynter, who, like Millais, was subsequently knighted, was another she could not refuse.

Still another painter who demanded that she sit for him was Edward Burne-Jones, Poynter's brother-in-law, who also received a knighthood late in the century. So many demands were being made on Lillie's time that she tried to evade Burne-Jones request, but he retaliated by serenading her outside her bedroom windows at dawn, informing the entire neighborhood that Mrs. Langtry was a heartless vixen and an enemy of art.

Lillie capitulated, and the Burne-Jones portrait of her is one of the most famous ever made.

In the first year after Lillie's discovery, eleven oil portraits of her were painted, a record that no one before or since has equaled. The real wonder is that she found — or made — the time to sit for so many artists.

Many others claimed her attention, too, and some went to great lengths to capture her interest. Perhaps none was as inventive as Lord Hartington, who interrupted his own formal reception at his ancestral home, Devonshire House, to climb, in his formal attire, into a lily pond on the grounds. He pulled out scores of water lilies and piled them in the Langtrys' rented carriage, much to the amusement of Lillie and the other guests.

Edward Langtry's reaction on this occasion was recorded by his wife. He was not entertained, and on the drive back to the flat he threw the lilies out of the coach window. To his dismay a crowd formed, and hundreds followed the coach, fighting for souvenirs of the Jersey Lily.

One of Lillie's most persistent admirers was Captain Allen Young, an explorer who had made three unsuccessful attempts to reach the North Pole. Regarded as one of the dashing bachelor blades of the Victorian era, Young was a close friend of the Prince of Wales. He was also a tireless publicity seeker, and even Edward Langtry, who objected to Young's proximity at every social function, eventually learned that the man was harmless, and pursued Lillie only because of the gossip he created.

Lillie knew she was a full-fledged celebrity when a letter from her mother informed her that her photographs were being exhibited in the windows of Saint Helier's shops.

Overnight fame had its disadvantages, Lillie soon discovered. She could no longer go out for a walk with Edward, much less go shopping alone, without being followed by a large crowd. On three occasions total strangers came up to her, kissed her and raced away again.

One day, wanting to vary her appearance somewhat, she wound a band of velvet around her head and stuck a feather in it. By the following morning, every milliner in London was advertising the sale of the "Jersey Lily toque." And innumerable signs in the shop windows of innumerable London hairdressers informed potential customers that their hair could be arranged, for a reasonable fee, in a "Jersey Lily knot."

What was astonishing about Lillie's sudden rise to fame was that everything she did was completely respectable, sanctioned by society. She was an honorable, married woman, and was escorted everywhere by her husband. She engaged in no affairs, and although she may have flirted mildly with various dinner companions and dancing partners, she did nothing that could have offended even Queen Victoria herself.

Beauty alone was responsible for Lillie Langtry's renown. Her photographs found their way into the Paris press, and the readers of American newspapers soon became as familiar as the British public with her features. Within a year of her discovery at Lady Sebright's party, she had become the most dazzling of all the Professional Beauties in London.

Only twenty-four years of age, she was not yet satiated, and felt no need to accomplish anything in her own right. Besides, she was enjoying herself too much. Most of her new friends in high society were shallow, it was true, but there were other people she found fascinating.

William Morris, the noted Oxford professor, who was one of the most prominent authors and critics of the age, always sought her out when he attended London dinner parties. He was responsible, Lillie said, for the vast knowledge of contemporary literature she acquired.

Dante Gabriel Rossetti, the poet and artist, painted her portrait, and she became friendly with him, as well as with his Bohemian poet sister, Christina. Although the Rossettis were middle-aged, they were young in spirit, and Lillie delighted in the literary arguments that raged through the night.

Although it is true that Christina Rossetti dedicated a short "Hymn to Beauty" to Lillie, there is no evidence to indicate that they became involved in a lesbian relationship. A number of rumors to that effect were heard after Lillie became notorious, but no facts are available to substantiate the whispers. A great lyric poet, Christina appreciated beauty, and saluted it accordingly. The rumors are reduced to absurdity when it is remembered that Lillie Langtry was interested only in men.

Another of her new friends was Algernon Charles Swinburne, the moody, brilliant poet of rebellion. Highly excitable, given to strong friendships and equally strong hatreds, Swinburne became attached to Lillie. His only romantic affair was a short-lived liaison with Ada Isaacs

Menken, the American actress, and he had no sexual interest in Lillie. Nor did she in him.

When Swinburne was in one of his manic moods, words poured out of him in torrents for hours at a time, and Lillie inspired him to become explosively verbose. Often, after attending an aristocratic party early in the evening, she would adjourn to the home of Rossetti or Whistler, and there, with Swinburne sitting at her feet, she would listen to him for the rest of the night.

"It was Swinburne," Lillie wrote many years later, "who taught me the meaning of real beauty, the beauty of words and the images they form."

Joaquin Miller of San Francisco had just arrived in London, and the unconventional American poet created a sensation of his own by dressing in garb suitable for spending a winter in the remote passes of the Rocky Mountains. He may have been the first to wander through the streets of the great city in buckskin trousers and a fringed leather shirt, with a leather headband keeping his long hair out of his eyes.

He became a minor celebrity of sorts, so it was inevitable that he and Lillie should meet, equally inevitable that he should become a Jersey Lily enthusiast. In fact, Miller, who lacked Old World sophistication, lost his balance and fell in love with her, a fact he revealed in a poem he sent to her. Lillie kept the poem, refusing to allow anyone else to see it, and many years later, when she visited Miller, his wife and their child in the American West, she returned it to him. It has never seen the light of print.

Walter Pater, the literary and art critic whose judgments were respected and feared by all of his contemporaries, met Lillie on a number of occasions and often conversed with her, although there is no evidence to indicate that they formed a close friendship. But the Jersey Lily did become well acquainted with Ellen Terry, who was generally regarded as the greatest actress of her day, and it was she who was credited with being the first to see there was more to Lillie than her beauty.

"That girl," she supposedly said, "is no one's fool. She has a rare intelligence, and some day she will surprise a great many people."

Two of Queen Victoria's children, Prince Leopold and Princess Louise, were friendly with many of the prominent authors and artists of the day, and Lillie met them at the flat of Frank Miles. She fascinated Leopold, who broke royal precedent by calling on her at the Langtry flat in Eaton Place.

On one occasion the Prince expressed such admiration of a pen-and-ink sketch of her just done by Miles that the artist presented it to him, and Leopold immediately took it to an art shop to be encased in a silver frame. These known facts gave rise to a story that may be apocryphal. Soon thereafter Leopold was confined to his bed by a head cold and cough, and his mother paid a visit to his sickroom.

Queen Victoria allegedly stopped short when she saw the sketch hanging on the wall, and demanded to know the identity of the woman.

The Prince told her.

Lillie's fame had penetrated the walls of the palace, and Victoria supposedly stared at the sketch for a long time. Then, according to the story, she dragged a chair across the room, climbed on it and removed the picture. At that time she had no reason to disapprove of the glamorous Mrs. Langtry, but may have thought it unsuitable for a sketch of a Professional Beauty to be hanging in the bedchamber of a member of the royal family.

One friendship which Lillie formed during the first year of her social triumph stood out above all others, and became a truly close companionship. Frank Miles' neighbor was a flamboyant young Oxford graduate who was two years younger than Lillie, a heavyset iconoclast who was exerting tremendous efforts of his own to attract attention as an author and personality. Oscar Wilde wore suits of exaggerated cut and color, and thought nothing of appearing in the streets of London in a pith helmet if the act created talk.

Whether he would have sought out Lillie in the first place had she not attained overnight fame is questionable. Always conscious of publicity values, he maneuvered so that her limelight reflected on him, too. What may have started as an attempt to advance himself soon developed into a lasting friendship, however. Wilde remained loyal to Lillie when her notoriety caused aristocratic London to drop her, and many years later, when his homosexual activities sent him first to prison, then into disgraced exile, Lillie was one of the few who refused to desert him, and not only publicly defended him, but helped him with loans she knew he would never be able to repay.

Wilde conceived an idea for publicity purposes, and it caused precisely the furor he had anticipated. He wandered through London carrying a single, large lily in his hand, and the meaning of the gesture was obvious to thousands who saw him. Cartoons showing him with the lily appeared in several newspapers, so he began to make the lily a regular part of his attire, always wearing one on his lapel. Although associated in the public mind with the Jersey Lily, the flower also became an integral part of his own appearance, and he continued to display one every day, up to the time of his trial and imprisonment.

Believing he could obtain still more publicity, Wilde began to write poems to Lillie. Unlike some of his colleagues, who preferred that their efforts remain private, he eagerly sought publication, and one of his works, "The New Helen," soon was printed in a newspaper, *The World*, which was edited by Edmund Yates:

> Lily of love, pure and inviolate!
> Tower of ivory! Red rose of fire!
> Thou hast come down our darkness to illume.
> For we, close caught in the wide nets of Fate,
> Wearied with waiting for the World's Desire,
> Aimlessly wandered in the House of Gloom,
> Aimlessly sought some slumberous anodyne
> For wasted lives, for lingering wretchedness,
> Till we beheld the re-arisen shrine,
> And the white glory of thy loveliness.

Wilde had the poem reprinted, along with several others, and presented Lillie with a copy. On the flyleaf he wrote, "To Helen, formerly of Troy, now of London."

Joaquin Miller was badgered so much by his friends that he wrote another poem for Lillie, and, after presenting her with a copy, made this one public. It read:

> If all God's world a garden were,
> And women were but flowers,
> If men were bees that busied there
> Through endless summer hours,
> O! I would hum God's garden through
> For honey till I came to you.

Life was not all poetry and adulation, however. On one occasion Lillie, who was almost totally ignorant of world affairs, made an error that created international laughter. In her favor, however, is the fact that she freely admitted the blunder.

A distinguished American, the bearded General Ulysses Simpson Grant, and his plump, inconspicuous wife were guests of honor at a dinner party to which Lillie was invited. Grant was accorded the privilege of escorting the Jersey Lily to the dinner table, and as they walked into the dining room, she froze all who heard her by asking, "What have you done since your Civil War, General?"

A number of witnesses said there was a gleam of humor in Grant's eyes as he replied, "Well, I've served two terms as President of the United States, Mrs. Langtry."

Not until Lillie had completed her first tour of the United States did the American people allow her to forget her mistake, and the newspapers in city after city invariably referred to it, relenting only when the editors and reporters had succumbed to her charms.

The successes of Lillie's social life were balanced by the steady deterioration of her marriage. Edward Langtry, who had no claim to fame other than his wife, grew increasingly exhausted by the endless, unchanging social whirl. Everywhere Lillie was the center of attention, and everywhere he remained in the background. Occasionally a compassionate host or hostess addressed a few remarks to him, and sometimes a well-meaning fellow guest asked how it felt to be married to the greatest beauty of the age.

It is apparent, even at the distance of a century, that the sex life of the Langtrys had dwindled to the vanishing point. Any Professional Beauty needed her rest, and Lillie maintained a schedule even more strenuous than that of the other attractive women who were in great demand. So she and Edward slept in separate bedrooms.

No one knows when this physical separation took place. But, within a year of Lillie's discovery, it was common knowledge that she had moved into a bedchamber of her own. No data is available to indicate whether one or the other was the instigator, or whether the change was made by common consent.

Within a year, too, Edward no longer acted as his wife's faithful watchdog. It would have been considered improper for her to have appeared without him at dinners, dances and other formal functions, so he always accompanied her on her nightly rounds, sometimes falling asleep in a chair when a Swinburne or a Wilde talked and postured for her benefit. In the daylight hours, however, Edward vanished, and Lillie went alone for her portrait sittings, to teas and luncheons and other daytime events.

One of the fixed events of literary and artistic London was the weekly Sunday breakfast given by James Whistler. The painter himself cooked such exotic, typically American dishes as flapjacks and sourdough biscuits, and the food as well as the company guaranteed that his flat would be crowded. Lillie not only became a regular at these functions, but was soon recognized as the queen of the group. Everyone who attended paid court to her, read poems dedicated to her and showed the progress he had made in his portrait of her.

Lillie relished her Sundays at Whistler's, but Edward Langtry flatly refused to accompany her. The unceasing, undiluted praise heaped on his wife had become sickening, and he preferred to sleep late, then turn to the solace of his whiskey bottle. It was an open secret now that Edward Langtry was drinking too much, and a number of Lillie's swains tried to sympathize with her.

But she remained loyal to her husband. She refused to listen to criticism of him, she said nothing that might be construed as antipathetic toward him, and she would not admit — to anyone — that he drank to excess. Any man who reasoned that the breakdown of her marriage made her more vulnerable to a new romance received no encouragement from the Jersey Lily herself.

At the end of Lillie's first year as a Professional Beauty, a marked change took place in her approach. Until now she had worn her black dress, made by Madame Nicolle of Saint Helier, to every social event she had attended. It had become her talisman, her trademark, and no one had ever seen her wear anything else.

Then, one night, Mary Cornwallis-West borrowed the dress to wear to a concert at Covent Garden being given by Adelina Patti. Lillie was indisposed, and Mrs. Cornwallis-West, the mother of three and reputedly a close friend of the Prince of Wales, hoped the novelty of appearing in the dress of a rival Professional Beauty would restore her to the limelight.

The dress was worn and tired, and perhaps Mrs. Cornwallis-West failed to treat it with the respect an antique deserved. She returned a dress that had literally come apart at the seams.

Lillie faced a social crisis of the first magnitude. She and Edward had been invited to a grand ball, being given within forty-eight hours, by Lord and Lady Dudley in honor of King Leopold of the Belgians, and it was also rumored that the Prince of Wales, whom she had never met, would attend.

So she went to a Mrs. Stratton, one of London's leading dressmakers, and promptly learned a valuable lesson. Mrs. Stratton was so pleased she had been given the opportunity to dress the Jersey Lily that, knowing her business would boom, she charged only a pittance for a magnificent Grecian-draped gown of white velvet. Edward was so delighted by the price that he told Lillie to buy several more gowns.

The appearance of the Jersey Lily in her first new gown was news, and she was so ravishing in the shrewdly chosen white that she created a sensation equal to that of her initial triumph. King Leopold, a short, swarthy man, was so entranced that he monopolized her for the better part of the evening, dancing with her repeatedly.

That week marked a definite but inexplicable change in Edward Langtry's attitude. Money, which had been one of his principal concerns, no longer seemed to matter to him. First he gave Lillie a regular clothing allowance. Then he voluntarily suggested they move to a larger flat, and seemed pleased when she found a two-story apartment on Norfolk Street, in one of the most fashionable districts in London. The flat was expensive, but he didn't seem to mind, and urged her to hire a second maid.

Lillie suspected, but could not prove, that several of her wealthy admirers were paying Edward to arrange her schedule in ways that would enable them to be seen more frequently in her company, at the expense of their rivals. She confided in Frank Miles and Oscar Wilde, who exchanged notes on the subject, thereby recording the matter for posterity. But neither then nor at any later time was Lillie able to confirm her suspicions.

Certain straws in the wind made her believe she was right, however. She unfailingly returned jewelry and other expensive gifts from her admirers, and Edward unfailingly became indignant when he learned of these attempts to buy her affections. But he displayed a far different attitude toward Moreton Frewen, a wealthy and dashing young aristocrat from Leicestershire. He appeared to be on friendly terms with

Frewen, and made no protest when the man presented her with a spirited horse named Redskin.

Ordinarily Lillie would have been quick to return the animal. But Edward's attitude gave her pause, and her own desire to own a horse finally overcame her. It had been a long time since she had ridden regularly, and she had missed the sport.

If Frewen had hoped he would have Lillie to himself on her morning rides, he was mistaken. So many men appeared to escort her that the group soon became known as Langtry's Lancers, and one of the most-repeated jokes in town was that Lillie's bodyguard was larger than the Queen's Household regiment of Grenadier Guards.

Frewen complained bitterly, and then took Edward off on a three-day fishing trip.

The relationships were becoming complex, and Lillie's friends grew worried. She had been safe enough while her husband had acted as her watchdog, but his changed attitude weakened her position, and she might not be able to resist the advances of every suitor who pursued her. There were so many, she was still young and impressionable, and they could see dangers ahead.

Lillie laughed at their fears. She was interested in all men, she told them, but wanted no romance with any, one man.

Their concern persisted, and Oscar Wilde wrote to Miles, "The nobility of human nature is confounded and mocked by our universal weaknesses, so I have cause to believe the Lily is ripe for adventure."

IV

ALBERT EDWARD, PRINCE OF WALES, THE SECOND child and eldest son of Queen Victoria and Prince Consort Albert, celebrated his thirty-sixth birthday in 1877, the year Lillie Langtry turned twenty-four. He had been married for fourteen years to Princess Alexandra of Denmark, who enjoyed tremendous popularity with people of every class in Great Britain.

The Prince himself enjoyed considerable sympathy, and his future subjects agreed that his lot was not an easy one. His mother was zealous, stern and devoted to duty, and although she expected a great deal of him, she constantly displayed a reluctance to give him any authority of consequence. Her whims, many of them arbitrary, determined the patterns of his life.

In spite of the handicaps that circumscribed his activities, Prince Albert Edward worked hard in the discharge of his obligations. His journey to India in the autumn of 1875, when he had traveled more than ten thousand miles and visited many Indian states, had been of the greatest political significance. Over a period of seventeen busy weeks he had met, charmed and impressed scores of rajahs, and succeeded so well in solidifying Britain's position in the subcontinent that, thanks largely to his untiring efforts, Queen Victoria was crowned Empress of India the following year.

Prince Albert Edward was the first member of his family to show an understanding of the "Irish question" that had plagued Britain for centuries, and in several visits to Ireland he had not only won a strong personal following, but had, by his example, persuaded the government to adopt a more enlightened attitude toward the people of the long-impoverished and oppressed island.

When at home the Prince of Wales made the innumerable public appearances expected of royalty, taking the place of his mother at most events, since Queen Victoria had gone into semi-retirement after the death of the Prince Consort.

The line of succession was assured. Between 1864, when Prince Albert Victor, later the Duke of Clarence, was born, and 1869, when Princess Maud Charlotte Mary Victoria came into the world, Princess Alexandra gave birth to five children, two sons and three daughters. The second son of the Prince and Princess of Wales eventually became King George V, following the unexpected death of his elder brother.

The British people generously forgave the future Edward VII his weaknesses, which were those of the aristocracy of his day. He owned a large stable of racing horses, and they placed bets on his champions, often making money on their wagers. They read avidly about the magnificent royal yacht on which he cruised, but did not envy him. After all, the ownership of a yacht the size of a small nation's largest warships was the prerogative of the future monarch of the world's wealthiest and most powerful nation.

Full-bearded and standing more than six feet tall, Albert Edward would have been handsome had he not been portly. He disproved Victor Hugo's contention that no Englishman knew or appreciated good food and drink. The Prince of Wales was not only a gourmet of formidable qualifications, but regularly consumed awe-inspiring portions. Many of his good friends, it was noted, were people who employed expert French chefs. And it was no secret that when the Prince of Wales made one of his informal, incognito visits to Paris, he invariably dined in the best restaurants, where he was quick to praise the quality of a superbly prepared dish.

It was an open secret in all classes of British society that Prince Albert Edward had a discerning eye for feminine beauty. Certainly his attitude was no worse than that of other bluebloods, even though it was no better.

The double standard was perfected during the Victorian era, and no one thought less of a gentleman if he strayed from home and hearth, provided his behavior was discreet and kept within the rigid bounds of propriety. The aristocrats looked down their long noses at those who kept mistresses, were entertained by courtesans or had affairs with actresses. Everyone simply looked the other way and pretended to be deaf, dumb and blind if one of high station confined his extra-marital dalliances to his own social class.

It was taken for granted in these affairs that no one would be allowed to be hurt. It was assumed that a lady who took a lover had the tacit approval of her husband, and in all probability their arrangement permitted him to do as he pleased, too. A special set of rules also governed the conduct of the wives of gentlemen who strayed. These ladies were expected to smile, to remain good wives and mothers, and to behave as though nothing had disturbed the even tenor of their marriages.

There were few ladies in England who smiled more steadily than Princess Alexandra. She had not only done her duty by giving her husband — and the Empire — five children in as many years, but everyone knew, after all, that royal marriages were conveniences of state and not immortal romances.

The precise extent of Prince Albert Edward's dalliances never became known. The Prince of Wales was a man set apart, and although one might gossip with one's dearest friends behind closed doors, one simply did not discuss the heir to the throne in large social gatherings. Furthermore, it was a tradition of the British press, abetted by some of the most stringent libel laws on earth, to maintain a total silence about the private lives of royalty.

Behind the heavy curtain of discretion, however, the Prince of Wales was believed to be an exceptionally active man. It was noted that when he spoke at length to a dinner partner or asked a lady to dance more than once in a single evening, she was invariably very pretty. The Cockneys of London had a saying that summed up his proclivities. "'is 'ighness," they said, "is a sure judge o' women and 'orseflesh."

Almost inevitably, the names of one or another Professional Beauty were linked with that of Prince Albert Edward at one time or another. Many of these rumors were false, and a number of ladies retired to the country for periods ranging from several months to two or three years when they had been falsely identified as his mistresses.

But there were others who did not seem to mind. An underground telegraph of extraordinary sensitivity was at work in London's high society, and when the Prince of Wales seemed to pay special attention to a Professional Beauty, she was invited to every dinner, dance and weekend house party at which he, too, would be a guest. The meaning of the sobriquet, "a friend of the Prince of Wales," was clear to everyone.

Oddly, ladies who had enjoyed this standing displayed no overt signs of jealousy when Albert Edward turned away from them. They had known from the outset that the relationship would be a fleeting one. What was more, the Prince of Wales never dropped a lady so hard that she felt bruised. He always remained attentive, courtly and pleasant, no matter how much time had passed since he had lost personal interest in her. She could not complain she was ill-used or had been neglected.

One of the favorite pastimes of social London after Lillie Langtry burst onto the scene as a Professional Beauty was engaging in speculation regarding what would happen when Prince Albert Edward met her. It was taken for granted that the Prince, with his unerring eye for beauty, would be quick to develop an interest in her. But those who knew Lillie best — or thought they did — were convinced she would reject any advances he might make.

She had remained chaste after being subjected to endless temptations for more than a year, and had spurned many men far more handsome and aggressive than the Prince. Regardless of her arrangement with the nonentity to whom she was married, she was still faithful to him. And she was quick to cut any man who became too persistent in his advances.

There were many who agreed with the irreverent Wilde's prognosis. The Prince was a mortal man, he said, and therefore would be smitten. Lillie would be flattered by his attentions, but he would never take a single step beyond the Langtry parlor. He would recognize her purity, and would be satisfied if he sat beside her at an occasional dinner party. This, to be sure, was the fate to which other men were consigned.

Oscar Wilde, however, was not only dubious, but showed the bad taste of discussing the subject in Lillie's presence. "I will predict, accurately, all human behavior," he said, "except that which governs the human heart. Man is constant in his infidelity, and woman puts him to shame because she is, by nature, fickle."

Lillie boxed his ears and refused to speak to him for two weeks. She forgave him, however, when he appeared outside her windows on Norfolk Street and serenaded her morning and night with endless verses of a jingle-like lament that he composed for the purpose.

What puzzled many in London society was that Lillie and the Prince of Wales had never met. Albert Edward was busy, some said, while others declared that his interests were occupied elsewhere. For whatever the reasons, his path and Lillie's did not cross. It was believed that they were sure to meet at the ball for King Leopold, but the Prince was forced to take to his bed with a mild upset that night, and sent his regrets.

The noted novelist, Marie Louise de la Ramée, who wrote under the name of Ouida, committed the indiscretion of remarking in public that the Prince was avoiding Lillie because he was afraid to meet her.

When the meeting finally took place, at the home of Sir Allen Young, it was totally unplanned. Lillie and her husband had gone there, after attending the theatre, for a supper party of only ten persons. Suddenly, in the midst of the meal, the Prince of Wales appeared, loudly demanding a dish of the lobster curry for which Young was famous.

Most of those attending the party were acquainted with the Prince; only the Langtrys were unfamiliar, and were presented to him. Lillie curtsied, the Prince nodded and then told a story. Anyone expecting fireworks was disappointed.

The Prince and Sir Allen exchanged light-hearted remarks. Other guests, who didn't know the future monarch as well, made efforts to appear less self-conscious. Even the usually silent Edward Langtry occasionally joined in the conversation. Lillie, according to later accounts, confined herself to a few innocuous pleasantries.

According to the vague reports that seeped out later, the Prince of Wales offered the Jersey Lily a compliment before he departed, saying something to the effect that she was far more beautiful than the photographs and portraits of her that he had seen everywhere. Then he took his leave, and the party broke up. Social London was disappointed, and considered the evening anticlimactic.

Soon thereafter, however, Albert Edward found a way to get in touch with Lillie. The details have never been revealed, and are literally unknown. Lillie maintained a lifelong silence on the subject, and the Prince never said a word, either. Perhaps he corresponded with her, or it may be that he arranged for one or more private meetings. Secrecy has surrounded the subject down to the present day.

It was at this juncture that a burly English manufacturer in his sixties, C. J. Freake, entered the picture. A product of the working class, the shrewd Freake had become a multimillionaire, and he and his wife were busy working their way up the social ladder. He had recently given a large sum of money for the establishment of a Royal Academy of Music, he owned a large home in one of London's most fashionable districts, and he was known to be a friend of the Prince of Wales.

Freake was one of a very few people whose company Edward Langtry enjoyed, and the two men frequently met for lunch. Freake was able to give the younger man advice on investments, and, according to subsequent speculation, it may have been Freake's help that enabled Edward to rent a larger flat, hire an additional maid and give his wife a substantial clothing allowance.

In the light of what happened in the months that followed, it has also been suggested that Edward Langtry received the beneficial financial advice in return for keeping his eyes, ears and mouth shut, and for accepting a situation that most husbands would not have been willing to tolerate. This nasty allegation, like so much that touched on the Prince of Wales, can be neither verified nor disproved. If there were such an arrangement, however, it undoubtedly was made by Freake himself. The Prince was a man of impeccable honor, and would not have been a party to any low transaction.

It is known that Mr. and Mrs. Freake became close friends of the Langtrys, at least for a time. Lillie had rarely entertained prior to the move to the new flat, but the correspondence of many people indicates that on at least two occasions she gave small dinner parties, and that the Freakes attended both of them.

Soon thereafter it was rumored that the glamorous Mrs. Langtry and the Prince of Wales were meeting fairly regularly for tea at the Freake home. No one ever saw them there, and the Freakes maintained a tight-lipped silence, but the story persisted. And when Lillie and the Prince met at various functions in the next few weeks, meetings that now took place regularly, it was obvious that they were well acquainted.

It is apparent that a transformation had taken place in the clergyman's daughter from Jersey. Until now, in spite of the furor she had created, she had remained faithful to her husband, and had succeeded in putting off her suitors with a smile. Now, however, everything was changed, and although she hadn't yet had an affair with the Prince, the mere fact that she was willing to meet him privately at the home of a mutual friend indicated that she would not be averse to illicit romance at an appropriate time.

At least some of the reasons for the changes that took place in Lillie are clear. She was still very young, in her early twenties, and the adulation of the art and literary worlds, as well as of the aristocracy, undoubtedly went to her head. She was living something of a dream life, far removed from the realities she had always known, and her perspectives had become confused.

The deterioration of a marriage that had never been very promising made her restless, and may have contributed to a new spirit of recklessness. It should be remembered that she had never been in love with Edward Langtry, but had seen him as an instrument of escape from Jersey into the outer world. When he had sailed into the harbor of Saint Helier on his yacht she had seen him as sophisticated and debonair, but he had subsequently been revealed to her as almost as countrified a cousin as she had been. Now she was associating with men who were truly worldly, who were making history in the arts, in politics and in the development of industry. Edward, still lazy, did nothing and had no discernible ambition.

It is significant to note, too, that the couple no longer enjoyed marital relations. So Edward alleged in the law courts years later, saying that he had not gone to bed with his wife from the time they had moved to Norfolk Street. Although Lillie was engaged in a bitter legal fight with him at that time, she made no attempt to deny the charge, admitting it by her silence.

Perhaps nothing better illustrates the transformation than her changed attitude toward clothes. Until now her wardrobe had been the least of her concerns, and her one black dress had sufficed for an entire London season. Overnight, however, she became the fashion leader of society. Once she discovered she could buy her gowns for a fraction of the price others paid, she invested steadily in dresses, hats and accessories.

For the better part of a half-century the Jersey Lily set styles and was responsible for fads. When she wore a pink dress to the Ascot races, pink dresses by the thousands suddenly proliferated. When she appeared on London's Piccadilly or New York's Fifth Avenue carrying a muff, women of every class bought muffs. Every generation has had its fashion leaders, but Lillie Langtry's assumption of the unofficial title of the world's best-dressed woman was extraordinary. She who had been indifferent to her own appearance displayed an infallible instinct for the dramatic, for ideas that had universal appeal and, above all, for what showed her off to good advantage.

It is impossible to say whether her talent had been latent, and was developed by her circumstances, or whether, as she did in so many things, she taught herself "clothes sense." Whatever the cause, the results were spectacular. The appearance of Lillie Langtry in something new and different was guaranteed to make newspaper headlines in a dozen countries, and she immediately had faithful imitators in all of them.

Lillie, more than anyone else, was responsible for the simplification of women's attire during the final portion of the Victorian age and the Edwardian era that followed it. Clothes had become overly ornate and fussy, it is true, but it was Lillie who sensed the need for a change, impatiently refused to follow the dictates of the time and repeatedly broke new ground.

"Man," she wrote from Monte Carlo several years after the end of World War I, when she was in her seventies, "wears what he pleases, and is guided by only two rules. He dresses for comfort, and to enhance his appearance. Woman is entitled to the same privilege, and if society won't give it to her, she must take it for herself. What looks attractive on someone else might be hideous if I wear it, and vice versa. Every woman is entitled to her independence. It is her right to dress conspicuously or modestly, as she chooses. It is her right to ignore the dictates of fashion and dress in a manner that is most becoming to her own character and personality. In these days when woman is being granted the vote everywhere, we hear she is at last man's equal, but she will not achieve true equality until she breaks the chains of fashion's tyranny and strikes out on her own."

At no time in her life did Lillie Langtry participate in the activities of the suffragettes, and in no interview or other statement did she express sympathies for their announced goals. But in her own life she set an example for other women who yearned for equality and freedom. As a girl in her early twenties, inexperienced and performing no function other than that of being an ornament, she was beginning to grope toward the ends that would make her an inspiration to other women as well as a living legend. Her iconoclasm and sense of independence in dressing as she pleased show posterity that this attitude, boldly expressed from the outset, was the beginning of what would prove to be an extraordinary career.

But it was her liaison with the future Edward VII that first brought her world renown, and she might have passed into limbo, like the other Professional Beauties of her time, had it not been for her celebrated affair. So it might be argued, at first glance, that Lillie relied on her femininity, and was similar to the mistresses of powerful, wealthy and prominent men since the beginnings of recorded history. How she utilized her position to create a life that was unique, influential far beyond the confines of London society, is what makes her story fascinating.

By her own admission, she had no thoughts beyond the immediate present after she and her husband moved to Norfolk Street. She was leading a hedonistic existence, basking in her momentary glory, relishing her popularity. She received many more invitations than she could accept, any change in her appearance caused thousands to imitate her, and the crowds that followed her in the streets grew larger week by week.

The first sign that Prince Albert Edward had developed a personal interest in her was a move devoid of subterfuge. When Lillie went out for her regular morning canter, the Prince appeared on horseback and joined her, forcing the members of the Langtry Lancers to fall in behind them. The word traveled with the speed of sound through the drawing rooms and salons of London, and was confirmed when the Prince reappeared on the bridle path the next day, and the next.

Wise hostesses who sought the triumph of entertaining the Prince of Wales made it their business to invite Mrs. Langtry to their dinner parties, receptions and dances. It soon became evident that, if Lillie wasn't asked, the Prince busied himself elsewhere. It was also noted that, except on those occasions when his official duties occupied him, he and Lillie never went to separate affairs.

The proprieties were always observed, of course. Lillie invariably arrived and departed with her husband, and the Prince came to supper parties and other affairs with a pair of his ever-present equerries. If he chose to escort Mrs. Langtry to the table, if he elected to dance repeatedly with her, ignoring other ladies present, that was his prerogative. But, as those with sharp eyes were quick to note, the Prince and the Jersey Lily never spent any time alone, never wandered off into a garden or conservatory.

The domestic arrangements in the household of the heir to the throne made it easy for the Prince of Wales to spend as much time as he pleased with the lady who fascinated him. Princess Alexandra accompanied her husband to all official functions; she never shirked her duty, nor did he. But the Prince and Princess of Wales led separate private lives. Alexandra felt at home in the court circles Albert Edward found stuffy, and she spent most of her time there, while he escaped to the gayer life of London society whenever possible. They had followed this routine for many years, so it was taken for granted that an invitation to the Prince of Wales need not be extended to the Princess, too. Many hostesses felt it was only proper to ask Alexandra to their parties, but none were surprised when she refused. Living in the best of Victorian traditions, Alexandra obviously expected her husband to go his own social way.

Life in the Langtry household changed drastically in accordance with the new circumstances. A carpenter was called in to build new closets for Lillie's expanding wardrobe. C. J. Freake was seen frequently in Edward Langtry's company, and, it was rumored, was responsible for literally all of the investments made by the Jersey Lily's husband. There were many men in social London who enjoyed fishing and sailing as much as Edward Langtry did, and he was often asked to go for an outing.

The wise London gossips quickly noted, however, that he was always on hand to take his wife to a social function. If he went off on an overnight trip, he left London only on a night when Lillie stayed at home and rested. She was careful to appear nowhere without him, and even the critics who envied the rapid rise of the Jersey Lily were forced to admit that her husband was devoted to her.

It was at this time, Lillie later indicated, during her legal squabbles with her husband, that Edward's drinking became a real problem. On a number of occasions, she declared, he became too intoxicated to escort her to a social event, thereby forcing her to send last-minute regrets to her hostess of the evening. It was no secret that he was drinking too much, but there were many who sympathized with him. Lillie had become too popular too quickly, and her conquest of the Prince of Wales was the last straw. Although she was still faithful to her husband, she had already developed a measure of notoriety, and her husband acquired partisans who, if they could find no positive good in him, at least felt sorry for him.

Lillie seemed to go out of her way to make news. She met Benjamin Disraeli at a government reception, and not only dared to joke with him, something that few wits of the day attempted, but actually twitted him. "Mr. Gladstone," she said, referring to his arch-rival, "tells me he has dizzy spells. What will cure them?"

"Nothing," Disraeli replied, "and long may he suffer them."

Every newspaper in London reported the exchange, and the penny press elaborated on the conversation, attributing many witticisms to Lillie. It is improbable that she uttered any of them.

The King of the Belgians created talk when he called on Lillie at nine o'clock in the morning, an hour when ladies of fashionable London were just waking up. Lillie felt she had to see him, and dressed hastily, then went downstairs for coffee with him. King Leopold was so enchanted he came back at the same hour every day for a week.

Finally the exhausted and exasperated Lillie smashed protocol by sending word to His Majesty that she was unavailable. London chuckled, and King Leopold took the hint. Thereafter he paid his calls in the afternoons, as befitted gentlemen dropping in for chats with ladies.

Lillie's sense of humor was suspiciously like that of her brothers when they had been schoolboys. One of her favorite stories, which she often told herself, concerned Lord Malmesbury, a diplomat who had retired to his ancestral estate in Hampshire. He sat Lillie on his right at a dinner party, and insisted that she pass publicly on the main dish before anyone else ate it.

As nearly as she could tell, the much-heralded dish was a mixture of minced chicken and chopped cauliflower, cooked in a white sauce. It was probably no better and no worse than countless other, unimaginative dishes she had eaten, but it was so hot that it burned her mouth, and tears came to her eyes.

"Well," Lord Malmesbury demanded, "what do you think of it, Mrs. Langtry?"

"It would be very good," Lillie replied calmly, "if it weren't cold."

Malmesbury was astonished, and, insisting that his chef had never erred, plunged his fork into the tureen and swallowed a large amount of the dish. Gasping and sputtering, he had to drink both wine and water before he recovered. He and his guests thought Lillie's little trick very amusing.

A serious incident marred the peace of that weekend in Hampshire. Lillie had just received a gift from the Prince of Wales, a brooch set with small diamonds, and wrote him a note to thank him. The brooch, although handsome, was not particularly expensive, and the Prince had distributed a number of similar items to various friends.

But Edward Langtry, who had been drinking, read a portion of his wife's note on the desk blotter she had used, and became wildly jealous, the first time he had been known to create a scene. Lord Malmesbury heard of the incident, and was annoyed with his staff, saying that his butler had standing instructions to burn all blotters daily.

Apparently Lillie reported the matter to the Prince when she and her husband returned to London. Immediately thereafter Langtry received a pair of initialed gold cufflinks as a royal gift, and arrangements were made for the Prince of Wales to act as his sponsor and present him to Queen Victoria at a formal court reception. It is a matter of record that Queen Victoria seemed impressed with Mr. Langtry, and engaged him in conversation for more than five minutes, which was unusual. Edward Langtry, it appeared, was mollified.

Arrangements also were made for Lillie to be presented to the Queen at one of Victoria's "afternoon drawing rooms" at Buckingham Palace. No lady was considered to have made her permanent mark until she had curtsied to the Queen, and Lillie had heard gossip to the effect that, because she had become so notorious, Victoria would not receive her.

Presumably Lillie reported the rumor to the Prince of Wales, and soon thereafter she received her invitation to the palace.

She had a new gown made for the event, of course, and the occasion was considered so important that her mother came to London from Jersey to help her prepare for it. One touch, characteristic of Lillie, was her own audacious idea. All ladies presented to the Queen were required to wear feathers in their hair, and it was currently the custom to appear in tiny feathers, which, Lillie learned, irritated Queen Victoria.

So the Jersey Lily decided to wear three enormous white plumes, which bore a suspicious resemblance to the three large feathers on the Prince of Wales' coat of arms. If her mother or anyone else tried to dissuade her, these efforts were unavailing.

Presentations bored Queen Victoria, who usually made only a token appearance at them, and then departed, leaving the Prince and Princess of Wales to do the honors in her stead. Lillie's name appeared near the bottom of the list on the day of her appearance, which may have meant that someone who disapproved of her hoped the Queen would be gone when she came into the drawing room to make her obeisance.

But Victoria was curious, and wanted to see the Jersey Lily for herself, so she stayed until the end of the audience. Those who watched her said her face remained expressionless, but that she studied Lillie closely, her eyes never wavering.

Princess Alexandra was present, too, sitting beside her husband, and there was a touchy moment when Lillie curtsied to them, but the Princess's smile was impersonal and calm. The Prince of Wales, untroubled by the presence of his mother and his wife, reacted as he always did, and made no secret of his pleasure as he looked at an exceptionally attractive young woman. The presentation was a success.

No one knows when Lillie became the mistress of the Prince. That was very much their own business, and they were discreet in the handling of the situation. Word appeared to seep out to others in their social circle, however, and when they were invited to weekend house parties at various manor houses, their suites were located, as a rule, in the same wing and on the same floor.

Whether Lillie was in love with the Prince at any time in their relationship is a matter of conjecture. She made only a few vague references to him in her autobiography, which she wrote in the early 1920's, and if the couple corresponded at any time, none of their letters have come to light. Hearsay evidence, presented by Lillie's friends and always unreliable, indicates that many who were fairly close to her believed she suffered no false illusions.

She was flattered by the Prince's attention, she undoubtedly knew that her position gave her increased standing in certain circles, and she accepted the gifts that he gave her. She was never mercenary, but Albert Edward was one of the wealthiest men in the world, and he had a predilection for expensive jewelry. The rings, bracelets, pendants and earrings he gave

Lillie were in spectacularly good taste, and became part of what grew into one of the world's largest private jewelry collections. For a woman who sought little in the way of material advantages for herself, at least at this stage of life, Lillie enjoyed a success that few others had ever equaled.

She must have known that her good fortune was temporary. The Prince was notoriously fickle, and had never maintained an interest in any favorite for more than a year or two. So it would have been short-sighted had she failed to realize that her own days were numbered.

Regardless of what she may have known, Lillie made the most of the time at her disposal. She and her husband spent part of the summer at Cowes, where they were the guests of Sir Allen Young on his yacht, the *Helen*, which was berthed adjacent to the slip occupied by the magnificent royal yacht, the *Osborne*, on which the Prince and Princess of Wales were enjoying a holiday with their children.

The Langtrys were frequent guests on the *Osborne*, where they met the King and Queen of Denmark, various members of the Austrian royal family, assorted German princes and the exiled Empress Eugénie of France, who was reputedly at that time the best-dressed woman in the world. Presumably Lillie learned something about clothes by watching her.

Edward Langtry was in his element on board ship. He struck up a friendship with Danish royalty, and every morning took the King and Queen for a ride around the harbor in a rowboat. He participated in many of the races, and came alive for the first time in many months. Then the Prince of Wales loaned the Langtrys one of his yachts, the *Hildegarde*, which was manned by sailors of the Royal Navy. Lillie, escorted by her husband, sailed off in style for a brief visit to Jersey.

Her parents were pleased to see her, and her stay with them was uneventful. Nothing is known about their reaction at this time to her relationship with the Prince of Wales.

Reverend Le Breton was not a worldly man, and it might not have occurred to him that his daughter was enjoying a relationship of a very special nature with the heir to the throne. The Dean's later reactions suggest that, at this time, he was innocently in the dark. Mrs. Le Breton well may have suspected that there was more to Lillie's situation than met the eye, but she, too, apparently said nothing. A number of friends and relatives came to see the Langtrys, and several small family parties were held, but they were modest affairs, and on one occasion a group went out to the cliffs for a picnic.

Tourists who happened to be visiting Saint Helier gathered in front of the rectory at all hours of the day, hoping to catch a glimpse of the celebrated Jersey Lily. But the neighbors stolidly went about their own business. No one wanted to display bad manners, and Lillie Langtry was not considered newsworthy in her childhood home. Many years passed before the good people of Jersey felt ashamed of the notoriety she had brought to the entire island.

So far, to be sure, Lillie's discretion had prevented the outbreak of any major scandal, but her attitude was already changing. By 1879 everyone in England was whispering about her, while the rest of the world shouted.

V

THE FUTURE EDWARD VII ESTABLISHED A NEW,
SURPRISINGLY bold pattern in his relations with Lillie
Langtry. Although he had enjoyed affairs with a number of
attractive ladies, he had been circumspect, and relatively few
people had been aware of his involvement. Public opinion was
still important to him, of necessity, but he seemed eager to let
the world know of his interest in the Jersey Lily. He showed
her off accordingly, as though eager to tell everyone she was
his mistress.

The Prince owned one of the largest stables of racing horses
on earth, and Lillie was devoted to the sport, so they appeared
together in the royal box at Ascot, then at Epsom Downs.
Track habitués grew accustomed to seeing them together. By
1879 the couple also appeared together daily on London's
bridle paths, and rode for an hour or two. Most of Lillie's
admirers had been discouraged by the royal attention she was
receiving, and no longer rode with her, so it became customary
for her to be seen with no one but the Prince of Wales, his
equerries following at a respectful distance.

Hostesses who extended to the Prince invitation to their
dinner parties, balls and country weekends learned it was wise
to submit guest lists to Albert Edward in advance. If the name
of Mrs. Langtry did not appear on the list, it was a foregone
conclusion that the Prince would not appear.

Lillie's international reputation rapidly acquired a new
dimension. She was no longer merely the reigning Professional
Beauty of London, but was dubbed "the favorite of the Prince
of Wales" by the world press. British newspapers maintained

their usual stiff-necked reserve, but even they managed to keep their readers informed by utilizing subtle means. Whenever possible they published at least a partial list of guests at various social functions, and the name of Mrs. Edward Langtry usually followed that of the Prince.

What surprised many was the fact that Lillie often appeared at official functions. No one deserved greater credit than Princess Alexandra, who not only tolerated the presence of her husband's mistress on these occasions, but received her with at least a surface display of cordiality. The legion of Alexandra's admirers grew larger.

Meanwhile Edward Langtry was fading farther into the background. He received many boating and fishing invitations, which he accepted with alacrity. It was obvious by now that he knew his marriage had become meaningless, and he no longer tried to maintain the facade that he and Lillie had erected. He continued to act as her escort on important occasions, where he arrived and departed with her, but he was leading a separate life of his own, and appeared indifferent to his wife's activities.

It is not surprising that he continued to drink heavily. A stronger man would have forced Lillie to behave, and if she had refused, would have left her! Edward Langtry did neither; closing his eyes to her situation, he was available when his presence suited her convenience, and he disappeared when his proximity would have been awkward.

The respectable ladies of London society were shocked by Lillie's blatant transgression of the rules that governed the conduct of ladies and gentlemen. They may have entertained similar feelings about the Prince, but he was beyond criticism, so their wrath centered on Lillie. While she maintained her position as the Prince's favorite, however, their voices were muted, and it was impossible for them to show their contempt for her. They continued to entertain her because they had no choice, but they were biding their time, and as Lillie demonstrated when a crisis finally occurred, she suffered no false illusions regarding their attitude toward her.

A new scandal suddenly gave the Jersey Lily an even worse name. Late in 1879 Crown Prince Rudolph of Austria-Hungary, the heir to the throne of the Hapsburg Empire, paid a visit to London. Only twenty-one years of age, the son of the Emperor Franz Josef was brilliant, handsome and emotionally unstable, as he demonstrated a decade later, when he and his mistress, Baroness Maria Vetsera, committed suicide at Mayerling, his hunting lodge.

By the time Rudolph paid his semi-official visit to London he had already acquired a reputation as a playboy, and his antics had not only made headlines throughout the world, but he had repeatedly drawn fire from his high-principled father. Prince Rudolph met Lillie Langtry at a ball given in his honor by Baron Ferdinand de Rothschild, and his reaction was predictable. From the moment he first saw her, he went wild.

He danced with her repeatedly, refusing to relinquish her to anyone else. The Prince of Wales was present, and presumably Rudolph knew of his relationship with the Jersey Lily, but such delicacies were of no matter to the smitten Austrian. Albert Edward, always the gentleman, pretended to be unaware of the younger man's infatuation, and Foreign Office officials who were present breathed more easily.

Lillie, however, was having her problems. During a brief lull in the dancing a friend whispered to her that the Austrian was leaving finger-marks on her pale pink dress. So, according to the story she herself told about the occasion, she requested Rudolph to don his white gloves when the dancing resumed.

He quickly demonstrated that his standards were not those of England. "It is you, Madame, and not I who sweats!" he declared.

There were additional repercussions when supper was served. Rudolph, as the guest of honor, was expected to escort the Baroness de Rothschild to the table, while the Prince of Wales and Lillie fell into line directly behind them. But the Austrian took Lillie's arm and, refusing to relinquish it, marched her off to the supper table.

Again Albert Edward demonstrated his own good sense. He smiled quietly, offered his arm to the Baroness and escorted her to her place. Perhaps his own strict upbringing made him tolerant of the youth's rudeness.

That was anything but the end of the matter. Each day thereafter Prince Rudolph paid a call at the Norfolk Street flat, and his advances were so bold, so insistent, that Lillie had to summon her husband from a fishing trip. Much to Edward Langtry's disgust, he was required to be present whenever Rudolph appeared at the flat.

"Lovely Lillie Langtry," the New York *Tribune* said, "has added another royal scalp to her fast-growing collection."

The English press was more reserved than the foreign newspapers, but nevertheless conveyed the idea to their readers that the heir to the throne of the Austro-Hungarian Empire was infatuated with the beautiful Mrs. Langtry. Those who read between the lines undoubtedly wondered if the Prince of Wales might intervene, and the foreign press speculated openly on the possibility. But the future British monarch was far too sensible, and pretended to be unaware of the furor.

Lillie herself was as innocent as she was furious. She had done nothing to encourage Rudolph, and wanted nothing to do with the young boor. On two occasions, which the newspapers duly noted, she was not at home when he called, but the Crown Prince of Austria-Hungary was less sensitive than the King of the Belgians had been. Refusing to accept the snubs, he continued to visit Norfolk Street.

So much appeared in print throughout the civilized world that the Austrian government became concerned, and Emperor Franz Josef called his son back to Vienna, abruptly and prematurely canceling the rest of his journey abroad. So Lillie was spared further embarrassment, but the damage was already done. The publicity had sullied her name, and there were many people in many lands who believed, wrongly, that she had added Rudolph to her string of royal lovers.

The incident had one beneficial result, however. The last of Lillie's swains became discouraged, and disappeared; it is unlikely that the Prince of Wales mourned their absence.

One of those who vanished from the scene was Moreton Frewen, who went off on a long business visit to the United States. On his arrival he was interviewed by reporters who visited his ship, and in the course of questioning it was established that he was acquainted with the Jersey Lily. Would he call himself her intimate friend? The New York *Post* dutifully reported his reply:

"Unfortunately, no."

Would he have wanted to become her good friend?

"I believe she is otherwise occupied."

Was Mrs. Langtry as beautiful as all who knew her said?

"Yes, I suppose she is."

Did the reporters detect a hesitation in his voice?

"Not really," Frewen said. "She is lovely, but I've found her a bit dull, since she's always surrounded by people. A lily, to bloom as it should, must be planted in its bed."

People on both sides of the Atlantic laughed, but Frewen didn't realize his blunder until he read the interview in the *Post*. He was horrified, and wrote Lillie a long letter of apology, telling her he hadn't intended his comment in the way it had appeared.

She was angry, and did not forgive him until she herself came to the United States several years later. At that time Frewen tried to resume his courtship, but it was too late, even though by then Lillie was unencumbered.

Sarah Bernhardt paid a visit to London in the autumn of 1879, and Oscar Wilde, always eager to capitalize on publicity, acted as her constant escort. Through him the great French actress met his friend, Lillie Langtry, and the two women immediately established a rapport that lasted for the rest of their lives. Their paths frequently crossed through the years, they corresponded irregularly, and each, in interviews with the press, always spoke of the other with great warmth and respect. But it could not have occurred to Lillie, when she first met "the Divine Sarah," that it wouldn't be long before she, too, would be earning a living on the stage.

In the spring of 1880 Edward Langtry went off on a month's yachting trip with Sir Humphrey Coyne, who happened to be a member of what was called "the Prince of Wales' set." Perhaps it was accidental that Lillie and the Prince made their boldest gesture during this time, but there were millions, in many countries, who refused to believe it.

Lillie announced that she was leaving London for the purpose of visiting her parents, and two days later she arrived in Jersey. But she remained there for only a few days, and then went on to Paris, where a suite had been reserved for her at the exclusive Hotel Bristol.

A portly, bearded English gentleman happened to be staying at the same hotel, and the Paris newspapers said his suite was located on the same floor. The Prince of Wales, traveling incognito as a private citizen, used the name of one of his equerries, and enjoyed a strictly private visit to the French capital.

He and Lillie were seen everywhere in the city together, while tourists gaped at them and well-bred Frenchmen pretended they were invisible. They danced together at Maxim's, and, it was said in the busy Paris press, kissed on the dance floor. They took carriage rides down the boulevards and in the Bois. They sat at sidewalk cafes and sipped liqueurs. And when they had nothing better to occupy them, they shopped; oh, how they shopped.

The Prince bought Lillie an entire new wardrobe at the house of Worth, the former dressmaker to the Empress Eugénie. They visited a number of jewelers, and the Paris press reported that Lillie was wearing two new diamond bracelets, a magnificent diamond and emerald ring, and a huge diamond and ruby brooch. Whether the Prince actually gave her these gems on this trip isn't known, but she owned and wore them for the rest of her life.

Nervous British Embassy officials hovered in the background whenever the couple emerged from the Bristol, and pretended to be part of the scenery. Lillie and the Prince led them on a merry chase. They bought perfume, visited the graves of Voltaire and Rousseau at the Pantheon, and made a trip out to Versailles to see the great palace of Louis XIV there. The huge palace was not in use; the officials of the Third Republic considered it a symbol of royalty they wanted to forget, and it was closed to the public. But a high-ranking officer of the French army was on hand, and, with a professor from the Sorbonne as a guide, the incognito English gentleman and his beautiful companion were taken on a special tour.

They attended the theatre on a number of occasions, and one night saw Sarah Bernhardt in one of her favorite roles, that of the queen in Victor Hugo's play *Ruy Blas*. After the performance she gave a supper party for them at her apartment.

The following night they dined at the home of Hugo. The greatest French author of the century, now seventy-eight years of age, had a justly acquired reputation as a ladies' man that made the Prince of Wales rank as an amateur. Recently recovered from a heart attack, Hugo had given up his countless amatory adventures at the insistence of his "official" mistress of almost a half century, and was leading a quiet life.

But he was still gallant, and had lost none of his wit. After toasting his incognito male guest, he offered a toast to Lillie, which immediately became famous. "Madame," he said, "I can celebrate your beauty in only one way, by wishing I were three years younger."

Lillie and her companion traveled north together as far the French coast. Then she went on to Jersey for another brief visit, while he crossed the Channel to England. A few days later, when Lillie returned home, a domestic crisis awaited her.

Edward Langtry had just paid a visit to his family in Ulster, and had learned, apparently for the first time, that his father heartily disapproved of the notoriety that Lillie was giving the family name. The elder Langtry had offered to assume all of his son's debts and give him a place in the business that would pay a handsome annual stipend, on condition that Edward divorce Lillie.

Edward Langtry had refused, and had left Belfast without speaking to his father again. Regardless of what he either knew or suspected about his wife, the very idea of divorce was anathema to him. Too little is known about him to venture an educated guess regarding his possible reasons for being violently and unalterably opposed to divorce. He was not a religious man, rarely attending church services, and he knew by now that he and Lillie had drifted far apart, yet he was adamant in his insistence that he would never divorce her or permit her to divorce him. Lillie reported his stand to her friend, Mary Cornwallis-West, who subsequently included the information in a book about the social life of the period.

It was at this time that Lillie Langtry was riding the social crest. Dressmakers gave her unlimited credit, she could no longer walk anywhere in the streets for fear of being mobbed, and every change in her costume created a new fad. At the age of twenty-seven, having accomplished nothing whatever in her life, she was the heroine of millions.

Even W. S. Gilbert had written a lyric about her which his partner, Sir Arthur Sullivan, had put to music:

Oh, never, never, never since we joined the human race
Saw we so exquisitely fair a face.

The end came suddenly, unexpectedly, thanks to a rare indiscretion that Lillie herself committed. She went to a costume ball given by Lord Randolph Churchill and his American-born wife, dressed as Pierette. To the surprise of no one, the Prince of Wales came as Pierrot, even though Princess Alexandra, who accompanied him, wore a different sort of costume.

Accounts of what happened that evening differ. Most appeared in various memoirs, some in correspondence, and no two are identical. No one, to be sure, talked for publication, and aristocratic London soon closed ranks to deny that anything untoward had taken place. Even Lillie, who created the storm, spent decades blandly denying that anything out of the ordinary had happened, and not until her last years did she admit the central facts to a few intimates.

Ordinarily Lillie drank sparingly, and some eyewitnesses who attended the costume party insisted that she couldn't have taken more than a glass or two of champagne. Others, however, said she consumed wine at a far more rapid rate than was her custom, and that she became intoxicated.

There was controversy, too, concerning her relations with the Prince that night. Some eyewitnesses wrote in their memoirs that both he and Lillie were in high spirits, and were teasing each other, but indicated the teasing went too far. Others, however, said they had an argument, and that Lillie eventually became exasperated.

But all accounts were agreed on what happened at the climax. Lillie Langtry reached into a champagne cooler, picked up a large chunk of ice and dropped it down the back of the Prince of Wales' ruffled Pierrot collar.

There was a limit to the familiarities that anyone could take in public with the heir to the British throne; and Lillie far exceeded the bounds of propriety. Perhaps no one was more surprised than Albert Edward himself. He stared at Lillie for a long moment, then turned on his heel and stalked out of the room. Princess Alexandra hurriedly followed him, and the other guests hastily departed for home. The party was ruined, and so was Lillie Langtry.

Not until the following day could the full import of what had happened dawn on Lillie. When she went for her usual canter in the park, she rode alone. No invitations were delivered at the Norfolk Street flat, but before the day ended, cancellations of various social engagements began to arrive. Dinner parties were postponed, arrangements for weekends were unavoidably changed, and even the usual at-homes were temporarily terminated. Lillie had gone too far, and society had dropped her with a resounding thud.

There were few aristocratic secrets unfamiliar to London's fashionable tradespeople, and soon the bill collectors descended on Norfolk Street. Dressmakers and milliners, shoemakers and glovers demanded payment at once, and Lillie, by her own admission, discovered she had been living far beyond her means.

Edward Langtry lacked the funds to pay all the bills, and was incapable of earning the money, so Lillie decided she would have to go to work herself. In her autobiography she indicates she was tired of living as a social parasite, which was probably true, but necessity played a part in her decision, too.

Her only friends now were the artists and authors who were indifferent to the standards of high society, cared nothing about the disapproval of Lillie shown by the Prince of Wales and his friends, and who continued to accept or reject individuals on merit. The painters, poets and actors of London rallied to Lillie Langtry's cause, and she remembered their unswerving loyalty for the rest of her days. From that time onward, all of her lasting friendships were made exclusively in artistic circles. Only one woman of social standing, Mary Cornwallis-West, Lillie's predecessor as "the favorite of the Prince of Wales," demonstrated the desire and courage to remain friendly with her.

Bands of the faithful gathered at Norfolk Street to consider the future. Frank Miles and a number of others thought Lillie could prosper if she opened one, then a chain, of Jersey Lily florist shops. James Whistler offered to give Lillie drawing lessons, and believed she could become an accomplished artist.

Mary Cornwallis-West and several others were convinced she could become an enormously successful dressmaker.

Oscar Wilde, at his persuasive best, told Lillie she would be mad if she contemplated any career other than the stage. She already possessed several exceptionally valuable assets. She was the most beautiful woman in Great Britain, perhaps in the entire Western world. She had been making headlines for years as a Professional Beauty, and therefore already had an audience that would be anxious to see her on stage.

While Lillie pondered, unable to make a decision, she was unexpectedly restored to the Prince of Wales' favor. Whether he got in touch with her himself, or whether an intermediary notified her that she was forgiven is not known. It sufficed that the invitations began to pour into Norfolk Street again, and the creditors agreed to wait for their money.

On the surface, at least, Lillie resumed the life she had been leading, but for her private purposes she had merely bought a little more time to make up her mind. She had learned from her recent experience, and was determined not to let it be repeated. Still thinking about the advice she had received, she was inclined to go into the theatre, even though she completely lacked experience on the stage.

Henry Irving learned that she was contemplating the idea of becoming an actress, and offered her a role in a new play that would open the 1880-81 theatrical season. The part was small, but important, and she would be shown off to good advantage.

Lillie hesitated, then declined. The disappointed Irving wrote that she was afraid she would disgrace him by being too amateurish, and that he had not been able to persuade her to change her mind.

Then nature intervened, and hastened at least one portion of Lillie's decision, forcing her to retire from society. She discovered she was pregnant.

VI

ALEXANDRA, PRINCESS OF WALES, PAID A CALL ON Lillie Langtry at the Norfolk Street flat, and a few days later she received a visit from Albert Edward, Prince of Wales. No significant details of either visit are known, although Lillie herself wrote in some detail in her autobiography that the Princess had come to see her.

Accompanied by her private secretary, Charlotte Knollys, the Princess refused to permit Lillie to leave her bed to curtsy, expressed the hope that her violet scent wasn't too strong, and showed the younger woman every consideration. At her direction the Royal Household Physician, Francis Laking, called on Lillie, and thereafter attended her.

Lillie made no mention, in her autobiography or elsewhere, of the Prince's visit.

Soon thereafter her immediate financial problems vanished. She received a check from the Prince's friend, Sir Allen Young, for two thousand pounds, which was the equivalent of ten thousand dollars the better part of a century later. Presumably it was, for the sake of propriety, called a "loan"; but Lillie actually considered it a loan, and eventually repaid Sir Allen every penny. From then until the end of her life she refused to be indebted to anyone.

Edward Langtry had gone off on a two-week hunting trip, and Lillie moved quickly. She wrote her husband a brief note informing him she was leaving him. Since they had not slept together for more than a year, she made no mention of her pregnancy.

The funds supplied by Sir Allen easily took care of Lillie's creditors, but her plans made it necessary for her to give up the London flat, so she arranged through Mary Cornwallis-West for the furniture, rugs, bric-a-brac and drapes at the Norfolk Street quarters to be sold at auction. Then, with her friend accompanying her to the railroad station, she departed without fanfare for Jersey.

Mrs. Cornwallis-West passed the word that Lillie had "retired," and hinted that a marital break was responsible.

The news first appeared in a small London society paper, the *Figaro*, on October 2, 1880. Two days later *The New York Times* reprinted the London article in full under a headline, RETIREMENT OF MRS. LANGTRY FROM SOCIETY. Other newspapers around the world also carried every scrap of information available.

Edward Langtry was unavailable to the press, and refused to comment.

On November 6, 1880, *The New York Times* ran another story:

> Mr. and Mrs. Langtry have given up their London residence, and for the present Mrs. Langtry remains in Jersey. Is beauty deposed, or has beauty abdicated? The result on London society will be the same. Public pets may be objectionable, but few could so well have survived the ordeal of public admiration and preserved so much of the natural good-hearted woman as Mrs. Langtry.

Reverend Le Breton was in the process of leaving Jersey at the time of his daughter's arrival. Or, has been suggested, it may be that the news she brought with her caused him to seek a transfer. In any event, he announced that he was suffering from the infirmities of advancing age, and could no longer perform the duties of Dean of Jersey. Therefore he was transferred to a smaller church, in London, and took up residence in the Marylebone Parish. Mrs. Le Breton remained in Jersey for a time with her daughter.

The next months of Lillie Langtry's life are a complete mystery. Whether she remained in Jersey and gave birth to her child there, or whether she moved elsewhere during her confinement has never been revealed. It has been rumored that she went to a small estate owned by Mary Cornwallis-West in Wales. It has also been suggested that she went to Paris, or to Lille or to Rouen.

No records of the infant's birth or baptism appear in London, in Wales, or in Jersey. There are none in Paris or any of the smaller French cities. Enterprising newspaper reporters have, over the decades, scoured every official registry of both state and church, but after almost a century their efforts have revealed nothing.

It has long been assumed that Lillie's child was born in Jersey, presumably in either March or April, 1881. It was at about that time that Lillie rented a cottage near the Jersey cliffs, and was seen there with her mother and her maid, Dominique. It was there that word first seeped out concerning the birth of her baby.

The baby was a girl, and was called Jeanne Langtry. Her mother sometimes referred to her as Jeanne Marie, and when she became an adolescent she spelled her name Jean. Her existence was known to few, and was confirmed by still fewer.

London society, which would have drawn its own embarrassing and complicating conclusions, knew nothing of her existence. The world press was aware of still less, and even the artists and authors who had demonstrated their friendship for Lillie were kept in the dark.

The people of Jersey who stumbled onto the secret kept their mouths shut. "My mother," said a lady who still resides on the island, "told me that, as a child, she played with Jeanne Langtry, but it was an unwritten law that her name was never to be mentioned to outsiders. I was grown before she told me the secret, and I don't like to talk about the whole matter myself. We may hold our own opinions of Lillie Langtry, but when we're dealing with the rest of the world, we're loyal to our own."

One person, above all, had no idea of the baby's existence. Edward Langtry was in a deplorable condition. Dropped by aristocratic London the day his wife disappeared, he was a lost soul. The auctioning of the Norfolk Street furnishings had revealed his unfortunate financial condition, he had no friends of his own, and his drinking caused even those who felt sorry for him to part company with him.

He could have caused too many problems had he been aware of Lillie's secret, but he was far removed from London society, and none of the whispers that made the rounds reached his ears. He received a tiny allowance from his father, lived in a cheap London rooming house, and, a broken, humbled man, spent his days drinking. He was one of the last to hear about Jeanne.

Battered though Edward Langtry may have been, he refused to compromise the principles he considered basic, and would not grant Lillie the separation she wanted. It was commonly believed that Lillie, the daughter of an Anglican clergyman, opposed divorce, although she had already initiated the persisting efforts that she found so difficult to achieve. But it was Edward who would not allow her to divorce him and who would not take action against her. Nothing budged him, and Reverend Le Breton wrote to his daughter from London, "I spent an uncomfortable hour with Edward today. He was in his cups, and blames you alone for the failure of your marriage. You would be wise to put aside all thoughts of divorce, which he will not contemplate."

Lillie undoubtedly knew she would have to rebuild her life without thoughts of remarriage within the near future. She also knew that her limited funds were being spent too rapidly, and that she faced the problem of earning a living, which she couldn't do in Jersey. So she hired a governess for the baby, and her mother, who had gone off to join Reverend Le Breton, promised to spend as much time in Jersey as she could.

There was only one place Lillie herself could go, so she traveled with her maid, Dominique, to London, and engaged a small suite of modest rooms for herself in Ely Place. The ladies and gentlemen of high society had no idea she had returned, and she had no intention of getting in touch with any of them. She called on Millais, Wilde and Miles, and confided to them that she intended to become an actress.

Through these friends she received several offers, the most lucrative of them a tour through the United States. But she had received no training, and knew she would be paid only because of the notoriety attached to her name. So she refused, and told her friends she sought the experience that would enable her to become a professional actress.

Through Oscar Wilde she met the woman who would influence the rest of her life. Henrietta Hodson Labouchère was a tiny woman, as energetic and ambitious as she was wiry. A former dramatic actress who had achieved a minor reputation in secondary roles, she was married to Henry Labouchère, a Member of Parliament, ardent follower of Gladstone and editor of a small, liberal magazine called *Truth*. The domestic tranquillity of the Labouchère home was ruffled by Henry's eccentricities and devotion to politics, as well as by his wife's burning desire to create a life of her own.

Henrietta had enjoyed a fair success by giving dramatic lessons to several budding actresses who had managed to find roles on the London stage, but she wanted far more. Her great desire was the creation of a theatrical company she would manage, and through Lillie Langtry she saw the possibility that, in due time, such a company might be formed.

Lillie agreed to work with her, and went to the Labouchère home at Twickenham-on-Thames, where a charity performance of one-act plays would be given on November 19, 1881. Living in the Labouchère house, Lillie rehearsed a half-hour play, *A Fair Encounter*, in which Henrietta played the only other role.

The performance was held, as scheduled, in the Twickenham town hall, and a number of Lillie's artistic friends came out from London to cheer her. They told her she exhibited the potential of an actress, and so did Henrietta, who insisted on preparing her for a bigger role before a more demanding audience.

Lillie returned to Ely Place, and found that social London had learned of her return. On several occasions the Prince of Wales called on her, but Lillie refused all society invitations. She was serious about creating a genuine career based on talent and hard work, and would not be distracted.

Edward Langtry also discovered she was in the city, and after getting in touch with her through her solicitor, George Lewis, he came to see her. The hour's visit was a frustrating waste of Lillie's time. Her husband not only rejected her demands for a divorce, but tried to insist that they reconcile, which Lillie refused. He still had no idea she had given birth to a daughter more than a half year earlier.

A number of theatrical managers offered Lillie roles in forthcoming attractions, but she was not yet ready to accept any of them. She wanted recognition as an actress, not as a former Professional Beauty, and needed more experience.

The indefatigable Henrietta Labouchère saw that she got it. Acting as her manager, Henrietta obtained a role for her as Kate Hardcastle in a charity performance of *She Stoops to Conquer*, which would be held for the benefit of the Royal General Theatrical Fund at one of London's best theatres, the Theatre Royal in the Haymarket. A number of England's best actors and actresses had agreed to take parts, and the capabilities of the amateur would be tested to the limit.

The news that Lillie would appear in a leading role resulted in a rush for seats, all of which were sold long before the performance was given on December 15, 1881. At the age of twenty-eight, Lillie Langtry was launching her career.

Realizing that the critics and reporters from London and foreign newspapers would be present, along with scores of her former aristocratic friends, Lillie worked incessantly with Henrietta to prepare herself for her role, and, according to her own account, she spent ten hours out of every twenty-four working with Henrietta — after leaving the theatre, where she had already rehearsed for another ten.

The Prince and Princess of Wales occupied the royal box on the night of the performance, and the stalls were filled with members of the nobility, as well as representatives of the domestic and foreign press. To the astonishment of everyone present, Lillie was more than adequate. Although lacking in theatrical experience, she showed an instinct for the stage, and equally important, projected a strong and appealing personality across the gas footlights.

As the *Times* of London would say in its review, "Mrs. Langtry was not only lovely, which we expected, but surprised us by displaying a potential as an actress."

"She will become a star," the *Daily Telegraph* would declare, while the *Pall Mall Gazette* would take a critically sober approach: "The standing of Ellen Terry has not been threatened, nor will it be, but Mrs. Langtry will become an expert in the art of playing comedy."

Princess Alexandra led the large group that hurried to Lillie's dressing room after the performance, and placed a rare, impulsive kiss on her cheek. The Prince of Wales, close behind his wife, was even more enthusiastic. Oscar Wilde announced that he would write a play for the budding star, and Millais extracted a promise from her to pose for a new portrait in costume.

In all, Lillie achieved a triumph beyond her hopes. Only in high society circles had she placed herself beyond the pale. By becoming an actress she had forfeited her place in aristocratic ranks, regardless of the gesture made by the Princess of Wales. The good, aristocratic ladies would have been shocked to discover that Lillie Langtry no longer cared.

The managers of the Haymarket offered her a small but important part in a melodrama, *Ours*, by Tom Robertson, which was opening the following month, and Lillie promptly accepted. She went into rehearsal thirty-six hours after appearing in *She Stoops to Conquer*, and the play opened January 19, 1882. Lillie took only one day of rest, Christmas, when she dined with her parents at the Marylebone rectory. Presumably she learned from Mrs. Le Breton, who had just returned from a trip to Jersey, that Jeanne was thriving.

Clergymen of the Anglican Church were not enthusiastic supporters of the theatre in Queen Victoria's day, but

Reverend Le Breton evidently gave his daughter his full support. He attended her first charity performance at the Haymarket, and thereafter never missed one of her opening nights, attending each of them faithfully for the rest of his life. It has been suggested that his shame caused him to retire from his posts in Jersey, and to take a new parish, where he was relatively unknown. But at no time did he raise his voice against Lillie, nor did he indicate in public actions that he disapproved of her conduct.

"The loyalty of my parents," Lillie wrote years later, "sustained me in my darkest hours."

The darkness was beginning to lift. She was being paid the substantial salary of two hundred and fifty pounds per week, which enabled her to support herself and her child, start to repay Sir Allen Young and replenish her wardrobe, which was her greatest publicity asset. The newspaper reviewers were critical of *Ours*, but treated her with kindness, and her future on the stage seemed assured.

Her personal life, however, was becoming complicated. No longer protected by even the semblance of a marriage to Edward Langtry, she became fair game for every London man-about-town. The aristocratic ladies might shun her, but their husbands felt inhibited by no restrictions, and Lillie's dressing room was filled every night with flowers and other gifts. But she refused to accept engagements with anyone, and when she invited someone to her flat for a pre-theatre supper, she made certain there were other guests present. She was studying too hard to permit a late-night social life, she said, and would go out with no one after the evening's performance.

No one taught Lillie how to handle men, and she needed no instructions, but relied on her own instincts.

She received advice from one person, Prime Minister Gladstone, who came backstage after a performance to visit her. And for the rest of her life she followed, to the letter, the suggestions he gave her. "Mrs. Langtry," she reported him as saying, "you have become a truly public person, so you will be attacked, maligned and slandered, in your professional life, and in your personal life as well. Never reply to your critics! Never explain, no matter what you've said or done! If you attempt to defend yourself, you'll keep alive a controversy. As the French say, speech is silver, but silence is golden."

When *Ours* began to falter at the box office, the management of the Haymarket revived *She Stoops to Conquer*, and Lillie again played Kate. Uncounted thousands of Londoners wanted to see her, as did vast hordes of strangers in the city, so the two plays were alternated, and both did capacity business.

Henrietta Labouchère, who was still guiding her pupil, not only worked with Lillie for several hours every day, teaching her diction, movement and the myriad of technical details an accomplished actress needed, but drilling her in the reading of scores of roles. She was merciless, a taskmistress who never tired, and Lillie soon loathed the sight of her, but knew she needed Henrietta, and continued to depend on her.

It was Henrietta who refused to allow the Haymarket to give the Jersey Lily star billing, claiming she wasn't yet ready for it, and it was Henrietta who put off the provincial managers who were offering the budding star large sums for a tour.

By the summer of 1882 Lillie was still selling out at the Haymarket, but a change in Lillie's personal situation made it necessary for her to earn larger sums of money immediately. Edward Langtry was responsible for the new crisis in her life.

He had been coming to see her regularly, sometimes at the theatre, sometimes at her flat, and invariably begged her to take him back. Perhaps Lillie pitied him, but she could feel nothing else for him. His drinking had become a chronic problem, he looked seedy, and he was incapable of obtaining even menial employment. His father, hoping that stern treatment might cure him, cut off his allowance, and Edward was literally penniless.

He went at once to Lillie, explained his situation to her and demanded money. If she refused to give it to him, he said, he would make trouble for her. The nature of that trouble is not delineated in the correspondence of Lillie and her solicitor, but, by reading between the lines, it is possible that Edward intended to create a nuisance by revealing more than was proper concerning Lillie's relations with the Prince of Wales.

Whatever the threats may have been, Lillie capitulated, at least to an extent, but insisted on certain terms of her own. She agreed to pay Edward a monthly stipend, on condition that he never come to see her again. Should he break the agreement, she would have the right to cut him off.

The provinces were beckoning, and Lillie needed the money, so Henrietta put her own long-range plan into effect. Lillie would act as her own producer, ostensibly, but Henrietta actually would be in charge. They would form their own company, and Lillie would appear in four plays, none beyond her acting capacities. She would do Kate again, as well as the lead in *Ours*; she would have the chance to show off her legs as Rosalind in *As You Like It*, and would do Tom Taylor's light comedy, *An Unequal Match*.

In making these selections Henrietta demonstrated her understanding of both the star and those who would pay to see her. Lillie's talents would not be strained beyond the limits of her circumscribed experience, and the provincial audiences, anxious to gaze at the Professional Beauty about whom there had been so much talk, would have ample opportunity to revel in her appearance, but would not be required to think.

Lillie opened the tour in Manchester, playing in *She Stoops to Conquer*, and enjoyed an opening night triumph beyond the scope of most actresses' imagination. The audience cheered so lustily she was forced to take twenty-three curtain calls, the entire stage was filled with baskets of flowers, and her carefully rehearsed little speech of thanks was drowned by the roars of her admirers.

An enormous crowd gathered at the stage door, and became so enthusiastic that police reserves had to be summoned; Lillie was not allowed to leave the theatre until order had been restored. Then she saw that the horses had been unhitched from her carriage, which was being pulled by two dozen of her most enthusiastic admirers. Henrietta wisely refused to ride with her, and Lillie went off alone, her carriage followed by a huge mob of shouting torchbearers.

The men pulling the carriage demonstrated a complete lack of judgment, and lost control of the vehicle at the top of a hill. It shot down the street, narrowly missing several pedestrians and some other carriages, and finally came to rest against the side of a building. Lillie was badly frightened, although miraculously unhurt, and managed to smile as the crowd surged around her again. The carriage was hauled back to the hotel entrance, and she had to mount the roof and make a brief, graceful speech before the throng would release her. Manchester had never seen such an opening night.

Every performance in Edinburgh was sold out, and the success was repeated in every city of the Midlands and North. Then, after Lillie reached Edinburgh, the hot hand of scandal scalded her again, although she was blameless. The Prince of Wales, who had sent her flowers for each of her opening nights, wrote her a telegram requesting that she return to London for two days. A state dinner was being given for a prominent African tribal king whose homeland was under British protection, and the monarch had expressed a desire to meet the fabulous Jersey Lily. Albert Edward was delighted to make whatever arrangements he could.

Lillie received the telegram during her Saturday night performance, and apparently it did not occur to her to reply that she could not abandon her play. She had received a royal command, and intended to obey it. But, as she soon discovered, there was a serious obstacle that threatened her plans. The Scots were strict in their observance of the Sabbath, and no trains left Edinburgh for London on a Sunday morning.

But Lillie refused to be deterred, and hired a special train for the purpose, paying the sum of one hundred pounds, which, in a later era, seems ridiculously cheap. But in her own day not even millionaires hired special trains, and the world was stunned. British and Scottish newspapers printed the story, saying she returned to London for the state dinner, but making no mention of the Prince's request. The American and Continental press were less restrained, and the name of Lillie Langtry once again was coupled with that of the Prince of Wales.

The state dinner must have seemed anticlimactic, but it went off smoothly. The following day Lillie returned to Edinburgh, after canceling only one performance. There wasn't a vacant seat in the theatre for the rest of her stay.

One man in the audience who watched a number of performances and liked what he saw hadn't yet met Lillie. Henry E. Abbey, one of New York's more enterprising theatre owners and producers, had been in private correspondence with Henrietta Labouchère, and had crossed the Atlantic for the purpose of making his own judgments. Now he made an offer: Lillie would pay the salaries of her company, and he would give her fifty percent of the gross.

The offer was good, and Henrietta urged her pupil to accept, but Lillie was learning show business, and held out for sixty-five percent, with Abbey guaranteeing all traveling expenses, including those from England to America. After several days of haggling, the producer capitulated. "Mrs. Langtry," he wrote the following year, "is as tough a businesswoman as she is a lovely lady. She may smell of a delicious perfume, but nothing creases her hide except dollar bills."

Shortly before the news was announced that Lillie intended to invade the United States, another storm broke. Lillie created a new precedent by being the first woman to endorse a commercial product. The Pears Soap Company paid her one hundred and thirty-two pounds for signing a statement to the effect that she owed her flawless skin to her regular use of the product.

Ladies of quality were horrified, and it was said in high circles that Mrs. Langtry sold herself with the abandon of a prostitute. It would be more than a decade before impoverished aristocrats followed the Jersey Lily's example and began to endorse commercial products. As for Lillie, she calmly pocketed the money, and later wrote that she had requested the odd sum because she happened to weigh one hundred and thirty-two pounds at the time.

The news that she was going to America was too much. She had been a curiosity in England, but she would be exhibiting herself on the far side of the Atlantic before audiences attracted only by her notoriety. Lillie ignored the criticism, and contented herself with the knowledge that, if successful, she could earn as much as a quarter of a million dollars.

Henrietta prepared swiftly and shrewdly for the new British invasion of the former colonies. She hired a small company, which included her sister, Kate Hodson, an actress of considerable experience. She rented the Imperial Theatre in London for purposes of brief try-outs, and prepared a repertory of three plays. Lillie was already familiar with two of them, *As You Like It* and *An Unequal Match*. The third, *The Honeymoon*, was a frivolous work in which the star would be required to do little except look lovely and speak simple lines. Henrietta was taking no chances, and didn't intend to stretch the talents of the Jersey Lily.

On September 30 the trial engagement opened at the Imperial, with the Prince and Princess of Wales in attendance. Their presence made it necessary for society to buy tickets, too, and the aristocrats who had been damning Lillie had to swallow their harsh words and their pride. The engagement ended two weeks later, on September 13, and after the performance the Prince of Wales gave a sumptuous farewell supper in Lillie's honor. The ever-discreet British press made no mention of the event, but the publicity-wise Abbey saw to it that the American newspapers learned the details of the party, and hundreds of columns appeared in print throughout the United States while Lillie was on the high seas.

She sailed from Liverpool in October 14, and was scheduled to reach New York nine days later. The *Arizona* was an American vessel, flagship of the Guion Line, and Lillie elected to travel on it as a gesture certain to please her chauvinistic hosts. Her quarters were adequate, but she spent little time in her suite. She dined at the captain's table, and was surrounded by admirers when she walked on deck, took tea in the salon or merely stood at the rail, looking at the sea. In fact, Henrietta found it difficult to disengage her long enough to participate in brief rehearsals with the members of her company.

The New York to which Lillie Langtry was traveling was a brawling, bustling, contradictory city. So many immigrants were passing through her gates that no one knew her population in the autumn of 1882, although the census of 1880 had credited her with more than two million inhabitants. The center of town was Twenty-third Street, but the city was expanding northward on Manhattan Island at a rapid rate, and land was already so valuable that new buildings were as high as eight to ten stories.

Because land was so expensive, even the wealthy lived in quarters that would have been considered cramped by the English aristocracy. The most prominent families lived in brownstone houses of ten to fifteen small rooms, with tiny yards and gardens that opened onto the rear.

The poor, like the impoverished everywhere, were far less fortunate, and in New York they suffered from particularly inadequate housing. More than one million immigrants from Europe were pouring through the city every year, and many of them stayed, so it was impossible to construct new dwellings fast enough to accommodate them. It was common for entire families of eight to twelve people to crowd into a single room, and consider themselves lucky that they had found any quarters at all.

The contrasts between the classes were marked. The poor lived in semi-starvation, but the wealthy dined in restaurants where the menu was remarkably varied, and where the portions were so large that visitors from abroad were amazed. Two of the most popular were Delmonico's, an ornate establishment where the rich and socially prominent dined, and Pfaff's, which rightly regarded itself as an institution.

More than a restaurant, it had become an informal club for people in the literary and theatrical worlds. Actors and actresses could dine there without being subjected to harassment by an admiring public, and would be sure to meet playwrights, producers and directors there. Several book and newspaper publishers had regular tables, as did a number of authors. The management was loyal to its clientele, and the house quietly carried those who lacked funds. Walt Whitman had eaten there for many years, even when his wallet had been empty. And Ada Isaacs Menken, who had achieved theatrical notoriety, if not renown, by riding through an auditorium strapped to the back of a horse while wearing flesh-colored tights, had made Pfaff's her second home.

The arts were booming in America, and New York was leading the way, which frequently differed from that of the Old World. American authors and playwrights were striking out on their own, ignoring the trends in England and on the Continent, and such dramatists as Dion Boucicault, although Irish-born and trained in the London stage, thought of himself as American and actually exerted a strong influence on the English and European theatre.

Edwin Booth, the greatest of American actors, had made his profession respectable in the United States, and acted at his own theatre, which he built at Twenty-third Street and Sixth Avenue. He had played in London with Henry Irving, and in 1882 had just returned home from a triumphal tour of Germany, where he was regarded as the greatest actor of the age. He often teamed with Helena Modjeska, who was regarded as the first lady of the American theatre.

One of the newer influences in the American theatre was a director-dramatist-actor, David Belasco, a San Franciscan who was planning a move to New York. Although still in his twenties, he was already a legend in California, where he had directed three hundred plays, written more than one hundred and acted in almost two hundred.

Visitors from abroad often were startled by the lusty vigor of New World living, and were disturbed by relative indifference to English, French and other cultures. Charles Dickens, generally regarded as the greatest and most popular novelist of his age, had regarded the United States as barbarian. Oscar Wilde, who had been in the country since January, 1882, on a lecture tour, had written, "America is a land of unmatched vitality and vulgarity, a people who care not at all about values other than their own, and who, when they make up their minds, love you and hate you with a frightening, passionate zeal."

Wilde had returned to New York from the hinterlands he detested, and was on hand to greet Lillie. The day before her arrival he told the New York *World*, in an interview that was widely reprinted, "I would rather have discovered Mrs. Langtry than to have discovered America. You have asked whether she is indeed a beauty, and I can reply to such nonsense only by saying that you will see her for yourself. No, I will go farther. She is the most beautiful woman in all the world, and will be a beauty still at eighty-five. It was for such as she that Troy was destroyed, and well it might have been!"

On the morning of October 23, 1882, Henry E. Abbey and his partner, John Schoeffel, went out to the far end of the harbor in a rented boat to meet the Jersey Lily. Accompanying them were members of their staff, twenty to thirty newspaper reporters, Oscar Wilde and a brass band, which played "God

Save the Queen" as the boat drew up alongside the larger vessel.

Lillie awaited the company in the salon, and the first to enter was Wilde, who presented her with an enormous bouquet of white roses. He had selected white, he explained, because he had known the color wouldn't clash with her costume.

Lillie had dressed for the occasion in a severe, figure-hugging dress of dark blue, and had worn none of her jewelry. Her graciousness and charm overwhelmed the press, which had expected her to be haughty. She shook hands with each of the reporters, and she remembered their names, which impressed them. She exercised extraordinary patience during the mass interview, and answered all the questions except one.

"What do you think of America, Mrs. Langtry?" was the first, inevitably, although she had yet to set foot on New World soil.

Lillie fielded it smartly. "I have spent nine days on board an American ship," she said, "so I already know your kindness and your hospitality. I am enchanted."

"What is your opinion of American women?"

"I have often been told they are the most beautiful in all the world, and I am sure the reports are accurate."

"Have you seen the Prince of Wales lately, Mrs. Langtry?"

Lillie's composure remained unchanged, but she suddenly became hard of hearing. The question was not repeated, and the reporters refrained from asking others like it. The initial interview set a pattern, and thereafter, no matter where Lillie traveled, she suffered a hearing affliction whenever the Prince of Wales was mentioned.

The reaction of *The New York Times* was typical: "One may see a hundred as pretty on Fifth Avenue at any time, but if they could carry themselves with the ease, grace, and self-possession of Mrs. Langtry, they would be envied. She was asked all sorts of questions, sensible, idiotic, impertinent and irrelevant, and good-naturedly answered them all. She does not disappoint those who have been singing her praises."

A large suite had been engaged for Lillie in a quietly elegant hotel, the Albemarle, which was located on Madison Square, a short distance from the Park Theatre, where she would appear. Sarah Bernhardt had used the same suite on her last American tour.

More reporters came to the hotel, and again Lillie dealt with them patiently and graciously, answering questions for more than two hours. Wanting to see something of the city, she went out for a drive with Henrietta that afternoon, and to her astonishment was immediately recognized. Her coach was followed by such a large crowd that traffic on Fifth Avenue became snarled, and the police had to rescue her from her admirers. Then she visited the Lord & Taylor dry-goods store on Broadway, and a near riot made it impossible for her to do any shopping. She was taken to the manager's office, and a squad of policemen escorted her back to the hotel.

Abbey had done his work well. There were posters advertising the appearance of the Jersey Lily everywhere, and Henrietta, who could move around freely, reported that there were photographs of Lillie in literally hundreds of shop windows.

The flourishing song-writing industry tried to cash in on Lillie's popularity, and a numbers of composers had turned out waltzes, marches and polkas in her honor. "The Jersey Lily Waltz," by one Henry Le York, eventually became one of the most popular songs of the 1882-83 winter.

A dinner was given in Lillie's honor on her first night in New York by Pierre Lorillard, a financier whom she had met in London, and she found Delmonico's as sumptuous as any Old

World restaurant. "The Americans," she wrote to her parents, "do not eat buffalo steaks and bear meat. The food here is superb, but I find the portions so large I shall gain weight unless I exercise great care in my diet."

One unpleasant incident, minor but irritating, marred Lillie's American welcome. At Delmonico's she saw several members of high society whom she had met some years earlier in London, and spoke to them. But the good ladies snubbed her royally, a reminder that she was now beyond the pale of New York's aristocrats, just as she was no longer received in many of London's best homes.

But there were limitless compensations, not the least of them the generosity of American business. A wine importer delivered a case of champagne, and all he asked in return was that she order a bottle at a restaurant. Two competing piano manufacturers insisted that she accept their products, and asked nothing in return. Dressmakers who had, somehow, managed to learn her precise measurements, inundated her with gifts of gowns, and begged her to wear them. Milliners, shoemakers, glovers and corset makers did the same. The proprietors of restaurants invited Lillie to dine in their establishments as their guests. The owner of a fleet of hansom cabs put a carriage at her disposal for the duration of her stay in New York. America was pouring her products in Lillie's lap from a horn of plenty.

There was such a great demand for tickets to her opening in *An Unequal Match* on October 30 that Abbey conceived of an unprecedented stunt. On the night of October 24 an auction for all opening night seats except those to be used by the newspaper drama critics was held at the Turf Club Theatre on Twenty-sixth Street. The usual price for orchestra seats was $2, for the balcony $1 and for the gallery 50c. Lillie made the front pages when a front box sold for $325, and a group of ardent theatre-goers from the Union League Club bought a block at $17.50 per ticket. The cheapest orchestra seats sold at $10, those in the balcony brought $5, and $3.25 was paid for gallery seats. Not even lively New York had ever witnessed such a spectacle.

The wily, hard-bitten James Gordon Bennett, publisher of the New York *Herald*, assigned a reporter to cover literally every minute of every day in Lillie's life. Recognizing the publicity value of a limitless stream of stories, Lillie allowed the reporter, Bury I. Dasent, to accompany her on her rounds whenever possible. Dasent promptly fell in love with her, and his stories were ecstatic.

He was also an enterprising newspaperman, and one day he played a major role in the making of history — of a sort. As part of the publicity build-up for her theatrical appearance, Lillie was asked to sell tickets for a dinner at Sherry's restaurant that was being given for charity.

At Dasent's suggestion Lillie went down to Wall Street, with the reporter accompanying her. Streets were crowded and narrow in the financial district, and such a huge throng gathered that the police were called in to extricate Lillie.

She went into the Stock Exchange, where Dasent guided her to the balcony. Word of her presence spread quickly, and transactions on the floor below were forgotten as members and their staffs hurried to vantage points. Lillie's presence was announced, and precedent was smashed when transactions on the Exchange were suspended long enough for formal greetings to be extended to her.

Dasent did not record her words of thanks, but the following day's *Herald* featured a banner headline: MRS. LANGTRY PANICS WALL STREET.

Still not satisfied with his efforts, Dasent suggested that Lillie sell some tickets for the charity affair to the most powerful financier in the country, J. Pierpont Morgan. Lillie was agreeable, Morgan was obviously curious, and she was admitted without delay to his private office. Needless to add, he purchased a number of tickets.

But Lillie remained circumspect, and Dasent could not persuade her to reveal for publication the details of the conversations in the inner sanctum. "We have many mutual friends," she said, "and I find Mr. Morgan a delightful man."

Dasent scored another beat several days prior to the scheduled opening. A cablegram was delivered to Lillie at the hotel while she was rehearsing at the theatre, and it was delivered to her there by the thoughtful management. Dasent happened to be sitting next to her when she opened it, and saw it was from the Prince of Wales. He told the *Herald* readers that much, but was in no position to reveal any additional details.

Forty-eight hours before the opening, a fire destroyed the Park Theatre, and for a few hours it was feared that the catastrophe would force a postponement of the Jersey Lily's American debut. But Abbey was able to rent another theatre, Wallack's, and the accident became something of a blessing in disguise, as it was larger than the Park, which made more seats available.

The President of the United States, Chester A. Arthur, had been sent a pair of seats by a thoughtful Abbey, but the pressure of government business kept him in Washington, so he sent his regrets, along with his son, Chester, Jr., to represent him. Others in the first night audience included members of some of America's most prominent families, among them Vanderbilts, Goulds, Belmonts, Lorillards and Cuttings. Another spectator, who would play a major role in Lillie's future, was the lean, eccentric attorney, Abe Hummel, who had successfully defended some of America's most notorious criminals.

Someone else in the audience did not go unnoticed by the press. Her name was Lillian Russell, and she was twenty-one, eight years Lillie's junior. She had made her own theatrical debut the previous year, and although her talents were dubious, she was the American entry in the international beauty sweepstakes. Her admirers called her the loveliest woman on earth, and not until they saw Lillie did some of them desert her. It was duly reported to a waiting world that the exquisite Miss Russell was poker-faced, did not applaud and refused to express a public opinion of her rival. She did not return to her seat after the last intermission.

Dasent's interview with Lillie on the subject could not have endeared her to her competition. "What is your opinion of Lillian Russell, Mrs. Langtry?" he quoted himself in his *Herald* article.

"Who?"

"She is an actress, and is regarded as very beautiful."

"We haven't met," Lillie said, and that was the end of the matter.

Oscar Wilde had been hired by the *World* as a guest reviewer, and representatives of all the other New York newspapers were on hand. So were critics and reporters from many other parts of the United States, among them newsmen from Chicago, Philadelphia, Washington, Pittsburgh, Cleveland, Cincinnati, Boston, Hartford, St. Louis and other cities. In all, Abbey revealed, he had been forced to put aside an unprecedented two hundred and fifty seats for representatives of the press.

The opening night receipts were almost seven thousand dollars, a record in the American theatre, and a long line at the box office assured the Jersey Lily of success, regardless of the critics' verdict. Two large horse-drawn wagons were already standing in the alley outside the stage door, both loaded with floral tributes to the actress who hadn't yet demonstrated her talent to an American audience.

No one, including Lillie herself, had any idea that the curtain would rise on a new era, and that for the better part of the next five years Lillie Langtry would spend virtually all of her time in the United States, and would become an American citizen as well as a national institution. A town would be named after her, she would become independently wealthy, and a turbulent love affair would bring her fresh notoriety. She would suffer heartbreak, and in almost miraculous growth, would achieve a stature as one of the best actresses of her era. Life would never again be dull for the one-time nobody from Saint Helier.

VII

WILLIAM WINTER OF THE NEW YORK *TRIBUNE* was
the dean of American drama critics. Scholarly, erudite and
profound, he had been the most important member of his
profession since the end of the Civil War, when he joined the
Tribune staff. The author of a long list of books on the theatre,
he had been the first to recognize Edwin Booth as a great
actor, the first to hail the sensitivity of Modjeska, the first to
call Sarah Bernhardt incomparable. His reviews were respected
in England, France and Germany as well as in all parts of the
United States, and had he given Lillie Langtry a harsh review,
her success would have been short-lived. To the astonishment
of those who believed her an inferior actress, he treated her
with unexpected, gentle sensitivity:

> It is unfortunate that Mrs. Langtry has chosen to appear in
> her American inaugural in a play that shows its age, since her
> own youth and vitality are among her greater assets. On the
> other hand, she may have been wise not to attempt too much.
>
> The crudities of her performance were obvious last night,
> although I may not be regarded as a gentleman for telling the
> truth. However, her freshness, charm and promise are equally
> great, and it is to be hoped that she will make progress in her
> elected profession. If she does, she will be hailed as an actress
> with the enthusiasm that now trumpets her appearance as a
> great beauty.

Some of the other reviews were equally ambivalent. The
Times complimented her beauty, but damned her acting with
faint praise. Bennett's *Herald* was reserved, and so was his

evening newspaper, the *Telegram*. The *Post*, the city's oldest newspaper, called her performance "the work of a clever, attractive amateur who has been subjected to a brief course of intelligent training."

Oscar Wilde, writing in the *World*, pulled out all the stops, but said little about Lillie's acting ability, whose limits he thoroughly understood. In a portion of his three-column article he said:

> It is only in the best Greek gems, on the silver coins of Syracuse, or among the marble fringes of the Parthenon frieze that one can find the ideal representation of the marvelous beauty of that face which laughed through the leaves last night as Hester Grazebrook.
>
> Pure Greek it is, with the low grave forehead, the exquisitely arched brow; the noble chiselling of the mouth, shaped as if it were the mouthpiece of an instrument of music, the supreme and splendid curve of the cheek, the augustly pillared throat which bears it all.
>
> The character of Hester requires no small ability on the part of the actress who sustains it.
>
> If I was to express the opinion, in which I think all who were present last night might well honestly agree with me, it is that Mrs. Langtry went through the phases with taste, feeling and force. I do not see what higher commendation I can pay her.

In all, the reviews were better than any that Lillie had received in London, and she could not have been too badly disappointed. But she was anxious to repair her image, and chose the most forthright route. Her decision caused an argument with Henrietta Labouchère, who disagreed with it, so Lillie proceeded on her own. Her increasingly frequent quarrels with Henrietta dated from this incident, but if they hadn't fought about reviews, Henrietta probably would have found something else. As her husband wrote to Lillie from London, "I marvel at your ability to remain on good terms with that termagant, who is not happy unless she is creating misery for someone else."

Lillie's idea was simple. She wanted to meet Winter by "accident," and then charm him. Henry Abbey believed that nothing could be lost, and saw the potential of a gain, so he arranged a dinner engagement with the critic at Pfaff's. Lillie "happened" to be dining alone a few tables away. It was typical of the restaurant that no one paid any attention to anyone else. Virtually everybody who dined at Pfaff's was a celebrity, and it was the strict custom to mind one's own business.

William Winter made no objection, however, when Abbey discovered Lillie sitting alone, and suggested that she join them. The lovely young woman who had melted the reserves of the stern Gladstone required less time to make Winter her friend. Her wit and intelligence surprised him, her beauty numbed him, and he was flattered beyond measure by her breathless attention.

What was motivated for business reasons became a far different relationship. Lillie and the austere Winter developed a genuine fondness for each other, and were close friends for the rest of their lives. It was almost irrelevant that, thereafter, Winter unfailingly gave Lillie's stage appearances his most glowing reviews.

Shortly after Lillie's opening in New York she met the man who would mean more to her than anyone else she had ever known or would know. Many years later, in her sixties, she told Somerset Maugham that he had been "the great love of my life."

Frederick Gebhard, Jr., soon known as Freddie to the newspaper readers of two continents and the British Isles, was twenty-two when Lillie met him, which made him seven years her junior. He was tall, with black hair and dark eyes, and had the magnificent physique of an athlete who swam, played tennis, rode, boxed, fenced and handled a sailboat.

The son of a Baltimore dry-goods merchant who had died several years earlier, Fred had inherited a fortune conservatively estimated at five million dollars. Most of his contemporaries believed he enjoyed an annual income of approximately $80,000 to $100,000. He had considerable social standing in New York and Baltimore, but had never played an active social role. Until he met Lillie he was rather retiring, and hostesses with eligible daughters had found it difficult to lure him to their homes.

Some of the more romantic reporters covering the continuing Lillie Langtry story claimed that she and Fred fell in love at first sight, but they were exaggerating. Fred fell in love with Lillie, but she was indifferent to him, and he was forced to pursue her. He invited her to go riding and ice-skating. He took her driving and went with her on long walks. He dined alone with her, sometimes at the fashionable restaurants, sometimes at German beer gardens and other middle-class hideouts where she might escape public recognition.

The enterprising Dasent discovered that Fred purchased a necklace and bracelet of matching diamonds for Lillie at Tiffany's, and enlightened the *Herald*'s readers with the details. He sent her the gems in a huge bouquet of flowers, and she did not return the gift. Overnight Fred Gebhard was catapulted into international prominence, much to his annoyance.

He had been brought up to believe that a gentleman lived quietly, avoiding the limelight, but it was impossible to remain anonymous when one associated with Lillie. They were mobbed when they went walking or ice-skating. Sometimes all the diners in a restaurant seemed to descend on their table at the same time. And whenever they went anywhere, one or more newspapers commented. Fred hated the press with a passionate hatred.

He didn't get along, either, with Henrietta Labouchère, who disapproved of him. Henrietta was no prude, but she thought it harmful to Lillie's image to be seen so frequently with the young millionaire. She wanted Lillie to spend more time rehearsing for *As You Like It*, which the critics would treat seriously. And she thought it wrong of Lillie to accept the expensive necklace and bracelet.

Lillie supposedly told her to mind her own business, that she had taken the gifts because she hadn't wanted to hurt Fred's feelings, and she insisted he meant nothing to her.

The reviews of *As You Like It* confirmed Henrietta's worst fears. America might be a sprawling, brawling country, but her people were highly moral, and apparently shared Henrietta's opinion that it was wrong for a married woman to be seen so frequently with a dashing young bachelor. The reviews reflected this view, Henrietta believed. Whether her analysis was correct is less important than the fact that the reviews were the worst Lillie had ever received.

The critics agreed that she looked the part of Rosalind, but said that her portrayal was stiff and unnatural. The *Times* declared that Ellen Terry had remarked on the perfection of Lillie's diction, but added, "The role requires the services of an actress, not that of a pretty elocutionist."

Only William Winter was kind, and may have saved Lillie. He praised her beauty, grace and charm, but carefully refrained from commenting on the quality of her performance.

Henrietta Labouchère felt that her own professional standing was being injured, and issued an unprecedented statement to the press. The following day's *Herald* led the way in proclaiming THE LANGTRY SCANDAL. Mrs. Labouchère, Dasent wrote, "officially announced that she disapproved of Mrs. Langtry's proceedings in this country, had no further connection with her, personally, or with her theatrical engagements, and intends to return to England after visiting friends in Washington."

The details of what happened during the next twenty-four hours are not known. Lillie subsequently claimed that she offered Henrietta financial remuneration for her interest in their joint enterprise, but that her mentor refused to take any money. Henrietta, however, claimed that no offer was made.

The press enjoyed the bonanza. The United States was, indeed, a highly moral country in which the principles of Victorian morality were observed. So Henrietta was presented as a champion of virtue, Lillie as a fallen angel, and Freddie Gebhard was portrayed as a conniving seducer.

Lillie took Gladstone's advice to heart, and refused to comment.

But Fred Gebhard was less worldly, and made the mistake of writing a letter to the New York *Sun*, which he regarded as Lillie's principal tormentor. So angry that he wasn't logical, Fred's epistle made up in fury what it lacked in grammar and spelling. Mrs. Labouchère's departure, he said, was caused by the harmless gift of a basket of fruit he had made to Mrs. Langtry. Things had come to a pretty state of affairs if a gentleman couldn't make a token gift to a lady whom every man in America admired. He added:

> Mrs. Langtry could do no wrong, even if she wanted to, because she is watched by Mrs. Labouchère, by a younger

sister of that woman who is a better actress than she is a watchdog, which isn't saying much, by a Miss Pattison of Mrs. Labouchère's staff who never stops spying on Mrs. Langtry, and in my opinion she is jealous, by the manager of the hotel, by the hotel servants, and even by people on the staff of the Wallack's Theatre. I am willing to wagger [sic] that these spies are also on the payroll of the snooping Mrs. Labouchère. I challenge her to produce her own marriage certtificat, [sic] as proof that she has a right to criticize a lady who has done no wrong.

This remarkable communication was published on December 9, and the newspapers of the following day joined in the uproar. A member of the cast was found who defended the bewildered secretary, Miss Pattison, from charges of espionage. The reporters again besieged Lillie, who smiled pleasantly, gave them tea and refused to discuss anything but the raw, early winter that had come to New York.

In the excitement the reviews of *As You Like It* were forgotten. But the publicity made the public all the more anxious to see the Jersey Lily, and Abbey reported to Lillie that the advance sale at the box office for the next four weeks amounted to an unprecedented sixty-five thousand dollars. It was obvious that the controversy over Lillie's morals was better for business than the most splendid of reviews would have been.

Necessity caused a major change in the management of the company's American tour, and Lillie announced that she would take charge herself. Abbey protested that she lacked the experience, and offered to provide her with someone from his own staff, but she demurred. No one could look out for the interests of the Jersey Lily with the single-minded devotion that Lillie Langtry would show.

What developed out of need proved to be a proverbial blessing in disguise. Lillie demonstrated a natural aptitude for the handling of business details, and the rest of her career she knew no manager other than herself. She was as hard-headed as the men with whom she dealt, veteran showmen who were not impressed by either glamour or beauty.

A flair for publicity also led her to make another decision that was even bolder. Fred Gebhard, she told Abbey, would accompany her on the tour, which was scheduled to begin in Boston, and would act as her bodyguard.

The producer was shocked by the idea. No matter what her private morals, a married woman living in the 1880's could not travel around the United States with a wealthy, handsome young bachelor who made no secret of his love for her. Such things simply weren't done.

But Lillie was indifferent to gossip, and literally didn't care how much she might be criticized. As the boom in New York sales had just demonstrated, scandal was good for business. What she didn't need to spell out was that she found Fred good company, and undoubtedly enjoyed his gifts. From what he indicated to others — or what they said he indicated — he had not yet had an affair with Lillie, who was still holding him at arm's length.

It was at this juncture that one of the most celebrated and colorful Americans of the age began to play an important role in Lillie's life. Diamond Jim Brady, ostentatious, vulgar and generous, was a part-time stock market gambler, part-time businessman and self-styled railroad magnate. He always wore a huge diamond stickpin and cufflinks, and he gave his favorite gems to a remarkably large number of his friends. An inveterate party-giver, who thought nothing of inviting forty or fifty people to dine at Delmonico's or Sherry's, he was a teetotaler who compensated for his dislike of liquor by eating gargantuan meals.

He had met Lillie soon after her arrival in New York, and had already given her a large diamond ring and a diamond brooch, asking nothing in return except the privilege of being seen in her company at the restaurants he frequented. In a later time he would have been called a celebrity hunter who acquired a renown of his own by virtue of his association with the famous.

It was Brady who told Lillie that someone of her stature could not go on tour in the ordinary railroad accommodations available to ordinary people. She needed a private railroad car, and he obtained the loan of one called *The City of Worcester*, which boasted a living room, three bedrooms and a private bath. Lillie enjoyed the luxury so much that she developed a taste for private railroad cars, with results that were spectacular. Those activities, however, were still in the future.

The actors who had accompanied her from England were badly upset by Henrietta Labouchère's defection, but it was Kate Hodson, Henrietta's sister, who saved the day. Announcing that she had no intention of abandoning the tour and returning home, Kate said — in print — that her sister was a lifelong troublemaker who couldn't get along with anyone. The rest of the company grew calmer, and accepted Lillie as the manager as well as the star of the tour.

A huge crowd gathered to see the Jersey Lily depart on board *The City of Worcester* in early January, 1883. At her side was Fred Gebhard, who threatened to punch several reporters who made the mistake of trying to interview him.

Boston maintained its traditional reserve, and only a few people were on hand when the train arrived there. That night a dinner was given in Lillie's honor at the exclusive Papyrus

Club, many of whose members were authors and artists, men with whom she always felt at home. The following night she opened her engagement at the Globe Theatre, and the audience responded so enthusiastically that she took ten curtain calls.

The newspaper reviews the following day were brutal, the worst Lillie had ever received. The critics said she was an amateur, criticized her acting as shallow and her performance as lacking in sincerity. She might be pretty enough, if one was attracted by her type of beauty, but her appearance on the stage was a sham and a disgrace.

Long lines that formed outside the Globe Theatre mocked the critics, however, and within forty-eight hours every seat for the two-week engagement had been sold. Lillie was rapidly learning that she was an attraction, no matter what the critics thought of her.

Quick to sense Boston's conservatism, Lillie acted accordingly. Fred dined with her in her hotel suite before the evening performance, and sometimes took her to and from the theatre, but made no public appearances with her. She was a model of discretion, and when she went sight-seeing, shopping or merely took a walk in the Common, she was escorted by one or another member of the British Consulate staff. The newspapers made virtually no mention of Fred's presence, and he remained invisible.

Philadelphia, the next city on the tour, cast aside its own traditional restraint with a loud whoop. When Lillie's train approached the city it was halted several miles from the station by the police, and the passengers disembarked in the yards. Such an enormous crowd had filled the terminal that the authorities could not guarantee the Jersey Lily's safety.

A challenge awaited Lillie in Philadelphia, and she met it eagerly. The best hotel in the city was the Bellevue, which took pride in its aristocratic clientele, and the previous year it had been very much in the news when it had denied Sarah Bernhardt the right to engage rooms there. The Bellevue did not cater to actresses.

Lillie would not consider the idea of staying anywhere else, even though Henry Abbey had warned her she might be in for trouble. But the management was quick to assign her a suite, and Fred Gebhard was given another. The hotel considered the social credentials of both Mrs. Langtry and Mr. Gebhard impeccable, and it didn't matter that she was, coincidentally, a member of the acting profession.

The Boston experience was repeated. The critics attacked Lillie, but the public thronged to see her, and there wasn't a vacant seat in the theatre for her entire engagement.

She was discovering, however, that Fred's presence could be embarrassing when there was no chaperon on hand. She had been corresponding with her sister-in-law, Agnes Langtry, who had long admired her, and thought a great many problems would be solved if Agnes joined her. She sent an invitation by cablegram, offering to pay all expenses, and Agnes accepted by return cable, promising to come immediately.

The offer had been extended just in time to avoid additional trouble. A prominent member of the House of Representatives, Richelieu Robinson, made a virulent attack on Lillie in a speech delivered on the floor of the House. He accused her of demoralizing the American stage and corrupting American society, and suggested that she be deported. The time had come for Lillie to behave with greater discretion at all times.

The shy, retiring Agnes arrived just in time to accompany the troupe to Chicago. She had no idea why she had been summoned, but soon learned, because Lillie needed all the help she could get.

Chicago, the fastest-growing city in the United States, had already achieved the reputation it would maintain for the better part of another century. Tough and rude, pugnacious and incredibly energetic, it stood on ceremony with no one. Men fought for the sheer love of combat and shouted at attractive women in the streets. A dozen languages were spoken, fortunes were made overnight, and the race went to the swift, the strong and the bold.

Lillie had to endure a baptism of press crossfire when her train arrived. A reporter from the *Inter-Ocean* persisted in asking about her relations with the Prince of Wales, and not even her bland refusal to reply deterred him. Others questioned her closely about Fred Gebhard. Then she repaired to the Grand Pacific Hotel, where Fred occupied a suite directly above hers. Reporters took up a watch in the corridors, and Fred could not come to her sitting room for a meal without bumping into them. On several occasions only the intervention of the hotel management prevented a fist fight.

There were compensations, of course. Business was booming, in spite of the usual attack by the critics, and the entire engagement was sold out. Also, Oscar Wilde had given Lillie an introduction to the woman he had described as the most gracious hostess in Chicago, Mrs. Herbert Ayer. Later to be known as Harriet Hubbard Ayer when she started her own cosmetics business, Mrs. Ayer extended her hospitality, and the two women formed a friendship that lasted for the remainder of their lives.

There were other pleasures, too. Lillie went ice-skating every afternoon in Lincoln Park, but had to give up the sport at the request of the police when the crowds who came to watch her became too large and unruly to handle. She discovered the shopping in Chicago was good, and went out on a number of occasions to the dry-goods stores, but an unpleasant incident that occurred one afternoon put an end to those activities, too.

She went shopping that day, escorted by Frederick A. Schwab, Abbey's representative on the tour, when a mob surrounded them on the street. In an attempt to obtain souvenirs of the Jersey Lily, people began snatching at her hat, veil, gloves and the fur piece she wore around her neck. Schwab tried to protect her, someone struck him and he struck back. A riot was barely averted, a police squad arriving just in time to disperse the crowd and rescue Lillie.

An even more serious incident erupted at the Haverley Theatre on the night of the final performance. A small segment of the audience was unruly, and began to throw candy at the bald head of the orchestra conductor in the pit. Soon candy and other objects were being hurled onto the stage, loud shouts interrupted the performance, and Lillie, who was onstage herself at the time, ordered the curtain lowered. The near-riot was choked off, and only a few members of the audience asked for refunds. The others, presumably, had received their money's worth.

But the events in Chicago were relatively mild when seen in the light of what happened in St. Louis, where a series of incidents doubled Lillie's notoriety and created newspaper headlines around the world.

One morning Fred Gebhard joined Lillie in her suite at the Southern Hotel for breakfast; it should be noted that Fred was fully dressed, while Lillie was wearing a peignoir that the incident soon made famous.

Colonel A. B. Cunningham, one of the editors of the St. Louis *Globe-Democrat*, who had made a reputation for himself as a fearless reporter in his younger days, chose that hour to call on Lillie, seeking an interview. Her maid went to the door, and said that Mrs. Langtry could not receive callers.

Hearing voices in the sitting room, Cunningham pushed past the maid, and came upon Lillie and Fred at breakfast. His manner that of a public prosecutor, the Colonel questioned the couple about their relationship.

Lillie not only refused to answer, as was her custom, but would not permit Fred to reply. She was under no obligation to explain her private business to anyone, including the press.

The highly moral Cunningham returned to the *Globe-Democrat* office, and wrote a blistering article, in which he condemned Lillie as immoral, branded Fred Gebhard as her lover and urged the citizens of St. Louis to organize a boycott of her performances in the city.

His piece appeared in that afternoon's edition. Lillie, who had gone to the theatre to prepare for her opening performance that evening, did not see it. Fred read it, however, and was furious. He had the good sense not to mention it to Lillie, as he didn't want to upset her before her opening.

The couple dined together in her suite, and Lillie returned to the theatre. Fred, who was still fuming, went down to the hotel lobby to smoke a cigar. An excerpt from the next day's New York *Sun* tells the story that promptly made headlines from Maine to California, and from Edinburgh to Berlin and Paris:

> At half past 7 o'clock last evening Mr. Fred Gebhard, who has gained distinction through his acquaintance with Mrs. Langtry, was smoking an after-dinner cigar in the rotunda of

the Southern Hotel, when he espied Mr. A. B. Cunningham of the *Globe Democrat*'s local force standing near the west end of the office counter. He stepped up to Mr. Cunningham and an excited scene ensued, which attracted the attention of nearly all of the large number of persons who thronged the rotunda.

Changing a cane which he carried to his left hand, Mr. Gebhard shook his finger in Mr. Cunningham's face and called him an infamous liar. Mr. Cunningham also shifted his cane, and putting his hand in his trousers pocket, waved Mr. Gebhard off with his left, saying, "I don't want anything to do with you, sir," at the same time stepping backward.

"But I want to have something to do with you, sir. You are an infamous liar," said Mr. Gebhard, advancing again on Mr. Cunningham.

"Keep away from me, I don't want to have anything to do with you, sir," said Mr. Cunningham, continuing his retrograde movement eastward along the counter and waving the enemy off with his left hand while he still kept his right hand in his trousers pocket.

In this manner they proceeded around the corner of the counter, and down to the south end, the epithet being repeated several times by Mr. Gebhard, and Mr. Cunningham's conservative answer following each time. At one point Mr. Gebhard was led aside by a friend, who advised him to desist, as he had gone as far as he could in denouncing Mr. Cunningham publicly; but he was returning toward the latter when a policeman, who had been summoned by the clerk (Mr. Willard) interposed, and by Mr. Willard's order Mr. Cunningham was led from the hotel.

As Mr. Cunningham is a very powerful and active man, and as Mr. Gebhard is a vigorous six-footer weighing nearly 200 pounds, the spectators, who had expected to see a gladiatorial exhibition, were disappointed by the interference.

It is said tonight that Mr. Cunningham has challenged Mr. Gebhard to fight a duel.

Once again Fred Gebhard had jumped off the deep end, and millions enjoyed the splash he made. The affair built in intensity, and meanwhile the lines at the box office grew longer. Before the smoke finally cleared away, Lillie's engagement of two weeks was sold out.

The complications were endless, graphic, and for a time threatened to be serious. Cunningham was a veteran of the Confederate Army, and was known to be a crack shot, so it was no laughing matter when his friend, Tobias Mitchell, called on his behalf at the Southern Hotel and formally challenged Fred to a duel with pistols.

At Lillie's insistence, Fred hesitated. She knew, if he did not, that her career would be ruined in the event that one or the other of the contestants were killed in a duel.

The newspapers kept up the controversy. Members of various New York clubs, including the Union, Union League, Knickerbocker, University, Lotos and Manhattan, to all of which Fred belonged, were interviewed. Most said that he had already satisfied a lady's honor, and that no further action on his part was required.

The Midwest, however, supported Cunningham, and Fred was branded as a coward by the men interviewed in a half-dozen cities.

The whole incident was threatening to get out of hand, and some of Lillie's influential friends intervened quietly. Diamond Jim Brady, who knew everyone of prominence in the country, led the battalions of reason. Discreet calls were paid on Cunningham and on Gebhard by men of standing, and the affair ended on a deflationary note.

Questioned again about the duel, Cunningham would only say to reporters, "I freely admit to you that if I had wanted to fight, I had plenty of opportunity."

The reporters returned to Fred, who said, "I refused to pay any attention to the Colonel's challenge, as I had already denounced him."

He also revealed that he did not intend to accompany Mrs. Langtry beyond her next stop, Memphis. He had business interests in Colorado and Wyoming, he said, and his presence was required in the West.

Meanwhile the company playing the Olympic Theatre grossed a record of $31,539.80 for its two-week stay.

The press refused to forget Fred Gebhard, however, and he surfaced from time to time as Lillie continued her tour. He joined her for a few days in New Orleans. He reappeared in Milwaukee, where he hotly denied that he intended to become her personal manager. He showed up for twenty-four hours in Cincinnati.

Everywhere Lillie broke box-office records, and her personal share of the earnings, after paying the salaries of her company, amounted to more than six thousand dollars per week. No entertainer in history had earned such a sum, and several generations would pass before anyone equaled it.

Oscar Wilde was reunited with Lillie in Buffalo, where he had a lecture engagement, and their joint visit to Niagara Falls provided the ebullient Wilde with an opportunity to publicize himself again. "Every American bride is brought here," he said, "and must content herself with the sight of vast amounts of uninspired water. The sight of this waterfall must be one of the earliest, if not the keenest disappointments of American married life."

His quip when Lillie posed in front of the falls for the photographers provided copy in hundreds of newspapers the next day. "Mrs. Langtry," he said, "was photographed with Niagara Falls as an unpretentious background."

By the time Lillie reached Buffalo, she was having an affair with Fred Gebhard. The available evidence indicates they had not been sleeping together when she had played in St. Louis, so the liaison probably was joined in one of the other cities on the tour. There was no question, however, that they had finally become intimate.

Fred arrived in the city one evening while Lillie was performing at the theatre, and went straight to her hotel, intending to surprise her when she returned. It must be assumed that she was duly surprised.

An hour or two later Agnes Langtry, who occupied the bedroom on the far side of the sitting room in Lillie's suite, saw lights burning there, and went in to investigate. She was astonished and horrified to find the lovers drinking champagne, with Lillie dressed in her peignoir and Fred wearing pajamas.

Agnes departed before breakfast the next morning. She wrote Lillie a farewell letter that must have been scathing; it has not survived, but Lillie made oblique references to it over a period of many years. Agnes returned immediately to England, and disappeared into the anonymity from which she had emerged. Like her brother, she was naive, and like her brother, she had found the Jersey Lily too peripatetic to handle.

The tour ended late in March, and Lillie was now a woman of means, having earned a net of somewhere between $100,000 and $150,000 for herself. She was still the strongest box-office draw in the United States, and Henry Abbey was reluctant to see her depart for England. She readily agreed to extend her tour, and went into rehearsals with a play never before presented anywhere but in England, W. S. Gilbert's *Pygmalion and Galatea*, the familiar myth about a lovely Greek statue that came to life. She later claimed it had been her idea to do the play, while Abbey said he had been responsible.

Regardless of who deserved the credit, Lillie opened in it at the Fifth Avenue Theatre in late April, 1883, alternating the play with *She Stoops to Conquer*. All she had to do as Galatea was to look beautiful. The part required very little acting ability, but the New York critics treated her sternly, William Winter excepted. She spent six weeks in New York, then played short return engagements in Boston and Philadelphia. Then the time came for a major break in her life, a chance to get away from her increasingly complicated romance with Fred Gebhard, a chance to see her daughter, and a chance to improve and polish her talents as an actress.

VIII

IN JUNE, 1883, LILLIE LANGTRY ENDED THE
BUSIEST and most profitable season of her life. She was now
an established actress, in spite of the opinion of the critics, and
she was a box-office draw who would command respect from
theatre managers anywhere in the world.

She celebrated by allowing Fred Gebhard to give a dinner in
her honor at Tony Pastor's restaurant, and thereafter they
made the rounds of seaside resorts, among them Coney Island.
Then, her plans ambitious, she sailed for England a few days
later.

Lillie had a great deal to occupy her thoughts on the voyage.
Fred desperately wanted to marry her, and she herself was
deeply in love for the first time in her life. George Lewis, her
London solicitor, had written repeatedly that there was no
chance Edward Langtry would consent to a divorce, but Abe
Hummel had suggested a way out of her difficulties. She could
become a citizen of the United States, and then file for divorce
herself in an American court. She had promised to give the
matter thought.

Lillie stayed a few days in London, visiting her parents, and
there is no record indicating that she spent time with anyone
else. Her visit was private, and the press, so different from that
in America, respected her desire to be ignored. After three or
four days she disappeared and went on to Jersey, where she
saw her daughter for the first time in many months. She hired
additional servants to help the governess, and rented a
somewhat larger house. No one knows how long she stayed in

Jersey, but she probably spent about a week with Jeanne, who could walk, after a fashion, and was babbling pseudo-words.

On July 1 the Jersey Lily arrived in Paris, and astounded the theatrical world by enrolling in the Conservatoire of François Joseph Régnier, the leading dramatic teacher of his day. No one of Lillie's standing had ever reduced herself to the role of a student, but she was determined to win recognition for more than her beauty, and complicated arrangements had been made in advance.

Dion Boucicault, to whom she had confided her ambitions in New York, had written to Régnier, and the instructor had agreed to spend the entire summer working exclusively with Lillie. For three months he would handle no other pupils himself; he respected her desire for self-improvement, and had told her in a letter that he would do everything he could to help her.

Members of the Paris theatrical community hailed Lillie's arrival. Sarah Bernhardt gave a dinner for her, and the leading playwright of the day, Victorien Sardou, was the host at another. She was entertained in the Green Room of the Comédie-Française, and invitations by the score were delivered to her at the Conservatoire, but she sent her regrets to virtually everyone who wanted her as a guest. She had come to Paris to work, and didn't intend to waste time on frivolous activities. Her situation, as she well knew, was unique. Unlike the great actresses of the day, she had come late to the theatre, and was actually just beginning to learn her trade. At the same time, however, she was the most popular star of the era, and her name in front of a theatre guaranteed a tremendous sale. Certainly Lillie realized, however, that the novelty would wear off one day, that in time she would be judged on the basis of her talent rather than her beauty, and that even her notoriety would fade.

Régnier was a disciplinarian in his mid-seventies who had lost none of the energy that had made him renowned. Lillie was required to appear in his second-floor studio at 8:00 A.M., ready for work, and usually did not finish until late at night. Régnier drove her hard, but she drove herself even harder, and she quickly won the respect of the master.

One day Sarah Bernhardt dropped in at the Conservatoire to watch Lillie's lesson. Accompanying her was the great star of the Comédie-Française, Benoît Coquelin, then in his mid-forties, whose fame was already legendary. It had been said by impartial critics that his talents were greater than those of either Irving or Booth.

The chance visit brought miraculous results. The best actor and actress of the French theatre were so impressed by Lillie's determination and perseverance that they volunteered to play parts opposite her. Régnier and a delighted Lillie immediately accepted, and for a period of two to three weeks the Jersey Lily worked on the Conservatoire stage each day with Bernhardt and Coquelin, a priceless experience.

"Coquelin is extraordinary," Lillie said in a letter to Boucicault. "He says more in a pause than most actors can say in hundreds of words. He drops a hand, he raises an eyebrow, and one feels the controlled power of his gestures. As for Bernhardt, she is magnificent! I despair of becoming a real actress when I work on the stage with her, and I would gladly exchange my beauty, such as it is, for a soupçon of her great talent. I know I will never be a Bernhardt or a Coquelin, but must emphasize as best I can my own assets.

"I can make you one pledge, my dear friend. When I return to America I will not disgrace you or any of the others who have had faith. Even the assassins of the press will applaud me."

In spite of her heavy work schedule, Lillie found — or made — the time to buy a dazzling wardrobe from Jean Worth, son of the man who had founded the world's foremost dressmaking house. Each day, during the lunch hour, dressmakers and their assistants appeared at the Conservatoire carrying bolts of cloth, and each day Lillie submitted to fittings. She insisted that everything made for her had to be original, and that no copies be made for anyone else. She assisted in the creation of her gowns, and Worth later said that, had she not chosen a stage career, she would have become a successful dress designer.

She continued to prove, too, that she was a hard-headed businesswoman. Worth's clothes were expensive, and Lillie ordered more than fifty dresses, worth a king's ransom. But she paid only a fraction of what the dressmaker would have charged anyone else. She remembered the deals she had made in London when she had been a mere Professional Beauty. Now she was a theatrical star, whose costumes would be seen by thousands, and she arranged to give Worth program credit in lieu of cash for the better part of her bill.

A number of London managers were clamoring for a Langtry season, and Lillie was tempted to return to England, where she would be near her daughter and her parents, but she decided it would be premature to assault the London stage again. America was clamoring for her, and she could earn as much there in a week as she could make in a month if she played London. So she sent a cablegram to Henry Abbey, agreeing to appear in a new comedy by Daniel Frohman, *The Highest Bidder*, which he had sent her. The play was light, and her own role was not taxing, but would show her off to good advantage.

She needed two handsome leading men, and through friends in London engaged Arthur Elwood and James Pygott-Smyth, neither of whom she knew. The rest of her small company was also recruited in London, and Lillie agreed to cross the Atlantic with them at the end of September.

She gave a farewell dinner in Paris late in September, presenting Régnier with a diamond stickpin in the shape of a horseshoe, a symbol that Diamond Jim Brady had made famous. Then she vanished again for a few days, stopping in Jersey for a visit with her daughter before going on to London for a couple of days with her aging parents.

It was evident on board ship that there was a new Lillie Langtry in charge. Instead of sleeping until noon she assembled her company early every morning, and rehearsals of *The Highest Bidder* were well advanced by the time the ship reached New York.

There the usual crowd of reporters had assembled, and Fred Gebhard, who surprised the press by being restrained and almost friendly, was on hand, too. Arrangements had been made for Lillie to rent an apartment at 120 West Thirteenth Street that was owned by Harriet Hubbard Ayer, and in return for the gesture Lillie promptly endorsed Mrs. Ayer's cosmetics, which she was just starting to manufacture.

In late October the play opened in New York, and William Winter noted, at some length, Lillie's improvement as an actress. She showed greater depth, he said, her style was smoother, and she seemed far more sure of herself. The enthusiasm of the other critics for the Thespian talents of the lovely Mrs. Langtry was restrained, but at least they didn't treat her with the contempt they had displayed the previous year.

She had accomplished her immediate vocational goal, and was accepted as a professional actress.

Thanks to the apartment, she could lead a truly private life in New York. Fred Gebhard could come and go without being seen by reporters, and if Lillie gave a supper party, the list of her guests didn't appear in print the following day. Her stay in New York until January, 1884, was uneventful. And business remained good: she repeated her triumph of the previous year, and every performance sold out.

Lillie began her tour in Boston, and that was where the trouble began with Arthur Elwood, her leading man. A competent actor who lacked the qualities that made a star, Elwood erred by falling in love with his employer and co-worker. Lillie was accustomed to the spectacle that men made of themselves over her, and for a time was able to contain Elwood's offstage attentions.

But the actor became jealous of Fred Gebhard, and protested whenever Fred appeared somewhere on the tour. Lillie and Fred had learned the previous year that the publicity was adverse when Fred accompanied her, so they utilized their improved technique. She arrived in a city and was accorded due fanfare, then Fred appeared quietly the following day. The press was avoided, and there were no repercussions.

Elwood was always aware of Fred's arrival, however, and his acting suffered. He stammered onstage, he forgot lines, and he complicated the tasks of his colleagues. Worst of all, he went to Lillie's dressing room on a number of occasions and created scenes. This annoyed Fred, and in St. Louis, of all places, the city where the near-duel with Colonel Cunningham had created international headlines the previous year, a bitter backstage quarrel erupted.

Lillie had her hands full, but managed to quiet both men, and swore the other members of the cast to secrecy. Not one word about the incident leaked into print.

On April 26, 1884, while playing in Chicago, Elwood was discharged on the day his contract expired. He promptly returned to New York, and there filed suit, claiming that Lillie had agreed verbally to a ten-week extension of the contract. She was forced to return to New York to defend the suit, and had to suspend the tour for several days. In spite of the advice she received from Fred and others, she refused to hire an attorney, and defended her own case.

It was true, she told the court, that she had agreed to keep Elwood as a member of the company, but she had changed her mind when his acting became progressively worse. She made no mention of the actor's personal interest in her, and he also avoided any reference to that phase of their relationship. The court ruled in Lillie's favor, and the case was dismissed.

James Pygott-Smyth was elevated to the first male lead, another actor was hired for the second lead, and the tour was resumed, continuing until late June, 1884. Nowhere had there been an empty seat, and Lillie was richer by another $100,000 to $125,000. The most noteworthy aspect of the tour was that she played Denver, became fascinated by the West, and wanted to see more of it.

Lillie returned to New York, where every photographer of consequence took her picture, and then she went off to the Catskills with Fred to help him buy some horses for his racing stable. It was during this brief sojourn that she wrote to her solicitor, George Lewis, in London, expressing the desire to own a stable of her own, the first time she had mentioned the idea in writing. What made the matter memorable was her ability, within a few years of starting a career, to think seriously in terms of participating in the inordinately expensive sport of kings. It must have pleased her to know she had earned her own way, without financial help from anyone.

When she returned to New York, she faced still another lawsuit. The management of Niblo's Garden Theatre said she had missed a performance, which had made it necessary to offer refunds to patrons who had purchased seats for that evening. The theatre owners claimed she had not been ill.

What made the situation ticklish was the fact that Niblo's was represented by the exceptionally able Abe Hummel, while Lillie again refused legal representation. The press covered the case in full force.

Lillie freely admitted she had not been ill on the night in question, but insisted that her health had been "precarious," that had she not taken a night to rest, she would have fallen ill, and might have been forced to cancel many days of appearances. Hummel's questioning on the witness stand could not shake her, and she so charmed both the judge and the jury that the verdict was returned in her favor, MRS. LANGTRY BEATS HUMMEL IN COURT, the *Herald* trumpeted.

The long-range significance of the case was that Lillie and Hummel became friendlier, each developing an increased respect for the other. Immediately thereafter Hummel formally became Lillie's attorney, and represented her in all of her American legal and business dealings.

The time had come, Lillie decided, to attack London. She had two full seasons in the United States under her belt, and believed she was ready to be accepted as a serious actress by the British. Fred Gebhard didn't want her to leave, but she thought it was necessary for the sake of her career. He made plans to accompany her, but was dissuaded by Hummel and, through Lillie herself, by George Lewis, whose correspondence makes it clear that he felt certain Edward Langtry would never consent to a divorce if Fred's name should be linked with Lillie's in the British press.

So Lillie sailed alone for England in late August, 1884. She spent several days with her parents, and then went off for a month in Jersey, which she spent with her daughter in their rented house. Returning to London, she rented a handsome house at 86 Eaton Place, in one of the most fashionable districts.

Clement Scott, the author and influential freelance drama critic, was one of her friends and admirers, responding to the same treatment that had been accorded William Winter. Through Scott, Lillie established contact with one of the best leading men of the London stage, Charles T. Coghlan, who agreed to become her co-star in a season of repertory. Having established a core, Lillie set up a base of operations by renting the new Prince of Wales Theatre on Coventry Street, in the heart of Piccadilly, which was becoming the theatrical center.

If the appearance of Mrs. Langtry at a theatre named after the Prince of Wales was accidental, it was remarkably fortuitous. Certainly potential theatre-goers remembered the gossip about her and the Prince, and the name of the theatre did nothing to diminish her drawing power.

Whether Lillie and Prince Albert Edward actually saw anything of each other in private during the season that opened on January 24, 1885, has never been authoritatively determined. It is a matter of record that the Prince and Princess of Wales faithfully attended the opening performance of each play in the repertory, and the Prince returned to watch at least one or two performances of each play. On these occasions he invariably went backstage and visited the star in her dressing room.

A consensus of the opinions expressed by letter writers of the period is that Lillie and the Prince quietly resumed their affair. Albert Edward made his own rules, particularly when dealing with ladies; as for Lillie, Fred Gebhard was three thousand miles away, on the far side of the Atlantic.

There can be no question that, if she and the Prince decided to become intimate again, they had every opportunity, without interference or the knowledge of anyone. Lillie was taking no part in the activities of high society, thanks in part to the limited time at her disposal, so it didn't matter whether the Prince appeared at this or that dinner and sat beside her. Nothing prevented him from driving to her house after a performance, leaving his unmarked carriage in her private, inner coach yard, and departing later in the night without anyone in the neighborhood even realizing that she was entertaining a guest.

All that can be said for certain is that the name of the future Edward VII appeared frequently in Lillie's trans-Atlantic correspondence. "The Prince of Wales thinks my performance has improved since the opening," she told William Winter. "The Prince of Wales thinks Coghlan and I have achieved perfect timing," she wrote to Dion Boucicault. Whether she mentioned the Prince in her correspondence with Fred Gebhard is unknown but unlikely. Fred had sent her a magnificent diamond brooch for Christmas, and other gems crossed the Atlantic from time to time, too.

Had Lillie wanted to buy her own jewelry, she was rapidly acquiring the means. Her season was an unqualified financial success, and she sold out every night, just as she had in the United States. The staples of her repertory consisted of three plays. One was *Princess George*, a translation from the French of Alexandre Dumas, the younger. Her role was difficult, and she had chosen it deliberately, as a challenge. Some of the critics said she was not capable of playing the part, but audiences applauded her roundly in it every night, and there was no drop in box-office receipts, so she kept it in her schedule.

A second play was *The School for Scandal*, with Coghlan playing Charles Surface, and Herbert Beerbohm Tree, soon to win recognition as one of the great actors of the period, as Joseph. Not only had Ellen Terry played Lady Teazle recently, but any actress doing the part needed a polished, high comedy style. The critics were astonished by Lillie's performance, and without exception praised her. "Mrs. Langtry displays hitherto unsuspected gifts as a classical comedienne," the *Times* said, and the *Telegraph* added, "She proves herself an actress of genuine merit, even though her range may be limited."

It was the third play in the repertory that really established Lillie's reputation as a professional actress. It was Sardou's *Peril*, which Clement Scott translated into English at her suggestion, and it seemed to have been written specifically for her talents. She created a critical sensation in the role of a beautiful, charming lady of culture and means, and later, when she played the same part in the United States, the critics there echoed the praise of their London colleagues.

Eventually *Peril* became the heart of Lillie's repertory. It has been estimated that the play earned her $500,000 over a period of years. Scott became wealthy, and Sardou was her lifelong, devoted friend.

Lillie's success in London, under her own management, made it possible for her to take a bold step that the fear of gossip had previously prevented. She brought her child and governess to London, and for the first time Jeanne lived under the same roof with Lillie. In the presence of outsiders the little girl learned to address Lillie as "Aunt."

The proximity to Reverend and Mrs. Le Breton made it possible for the child's grandparents to spend a great deal of time in her company, too. The clergyman was suffering from failing health, but Mrs. Le Breton, who always attended her daughter's opening night performances and frequently was seen shopping and riding in a carriage with her, was in good health, and devoted a great deal of time and care to the child.

Fred Gebhard frequently wrote that he wanted to visit London, but Lillie held him off. She was advised by George Lewis that Edward Langtry, happily collecting the monthly allowance Lillie sent him, had resumed his previous life in Southampton, where he spent his time boating and fishing. There was just one significant difference in his habits: he was drinking even more heavily now, and would become ugly, creating unfavorable publicity, if he learned that Lillie had an ardent American suitor.

There was more than enough unfavorable publicity caused by two of Lillie's high society friends on July 23, 1885. Her swains were the thirty-six-year-old Sir George Chetwynd, High Sheriff of Warwick, who was married to the daughter of the Marquess of Anglesey. The other was the twenty-eight-year-old Lord Lonsdale, whose wife, the former Lady Grace Gordon, was the daughter of the Marquess of Huntley, and was one of the few society women with whom Lillie had kept up a friendship after abandoning her career as a Professional Beauty.

The nature of Sir George's relationship with Lillie was very clear. He ardently wanted to have an affair with her, and she was equally determined to hold him at arm's length. She had no male protector to intervene on her behalf, but needed none. The Jersey Lily could handle men. Lord Lonsdale was the weapon she chose to fend off Sir George, as she knew that he, too, in spite of her friendship with his wife, would become romantically inclined if she encouraged him.

It was her plan, according to what she subsequently told George Lewis, and corroborated in talks with Oscar Wilde and his bride, Constance, to play off Sir George against Lord Lonsdale. She made separate arrangements to meet each of them at the same place on the same day, and hoped that Sir George, in particular, would become discouraged when he realized he had a rival.

Lillie may have less than good common sense when she chose London's most fashionable promenade, Rotten Row, for her double rendezvous. Everybody who was anybody rode or walked there daily between noon and two o'clock in the afternoon; it was the place to see and be seen, to gossip and remain active in the social swim. Behaving like a character in a farce of the period, Lillie told each of her admirers that she would meet him at 1:00 P.M. beneath the statue of Achilles that stood in Rotten Row.

She arrived a quarter of an hour early, heavily veiled, and stood on the far side of some bushes. Although she knew a number of people who walked or rode past the spot, no one recognized her.

Sir George and Lord Lonsdale, both on horseback, arrived more or less simultaneously. The press accounts of the precise sequel of events are somewhat garbled, but some indicate that the two men began to quarrel at once, each knowing, in some mysterious and unexplained way, that the other was waiting for the Jersey Lily. According to a number of more logical stories, they chatted amicably for several minutes, until one or the other revealed that he was meeting Mrs. Langtry.

At that point the quarrel started, and one hot word led to another that was still louder. A crowd began to gather. All of the newspapers indicate that Sir George was the first to lose his temper. "Stay away from my Lillie!" he shouted, or it may have been, "Don't meddle with my Lillie!"

Whatever his words, he accompanied them with a blow, delivered with his riding crop, that knocked off Lord Lonsdale's hat. Then, before the astonished nobleman could recover, Sir George hit him again.

His lordship reacted violently, and returned the blows, striking with such abandon that both horses began to buck. The crowd fell back, giving the combatants as much room as they needed. Presumably the veiled Lillie continued to watch from a distance.

The horses became so unruly that both men were forced to dismount, and the battle continued on foot. They freely traded punches, and finally wrestled on the ground, like two small boys engaging in a free-for-all. The burly Sir George managed to twist an arm around his opponent's neck, and was pummeling him in the face when the fight was halted by the Duke of Portland and a squad of hastily summoned mounted policemen.

Even the most austere London newspapers printed sedate articles on the affair the following day, and the ha'penny press went wild. The combatants, the newspapers said, were sent to their respective homes in closed carriages. Because of their prominence the police discreetly decided not to bring breach of the peace charges against either.

Within twenty-four hours Sir George reappeared in public, rode his calmed horse in Rotten Row, and dined with friends at one of his clubs. His only scar of battle was a bruise mark on his nose. But Lord Lonsdale remained at home, in seclusion, for more than a week, and did not reappear until his wounds healed.

The repercussions echoed and re-echoed. The London press made the most of the fracas, as did newspapers throughout the world, and the publicity barrage did not add luster to Lillie's name. It helped the box office, however. She had planned to end her London engagement in mid-August, but the demand for tickets was so great she extended the run for a month.

Apparently reasoning that the worst had already happened, and that no publicity could be more harmful, Lillie sent Fred Gebhard a cablegram. Telling him to ignore the fight, which had no real significance, she asked him to join her as soon as possible so they could share the holiday she planned to take before going on tour in the provinces.

Fred had pride and a mind of his own, however. Refusing to be summoned at Lillie's convenience, he replied by cable that he was paying no attention to the press accounts, but that the complications of his business affairs made it impossible for him to leave the United States at that time. He was making it amply clear that he was not at Lillie's beck and call.

Other results of the fight were even more unpleasant. A number of London tradespeople, perhaps deciding that Mrs. Langtry was more vulnerable than she had been in some time, brought suit against her on the grounds that she still owed them money from the days when she had been virtually bankrupt.

The trial took place in October, shortly before Lillie was scheduled to leave on her eight-week provincial tour. The two-thousand-pound loan ostensibly made to her by Sir Allen Young was brought into the open, and a deposition from Edward Langtry was read into the record. He was in no position to pay the alleged bills, he said, "because I have no funds other than the annuity allowed me by my wife on the condition that I do not molest her."

The court ruled in Lillie's favor, and she had to pay the tradespeople no additional sums, but the revelation of her private affairs was embarrassing. She was particularly disturbed by the publication of the facts concerning the loan that Sir Allen Young had made her. Everyone who knew the explorer realized he had no fortune of his own, and those who realized he was a close friend of the Prince of Wales could draw their own deductions concerning the real source of the loan.

Lillie was convinced, then and later, that Sir George Chetwynd, who was no longer on speaking terms with her, was responsible for the harassment. She had made him look foolish in the Rotten Row incident, and he was trying to even the score, or so she wrote Fred Gebhard.

As usual, however, there were compensations. The fresh notoriety increased the demand for tickets, and thousands in York, Liverpool, Edinburgh and other cities clamored for seats. Lillie extended her tour for an additional four weeks, and did not return to London until a few days before Christmas.

She and her daughter spent the holidays with her parents, and early in January, 1886, Lillie went off to Paris for ten days on a clothes-buying spree. Her expensive, unique wardrobe had made her the acknowledged, if unofficial fashion queen of the world, and she had an image to maintain. Her only rival was the widowed Empress Eugénie of France, who maintained homes in England and on the Riviera. A quarter of a century older than Lillie, Eugénie offered her no real competition.

Virtually the entire visit to Paris was spent at the dressmaking house of Worth, where Lillie again designed many of the gowns that were made for her. She took a portion of her new wardrobe back to England with her, and it filled twelve large steamer trunks. Enough clothes to fill another ten trunks followed within a few weeks.

A day or two after Lillie's return to London, Fred Gebhard suddenly and unexpectedly appeared, giving her no advance notice of his arrival. Mrs. Le Breton, who happened to be visiting at the time, met Fred and like him enormously. Presumably the good clergyman's good lady knew nothing of the notoriety her daughter and Fred had attained.

In fact, Mrs. Le Breton moved into the Eaton Place house herself to act as a chaperone so Fred could stay there instead of lodging at a hotel. Ordinarily, as a wealthy, socially acceptable bachelor, the handsome Fred would have been welcomed by the British aristocracy. But the ladies who determined such matters, led by the American-born women who had married into the nobility, turned their thumbs down. Lillie Langtry was no longer acceptable in many of London's best homes, so her American lover was kept out in the cold, too. There is no evidence to indicate that Lillie and Fred felt hurt.

In the half-decade that had passed since Lillie had launched her theatrical career she had taken no prolonged holidays. Either she or Fred conceived the idea that she should take the equivalent of a grand Continental tour, and that he should accompany her as an escort-bodyguard. Presumably the couple presented the idea to Lillie's parents in some manner that made the tour sound respectable, because Mrs. Le Breton agreed to look after Jeanne during Lillie's absence, and maintained a spirited correspondence with her.

The services of a bodyguard on the tour, which began in February, 1886, were a necessity. Police reserves had to be called out in Brussels to extricate Lillie from a mammoth throng of her admirers. So many followed her in Amsterdam that she and Fred retired to their hotel, and had to do their sight-seeing at night. Even in blasé Paris, where Lillie had become a familiar sight, people gathered outside the couple's hotel, and near restaurant entrances, hoping to catch a glimpse of them.

In Geneva the lovers were ignored, and Lillie's tone was piqued when she wrote her mother that she had been unrecognized there. Like so many others who have grown accustomed to the limelight, she was unnerved by public indifference.

The welcome given her in Vienna more than made up for the lethargy of the Swiss. Proud of her own lovely daughters, the Austro-Hungarian capital turned out in force to greet the pride of the Anglo-Saxon world, and on her first night at the Sacher Hotel, Lillie was serenaded by a large band and a chorus of more than two hundred voices.

She quickly discovered that Crown Prince Rudolph, who had embarrassed her with his attentions in London, had not forgotten her. She and Fred were invited to dine with the Prince, and the following afternoon, while Fred presumably went sight-seeing on his own, the Prince took Lillie on a personally conducted tour of his palace.

The hour Lillie spent there was one of the strangest she had ever known. Dust covers were thrown over the furniture, and room after room was filled with enameled clocks; countless items of bric-a-brac and a variety of historical relics were preserved in glass cabinets.

Lillie made the mistake of remarking that the place looked more like a museum than a home.

Rudolph immediately began smashing cabinets and bric-a-brac with his walking stick. Working himself into a demonic fury, he broke priceless crystal chandeliers and clocks that could not be replaced. Two of his aides, who had been hovering discreetly in the background, were helpless to stop him, and he did not appear to hear Lillie's repeated pleas.

At last exhaustion forced Rudolph to halt, and he quietly led Lillie to a parlor for tea. Behind them an army of servants went to work clearing away the debris, and other chandeliers and bric-a-brac were brought up from the crammed cellars of the palace to replace what the Prince had broken. Lillie wrote in her autobiography that he had gone on the rampage in order to please her, and that she had never before been so frightened. She could not have been surprised, a few years later, when she read of Rudolph's suicide.

She and Fred returned to England early in April by way of Germany and seldom-visited Denmark, and she received royal receptions everywhere. Then Fred went back to the United States, and Lillie settled down for a quiet, five-month interlude with her daughter. This was one of the most relaxed periods of her life; she spent her days with Jeanne, rarely went anywhere at night and entertained infrequently. She wanted to spend an uninterrupted time with her daughter, and she knew, too, that she needed rest or her beauty would fade.

In September, 1886, she launched a new assault on the United States, accompanied by Coghlan and a carefully selected company. The American press was on hand to greet her in force, and she delighted many of the reporters when she greeted them by name. Fred Gebhard did not meet her at the ship, but waited for her at her hotel, and had a surprise in store for her.

He presented her with a gift, the deed to a house he had purchased for her. Located at 362 West Twenty-third Street, in what was at that time New York's most exclusive residential district, the house had been built by Clement Clarke Moore, author of the classic, "'Twas the Night Before Christmas." It was a small, exquisite mansion, with a long driveway, carriage lights and a mammoth double front door. Lillie immediately ordered a garden installed in the front yard, which was about fifteen feet deep, and then had to put in a high fence of grilled iron so her lawns, flowers and shrubs wouldn't be trampled by crowds of the curious, who gathered in front of the place each day.

Fred, ever generous, had also arranged that the place be decorated at his expense by James Mitchell, New York's most high-priced contractor and decorator. For the first time in her life Lillie was free to decorate a house as she pleased, without giving any thought to the expense, and she reacted accordingly. She had walls knocked down and rooms enlarged, she installed marble fireplaces with ornately carved mantels, and she put in marble bathtubs. The rumor that the faucets in her bathrooms were made of solid gold was false, however, and contrary to detailed press reports, she did not keep a menagerie of rare and exotic animals on the top floor.

Mitchell, later writing about the redecoration in the New York *Sun*, revealed that his task had been neither simple nor untroubled:

> The interior was to be finished entirely in highly polished walnut, and it had to be imported from a certain English forest. We were kept on our sharps for a year in getting the wood just the right grain, and then the interior graining and polishing was a tremendous job. This was a big commission for me. I worked on it day and night, and when we finished that beautiful walnut job, I was the proudest man in New York.
>
> But my troubles were only beginning. Mrs. Langtry looked over the work, but she seemed hardly to notice it. "The very latest thing in interior decoration," she said, "is hard, finished

white enamel. You will have to send to England for the right kind. I am sure you won't be able to get it here."

I tried to beg off, but she was accustomed to just waving her hand to get things done. I could have got it here, but it had to come from England.

It almost broke my heart when my men set to work, covering the walnut with this white, hard finish. I don't know where she got the idea, but at that time all the women were copying her hats and gowns and imitating her speech, and before long all the moguls in New York were smearing their houses with enamel.

Lillie's version of the matter, as explained in her autobiography, was simple. The grained walnut was beautiful, and would have looked appropriate in a country house that enjoyed the benefits of a great deal of sunlight. But town houses were cut off from the light, and her rooms looked dark and gloomy. The white enamel brightened them, so the extra labor and expense were well worth her while.

She played the same repertory that London had applauded, and the New York critics were even kinder to her than their English colleagues had been. William Winter called her an actress of the first caliber, the highest compliment he had yet paid her. The *Times* said she deserved and had earned her stardom. The *Post* announced that her acting was so superior the audience actually forgot her beauty. The Jersey Lily was being accepted as someone worthy of her profession, and audiences reacted accordingly. The sophisticated and theatre-wise applauded her as fervently as did the general public.

But her beauty was not forgotten. Lillie was now thirty-three years of age, but still looked ten years younger, and the press knew she not only drank champagne regularly, but that she and Fred Gebhard often gave parties that lasted the better part of the night. Lillie was a wonder, and the press asked her beauty secret one day during a mass interview in her parlor. Sensing headlines, she readily revealed it: she was a physical exercise addict.

She gave no details, and the press engaged in a series of happy fantasies. A paragraph in the January 5, 1887, issue of *Punch* illustrates the joy of the working newsman:

> "Mrs. Langtry's horror is adiposity, which she combats with dumbbells." So says the evening paper. Had the information been given with regard to any other woman, it would have been said — "She's afraid of getting fat and has taken to dumbbells." But fancy a fat lily. An adipose one is bad enough in all conscience. And a lily working with dumbbells. How Oscar must shudder.

The form of exercise Lillie preferred was not revealed until a year after her death, when a piece in the New York *Sun* finally told the inside story of her secret. She may have been the first woman to indulge in the sport that, the better part of a century after she began, came to be known as jogging. Every day, shortly after arising, she dressed in heavy woolens and had herself driven to some remote park or rural area, and, no matter what the weather, she trotted for a minimum of two miles.

What makes her activities remarkable is that, in her day, ladies were expected to be sedentary. "Laborers sweat, gentlemen perspire and ladies glow," was a saying of the period, and most women accepted it literally. The Jersey Lily, accustomed to violent physical sports in her childhood, paid no attention to the notion. In fact, she never minced and rarely sauntered. Her normal walk was a long, loping stride that she managed to achieve gracefully, and her friends jokingly said that a quiet stroll with Lillie exhausted them. She managed to keep her weight down, however, and either inadvertently or otherwise became one of the initiators of the youth cult that would grow into a major international industry.

Lillie found other ways to keep her name in print during the 1886-87 theatrical season, too. One was the celebrated card game played in a private room at Delmonico's, with Diamond Jim Brady as the host. The newspapers had been stressing an imaginary feud between Lillie and Lillian Russell for several years, and it may have been the limelight-loving Brady who conceived the idea of bringing the two great beauties together in a friendly game of cards.

They were the only women who participated, along with a number of men, one of them Fred Gebhard. Ladies did not play poker, much less in mixed company, but actresses were a special breed, and didn't care if they were criticized, particularly if the press coverage was broad enough.

Reporters and photographers besieged Delmonico's, but were not admitted to the room in which the game was being played. They would have to wait, they were told, until the play was finished. At last the inner door was opened, and the two most beautiful women in the world allowed themselves to be photographed together. Both were smiling, and their expressions were smug.

Even a reporter who knew nothing about cards needed only to glance in the direction of the table to discover the reason. Piles of chips stood in front of both women's places; they were the night's big winners.

The reactions of their male companions indicated that the men had not been gallant. Some were disgruntled, and one or two muttered that poker was a man's game.

The reporters asked the glamorous beauties to account for their evening's success.

"Miss Russell and I work for a living," Lillie said.

"We must earn every penny," Lillian Russell added, "so we take few risks."

Their reactions having been duly recorded for posterity, the great beauties went their separate ways, basking in the refulgent glow of heavy press coverage. Talk of a feud died away.

Lillie enjoyed her longest single run to date in her New York season of repertory, and did not close until late March, 1887. For several months she had been making plans for her most ambitious tour, which would take her to the shores of the Pacific, then back to the Atlantic. For the sake of personal convenience, the mitigation of discomforts and the desire to achieve maximum publicity, she wanted a private railroad car of her own.

Fred Gebhard offered to pay for the car, and arranged a meeting between Lillie and William D. Mann, the inventor and manufacturer of a sleeping car that, for a time, threatened the fast-growing supremacy of the Pullman car. Mann was a curious character. A colonel in the Union Army during the Civil War, he was, in addition to being an industrialist, a newspaper publisher who loved gossip so much that he often neglected his other interests to write innuendo-filled articles for his rather disreputable publications.

Lillie told Mann what she wanted, and he designed, then built a railroad car for her that was extraordinary. It was seventy-five feet long, and at either end was a platform of teakwood imported from the Orient. The rim beneath the roof was decorated with a bas-relief of brass lilies. The car was painted a color described as "Jersey blue," and the roof, which was curved, pointing upward at either end, was done in the heavy white enamel she loved.

The principal bedroom was upholstered in a rich, green silk, and every piece of furniture was padded to prevent injury when a moving train swayed, bumped and jolted. Adjoining the stateroom was Lillie's bath, with fittings of silver, her dressing room and a small sitting room, both of which boasted curtains of rose-colored silk. Beyond stood the parlor, a chamber filled with overstuffed chairs and a piano, and lined with bookcases. At the far end were two guest bedrooms, a maid's room, a kitchen containing the most modern cooking aids, and a pantry, complete with a large icebox.

Lillie named the car *Lalee*, which, she said, was the East Indian word for flirt.

The railroad car was the best publicity device she had ever developed. Tens of thousands of words were written about it over the years; it attracted attention everywhere, advertising the presence of its owner, and in city after city large crowds visited the railroad stations and yards in order to gape at it. Not the least of its many features was its special construction: there were thirteen layers of flooring and walls, and eleven of ceiling in order to make it crash-proof. It was also so heavy that it could not be routed over many bridges and other sections of questionable track, so Lillie frequently was forced to make long detours in order to reach a destination.

More than the tour and her expensive new toy occupied Lillie's mind. Abe Hummel had finally prevailed upon her to become an American citizen and obtain her divorce in the United States. She was proud of her heritage and reluctant to give up her English citizenship, but had grown desperate.

George Lewis had gone to Edward Langtry and offered him a generous lump sum if he would consent to a divorce, but the stubborn Langtry had refused, saying that no amount of money would be large enough for the purpose.

Lewis strongly advised against bringing suit in England. Lillie had left Langtry, which would tend to strengthen his position, and, in any event, a divorce there could be obtained only on the grounds of adultery. She had no evidence against her husband, but he could make life thoroughly uncomfortable for her. And if he questioned the paternity of her daughter, of whose existence he and the world knew nothing, the scandal could cause endless repercussions.

American citizenship appeared to be the only solution.

IX

LILLIE BEGAN HER TRANSCONTINENTAL TOUR IN April, 1887, and by the first of July she reached San Francisco. Everywhere the Langtry name guaranteed sold-out theatres, and the money poured in as rapidly as ever. There were inconveniences, of course. The *Lalee* attracted so much attention that Fred Gebhard could not travel with her, and had to precede her.

He reached San Francisco first, and immediately conferred with the attorney Hummel had engaged to represent Lillie there, W. H. L. Barnes. At his recommendation Fred approved the purchase, in her name, of a ranch near the city. Armed with the deed, the lawyer filed an application for citizenship on her behalf, and was sufficiently influential to arrange for the Federal records to be brought to his office so undesired publicity could be avoided.

The net result of this maneuver was the opposite of what he had intended. The ever-vigilant San Francisco press traced the missing records and ferreted out the story, much to the embarrassment of both Lillie and Barnes. When she appeared in Federal court on July 17, 1887, she was severely criticized by the presiding judge, which made additional press copy, but her citizenship was granted.

The news put her on the front pages again, and Americans applauded her move. But feeling ran high against her in Great Britain, where her motives were unknown, and several newspapers ran editorials suggesting that she would be wise not to reappear on the English stage because audiences would not forgive or forget her desertion of her native land.

The California property Lillie had purchased was no token plot, but a working ranch of more than four thousand acres. Whether she paid even a brief visit to the place is open to question. According to some accounts, she did not go near it, but the manager she hired, Charles W. Aby, later was the authority for the claim that she stayed there whenever possible during her sojourn in the West, and that she spent a holiday of several weeks there before starting on the return swing of her long journey.

Only a few facts about Lillie's ownership of the ranch are known. She purchased several racing horses while in California, and housed them at the ranch. Apparently it was her intention to fulfill her long-standing dream of owning her own stable, but distances were so great in the United States that she could not race her animals in the East and stable them in the West, so she finally sold all three horses. Eventually she also disposed of a portion of the ranch, keeping only the ranch house and some of the surrounding property. Being Lillie Langtry, she made money in the process. According to press accounts, she showed a profit of more than twenty thousand dollars.

Before departing on the eastward swing of her tour from California, Lillie appeared privately in the chambers of a California judge for the purpose of obtaining a divorce. On this occasion Barnes was able to ensure secrecy, and the press learned none of the details. Neither did posterity, because the records were lost two decades later in the great fire that followed the disaster known as the San Francisco earthquake.

Lillie's correspondence with George Lewis reveals the outlines of what happened. She testified that Edward Langtry had been unable to support her, that he had left her for long periods to seek his own pleasures, boating and fishing, and that, after declaring herself bankrupt, she had been forced to go on the stage in order to earn her living. Her divorce was granted.

In spite of the many precautions Barnes took, rumors of the divorce appeared in print during the following months, as did a persistent story to the effect that Lillie either had married or was on the verge of marrying Fred Gebhard. She was kept busy denying the allegations.

Why she didn't marry Fred now that she was free remains a mystery down to the present day. She was in a position to do whatever she pleased, and could have become Mrs. Fred Gebhard at any time she wanted. She was in love with Fred, who had demonstrated his fidelity and loyalty, and it was common knowledge that he wanted to marry her.

According to the dictates of logic, Jeanne Marie was the inhibiting factor. It must be remembered that Edward Langtry was not only unaware of the fact that he had been divorced, but he didn't know of the child's existence. By filing a nuisance suit of some sort in England he could stir up all kinds of trouble, and for the present Lillie preferred to let a sleeping ex-husband remain somnolent. What Edward didn't know couldn't hurt her, and she didn't want vicious gossip to harm her child.

She had already made extensive plans for the autumn, and had no desire to see them interrupted or dislocated. She was wealthy enough now to support her parents as well as her daughter, and her father had finally agreed to retire. Reverend and Mrs. Le Breton intended to come to the United States in a few months, bringing their granddaughter with them, and the family would live with Lillie in her New York town house. Gossip could wreck that plan, and would mar Jeanne's entire future.

The booking schedule was so tight that Lillie was forced to postpone a detour of many hundreds of miles. She desperately wanted to visit a tiny Texas cow town, remote from any major city, and made a solemn pledge to go there at the first opportunity. Ever since its founding twenty years earlier, the place had been known as Vinegaroon. This summer it had changed its name to Langtry.

One man was responsible for the supremely flattering metamorphosis, Judge Roy Bean, one of the most colorful of the Southwest's pioneers, who was in his mid-seventies. Bean was a rancher, and proprietor of the town's saloon. A marksman with both rifle and pistol, he had maintained order in his district for many years, and had been the combined mayor and chief of police. Now that the town had grown to more than five hundred persons, he had given up his administrative duties to become the judge of a circuit court that made its headquarters in Vinegaroon.

When Lillie Langtry had first come to the United States, Judge Bean had fallen in love with her photograph. The walls of his saloon were covered with her pictures and press clippings about her, and on her first tour of the country he had traveled to Chicago to watch her on the stage and to obtain the autographed photo that occupied a place of honor behind the bar. Now, presumably with the consent of the town's electorate, he had changed its name. Lillie would be honored in appropriate ceremonies whenever she chose to go there.

In the meantime, however, she was busy completing her tour and making extensive plans for the coming season. While still on the road, she received word that the trip of her parents and daughter was being postponed due to the serious illness of Reverend Le Breton. But his physicians were optimistic, and

Mrs. Le Breton urged her daughter not to make the long journey to England and to remain in the United States.

After reaching New York, Lillie went with Fred to Saratoga for a week to watch his horses run, and then returned to the city to make specific plans for the new season. Sarah Bernhardt had just arrived in the country for a tour of her own, and Lillie entertained her frequently. They posed together for formal photographs, and on one occasion clowned for the benefit of photographers, donning boxing gloves and pretending they were engaging in a fight.

Lillie now had acquired more money than she could handle herself. She was worth approximately $500,000, the equivalent of four times that amount the better part of a century later, and Abe Hummel, writing her a formal letter, suggested that he invest it on her behalf. The canny Lillie gave him a quarter of a million, keeping the rest aside for a rainy day.

The vehicle for the new season was an inferior play, *As in a Looking Glass*, which gave Lillie the opportunity to play a type of role that was new to her. Her part was that of a sadistic, domineering woman who used her beauty to tyrannize others, and was a departure from the sweet milksops she had previously portrayed. In order to bolster her company she hired one of the most handsome, dashing young male stars of the day, Maurice Barrymore. They struck sparks together onstage, although in private life Barrymore was happily married to the talented and lovely actress, Georgiana Drew.

The reviews confirmed what everyone connected with the enterprise already knew, that the Jersey Lily had produced the most resounding success of her career. "Mrs. Langtry is superb," William Winter wrote in the *Tribune*, and for once the other critics agreed wholeheartedly.

Lillie and Barrymore remained together the entire season, going on the road after completing a New York engagement that set new records. Their love scenes together were so realistic that, it was rumored, Fred Gebhard was jealous and threatened to challenge Barrymore to a duel. The story was absurd, but helped sell tickets.

When the company went on tour, Fred remained behind, allegedly renting Lillie's house from her. He joined her now and then for a few days, but he found the unending traveling of show business boring as well as tiring, and preferred to remain in New York.

The theatre was a gold mine for Lillie, but she struck silver elsewhere. Hummel had purchased some real estate for her in Carson City, Nevada, and a rich vein of silver, allegedly worth five hundred dollars per ton, was discovered on the property. The newspapers speculated that she could sell the plot for at least a quarter of a million dollars; she did sell, but only she and Hummel knew the price she obtained. She was rapidly becoming one of the world's most independently wealthy women, and was in a position to retire whenever she wished.

When the company reached Chicago in February, 1888, Lillie canceled several performances, announcing that she was ill. She was actually in good health, but received a cablegram from London informing her that her father had died. No one except Barrymore and a few other members of the company knew the truth, and she made no mention of her tragedy to anyone else, concealing it from her associates, the press and the public.

Lillie took her company to California, playing one week in Los Angeles and two more in San Francisco. Although still the proprietor of the ranch there, she was "too busy" to visit it, according to the newspapers. She would neither affirm nor deny reports that she intended to sell it, and her silence was consistent with the attitude she long maintained regarding her personal affairs.

When she returned to Manhattan in mid-June, 1888, she barely had time to get her Twenty-third Street house in readiness for her seventy-year-old mother and seven-year-old daughter, who arrived without publicity of any sort. In no time at all Fred Gebhard was seen on the bridle paths with Jeanne Marie, whom he also took to the zoo, the circus and other entertainments. Fred probably was fond of the child, but he may have had another motive, as well. Lillie was still stalling, refusing to be married, and he might have been seeking a new, persuasive weapon.

In July Lillie rented a house for the summer at Long Branch, New Jersey, for herself and family, and Fred Gebhard moved in with them. No attempts were made to conceal the arrangement, and the press immediately assumed that he and Lillie were married. It was inconceivable in the Victorian era that a man and woman not married to each other could dwell under the same roof, even though amply chaperoned by Mrs. Le Breton and "Mrs. Langtry's nieces," as the newspapers called Jeanne and her governess.

When Fred wasn't swimming with Jeanne, accompanying Lillie on her constitutional jog every morning and escorting her to various social functions every night, he was kept busy denying the persistent questions of reporters, who were convinced that he and Lillie had been married at some time during recent months. Lillie herself kept the subject alive by smiling enigmatically whenever she was questioned. She was continuing to follow Gladstone's advice, and saw no reason to change the principle she had adopted.

Another visitor spent a portion of the summer at the Long Branch house, too. Lillie's brother, Clement, had become one of London's leading barristers, and came to the United States at her request to review her entire legal and financial situation. George Lewis was on the verge of retirement, and Clement was taking charge of his sister's affairs in London.

Their subsequent correspondence reveals that Clement believed Edward Langtry should be notified that Lillie had divorced him in an American court. But Lillie refused to grant permission for him to be told, and would do nothing to cut off the allowance she was paying him, either. Life was relatively peaceful, and she wanted no explosion that would expose her private business to the world or injure her daughter. She was earning so much that the pitiful sum she paid Edward Langtry each month no longer meant anything to her.

Clement went to California, made a study of the ranch and returned East with the recommendation that it be sold. Abe Hummel agreed, and the property was placed on the market. The conservative Clement Le Breton and the flamboyant, aggressive Abe Hummel worked remarkably well together.

Before beginning her preparations for the coming theatrical season, Lillie departed from her previous procedures. She was so well established now that she no longer needed to look after the business management of her enterprises, so she hired a general manager, Frank C. Griffith, who was destined to remain with her for a long time. He was efficient and, equally important, sought no limelight for himself.

As in a Looking Glass went on tour again in September, and remained on the road until mid-December. Mrs. Le Breton and Jeanne Marie saw something of America by traveling with Lillie in the *Lalee*, and the party included a tutor for the little girl. Fred Gebhard stayed behind in New York, and did not join Lillie on the tour. Perhaps he was somewhat inhibited by the presence of Mrs. Le Breton and Lillie's daughter in the relatively confined quarters of a hotel suite. On the other hand, it is possible, as the newspapers were beginning to hint, that the romance was growing a trifle cooler. Even the most ardent of suitors may lose interest when the lady he wants as his wife turns a consistently deaf ear to his proposal.

As soon as Lillie returned to New York she plunged into her most ambitious project. No actor or actress acquired real stature until he or she played Shakespeare, and she had made up her mind to do *Macbeth*. Charles T. Coghlan would direct and play opposite her, and Lillie was listed as the producer.

She poured a fortune into the production, spending an unprecedented eight thousand dollars for costumes and scenery. The sum was considered so large that some of the newspapers criticized her before the opening, saying she intended to lull the critics and the public by drowning them in luxury.

Coghlan, who had played opposite Ellen Terry in two full seasons of Shakespeare, closed the theatre to outsiders during rehearsals. It was rumored that Lillie was encountering difficulty, that her role was too much for her, and the public held back for the first time since she had come to the United States. They would pay to see Lillie Langtry, looking and sounding like herself in a wardrobe by Worth, but they would not purchase tickets for Lillie Langtry playing Shakespeare unless the critics approved.

To the astonishment of the skeptical, the critics unanimously hailed Lillie's Lady Macbeth. "She was admirable and rose to greatness; she was grand and exquisite." William Winter set the tone, and the others vied with him in their use of superlatives.

After the performance Griffith, Lillie's new manager, was almost mobbed by ticket brokers who wanted seats, and had to take refuge in a private room at Pfaffs. The next morning there was a long line at the box office, and the New York *Sun* commented, "Those who purchased tickets because of the novelty of seeing Mrs. Langtry as Lady Macbeth will be rewarded far beyond their expectations. So great is the demand for seats that they are selling for as much as $6, which is triple the box-office price."

Lillie played four months on Broadway, then went on tour again until summer. The money continued to pour in, and her profits were enormous, but she gained satisfactions beyond those of increasing wealth. In the United States, at least, she was recognized as an actress of the first magnitude. Now the time had come for her to conquer England as she had conquered America. Besides, she was homesick for London, in spite of her American citizenship, and the time had come for her to replenish her wardrobe at the house of Worth, too.

In Chicago she tried out a new play called *Esther Sandraz*, a first effort by Sidney Grundy, a British solicitor who was associated with Clement Le Breton. She played another domineering beauty, and the critics and public agreed that she was wonderful in the part.

Griffith departed to book a tour of the English provinces, and then rent a theatre for a London run.

Late in the summer Lillie was forced to cut short her tour when she fell ill, and suffered her first serious disability. Her ailment was diagnosed as bronchitis, and her physicians sent her to bed. When she emerged from her house two weeks later for her first breath of outside air, photographers were on hand, and their pictures seemed to confirm the rumors that she might be forced to abandon her career. Those photographs were seen by millions of newspaper readers, and the righteous exulted: the wages of sin were unvarying. The Boston *Herald*'s comments were typical:

Those who saw Mrs. Langtry when she first came to this country hardly know her as the same woman now. She looked a blooming English Hebe then, her eyes still bright with youth, her complexion superb and her figure willowy. She looks old now, her eyes are dull, the crows have come to stay, her face is colorless, and her complexion is like that of all actresses after years of excitement and late nights and stage paint, and her figure is portly and unharmonious.

Fred Gebhard, still pugnacious, wanted to sue the newspapers, and expressed his opinion at a dinner party held at Sherry's restaurant. A half-dozen of the guests reported Lillie's reply: "My dear, one never sues or contradicts someone who always has the last word, and I assure you the press cannot be out-talked or out-maneuvered."

Paying no attention to the attacks, Lillie engaged a large suite on a Cunard liner, the *Servia*, for herself, her mother, her daughter, the governess, two maids and sixty-three pieces of luggage. Clement and Sir George Lewis, who had been knighted on the eve of his retirement, had written urging that Jeanne Marie should not come to London as yet. The time wasn't ripe.

So, when the *Servia* docked at Southampton, Lillie went straight to Jersey with her mother and daughter, and rented a house for them there before proceeding to London. The press was astonished and even her Bohemian friends were surprised when she greeted them with a lighted cigarette in her hand. The only women who smoked were prostitutes, and all others considered the habit one in which men alone indulged. But Lillie had started to smoke on stage in one of her roles, and was a steady smoker. To her belongs the dubious credit of being one of the first women, if not the first, to smoke in public, and to make smoking acceptable if not respectable.

One of Lillie's first callers was Oscar Wilde, who brought with him the manuscript of a play he had written for her. He called it *Lady Windermere's Fan*, and had assured her in a letter that the part was perfect for her. As one of her greatest admirers of many years' standing, he had tailored the role perfectly to suit her own personality.

Lillie was shocked to discover that her part was that of an upper-class woman who was the mother of a grown, illegitimate daughter. She became so indignant that she refused to read the play, and would not permit Wilde to leave it with her. Her ostensible reason for rejecting it was her contention that she was not old enough to be the mother of an adult daughter; her real reason, of course, was that it struck too close to the bone.

Her relations with Wilde became strained, and they were barely on speaking terms for more than two years. Wilde's feelings were assuaged when *Lady Windermere's Fan* became one of the greatest high comedy successes of the era. But it is reasonably safe to assume that Lillie did not regret her refusal to play in it.

She elected to present *As You Like It* at the St. James's Theatre, which she rented for the season, and her choice of the play was not accidental. She had been a semi-amateur when she had first appeared in it, but now she was a professional, and she wanted London to see the difference in her performance.

A few hours before her opening Lillie was bedded by a high fever, but insisted on performing. Her maid would tolerate no nonsense, however, and summoned a physician, who diagnosed the ailment as measles; the opening was postponed. But while recuperating and in a weakened condition, she caught influenza, and for ten days was seriously ill. The newspapers set up a watch outside her house, and to prevent chaos that would disturb the patient, her physician issued three bulletins on her condition each day.

The world press ran daily front-page stories, and when the flu was at the crisis stage, even the staid *Times* of London said in a headline, MRS. LANGTRY IS GRAVELY ILL, MAY BE SINKING. It was variously reported that Lillie was dying, that she had lost her hair, that she had retired from the stage and that she would be crippled for life. After two weeks, however, she began to come downstairs for her meals. The physicians demanded that she rest for a month.

She promptly rescheduled the opening of *As You Like It* for mid-November, 1889.

The news of her illness brought Fred Gebhard to London. It is probable that they had quarreled seriously before Lillie had left the United States: if they exchanged correspondence after her return to England, there is no record of it. But it was obvious that he still cared about her because he came to London during her convalescence.

Fred paid Lillie one brief visit which lasted no more than thirty minutes, then turned around and caught the next ship for New York. Neither ever revealed the disagreement that resulted in a permanent estrangement.

One rumor, which gained credence over the years, was probably too conveniently romantic to be true. According to this story, the Prince of Wales called on Lillie to wish her a rapid recovery, and was chatting with her in her second-floor sitting room when Fred Gebhard arrived unexpectedly and unannounced. Breaking the rules of protocol, Fred insisted on joining them. Then, always jealous, he made an ugly scene, and Lillie dismissed him, telling him never to return.

If there was a factual basis for this tale, none of the principals ever confirmed it. Nevertheless it remained in circulation for many years, and was accepted as true by many people supposedly in the know on both sides of the Atlantic. Regardless of what may have caused the break, Lillie had broken with Fred, and they did not resume their affair. Years passed before they met again casually, after Fred finally married.

When *As You Like It* finally opened, no one was surprised to see the Prince and Princess of Wales sitting in the royal box on opening night.

The critics were as lavish in their praise as they had been chary when Lillie had first appeared in the play. "Mrs. Langtry is a bewitching Rosalind," the *Times* declared. "The improvement in her acting is astounding, and must be seen to be appreciated; she is worthy of her stardom now," the *Telegraph* said. "Mrs. Langtry joins the ranks of the great Rosalinds," the *Post* told its readers. "Her performance is memorable."

The box-office response was enthusiastic, and the play sold out for the entire three months that it had been booked. Lillie immediately extended the engagement for an additional month. And, encouraged by her favorable reception, she purchased a house at 21 Pont Street.

The success of *As You Like It* caused Lillie to ponder her next move, and she made one of the shrewdest decisions of her career, deciding to produce Shakespeare's *Antony and Cleopatra*, with Charles Coghlan directing and playing opposite her. The greatest beauty of her age would be an irresistible magnet in the role of one of the celebrated beauties of all ages. Established now as a true star, she would also enhance the play with a lavish production in the style of the *Macbeth* she had done in New York.

The St. James's was too small a theatre for the huge sets she had in mind, so she leased the large Princes Theatre. The scenery and costumes cost so much that it was rumored she was on the verge of bankruptcy. She refused to comment on the charge, but Griffith, when approached by the press, merely laughed.

What caused the story was the fact that most of Lillie's assets were tied up in securities and real estate, and she was short of cash. Her credit standing was impeccable, however, and she obtained a small loan from a bank, then repaid it within one week of the play's opening.

As Lillie had anticipated, the bait of seeing her as Cleopatra brought patrons to the box office in droves long before the opening, and ten weeks of the run were sold out in advance. The critics were dubious, however, and Lillie approached the opening with apprehension. Cleopatra's glamour caused her no concern, but the role was complex, and would stretch her talents to the limit. Under Coghlan's imaginative direction she was attempting several new approaches to the part, and, symbolically, was even refusing to wear the black wig that had become traditional when any actress played Cleopatra.

The play opened on April 28, 1890, with the Prince and Princess of Wales, accompanied by several other members of the royal family, in their usual box. The sumptuous production overwhelmed the audience, and Lillie herself won the greatest applause of her career. She took fourteen curtain calls at the end of the performance, finally bursting into tears, which started another round of heavy applause.

"Mrs. Langtry is dazzling!" the *Times* said. "She is the finest Cleopatra of our time," said the *Telegraph*.

The play was Lillie's biggest hit, and played to capacity audiences through the rest of 1890. She did not close it until a few days before Christmas, and she enjoyed her longest run in it. Eventually it became a staple of her repertory, and Griffith, interviewed in the 1930's, estimated that it earned her more than one million dollars.

She could hold her own now with the great actresses of the stage, although she herself knew she was no Ellen Terry or Sarah Bernhardt. She told Prime Minister Gladstone, who frequently repeated the remark, "An actor must be like a politician. If he thinks of himself as too important or forgets his sense of humor, the public will desert him in favor of someone who has the saving grace of humility."

When *Antony and Cleopatra* finally closed, an exhausted Lillie went off to Jersey to join her mother and daughter. She stayed there with them for two months, and in early March of 1891 went off to Paris, taking them with her. She showed them the sights, and they joined her at dinners given for her by Sarah Bernhardt, Sardou, Coquelin and others. During the three-week sojourn she managed to spend many hours at the dressmaking house of Worth, however, and when she returned to an exceptionally wet London in April, 1891, she brought with her seventeen trunks filled with new gowns.

The weather may have been responsible, in part, for a brief but serious illness that forced her to postpone any thoughts of doing a new play. An attack of pleurisy sent her to bed for a week, and again the world press gave its readers an edition-by-edition account of her condition. When she recovered she decided to do no acting until the autumn, and instead turned to her favorite hobby, that of attending horse races.

As a direct consequence she became involved in the stormiest and most spectacular of her romances. Much later, in a remark to various friends that was widely quoted, she said,

"It served me right for being lazy. How I wish I'd been spending my days in the theatre, where I belonged!"

There had been many men in her life since her break with Fred Gebhard, but she had formed no serious attachment. Prominent members of English and American society escorted her to parties, to the theatre and to the races, but she developed no real interest in any of them. She was close to no one but other members of her own profession, authors and artists.

Then, while attending the races, she met George Alexander Baird, Baron Auchmeddon. Possessor of one of the oldest and proudest of Scottish names, he was the last of his line, and was one of the wealthiest men in Great Britain. His income, most of it from coal mines in Scotland, was estimated at more than a quarter of a million pounds per year.

Known as Squire Abingdon, a name he used as an amateur jockey, he was the darling of the penny press. His father had died when he had been a small boy, and he had led a completely undisciplined life. Twice he had been expelled by Eton, the most exclusive of English schools, and only because of his family's prominence had he been readmitted. He had attended Magdalene College of Cambridge University for the required three years, but had left without winning his degree. A rebel who had never worked a day in his life, he consorted with jockeys, prize fighters and prostitutes.

He gambled to excess, he turned his back on the high society of which he was very much a member, and his exploits frequently landed in print. Himself a boxer of note, he became pugnacious when he drank, and he consumed astonishing quantities of liquor. He was a brawler, an iconoclast who thumbed his nose at the world, a gaudy dresser, and above all, a hedonist who never looked beyond the pleasures of the immediate present. He was also a very short, slender man, no taller than Lillie, who weighed only ten pounds more than her one hundred and twenty-eight pounds.

Baird had seen her as Cleopatra, and introduced himself to her by presenting her with betting slips on two of his horses, which were running that day. She tried to refuse, but he started to make a scene, and in her embarrassment she kept the slips. Both horses won, and she tried to return the one hundred pounds she had suddenly acquired. Baird accepted on condition that she accompany him to dinner, and he succeeded in spending the entire one hundred pounds that evening.

A psychiatrist might find it interesting that Lillie was older than all three of the most important men in her life, the Prince of Wales excepted. It can be said with considerable justice that she spent her entire adult life clinging to her own youth. Beauty had made her famous, and she saw to it that she remained beautiful. One way was to form attachments to younger men.

Certainly those men didn't think of her as an older woman. Thirty-eight years of age when she met Baird, she still looked like a girl in her mid-twenties. No one thought of her as maternal, and her beauty was still unblemished. Men like George Baird and Fred Gebhard were drawn to her for the same reason that those of other ages found her fascinating, simply because she was incomparably lovely.

The Squire owned a stable of racehorses and another of prize fighters; it was his questionable ambition to have the winner in at least one major horse race somewhere on earth every day, and to develop a heavyweight who would take the crown of John L. Sullivan.

For a number of years the Squire had been seen in public with a succession of remarkably ripe young actresses, most of them plump blondes with highly questionable reputations and very wise eyes. High society had looked the other way, and his elders had commented that these women were an improvement on the obvious trollops with whom he also consorted in the less fashionable parts of town.

Occasionally, when drunk, he became the victim of an unusual myopic delusion, and thought his mistress of the moment was one of his sparring partners. A number of his affairs had ended abruptly after the unfortunate young woman had suffered blackened eyes and other, assorted bruises. One actress, the blond Gladys Leslie, whose Thespian talents had won her few roles, had charged him with assault and battery after an evening on the town, and he had been forced to settle out of court.

The previous year he had been a principal in one of the lawsuits of the century. Eyebrows had been raised when a socially prominent member of the nobility, the Marquess of Aylesbury, had married a lissome dancer, Dolly Tester, but he and his family had been so prominent that society had been forced to accept her. One day about a year and a half after her marriage the new Marchioness had "eloped" with Baird, but had returned after he had threatened her while intoxicated. The Marquess had filed suit against the Squire, and had collected damages to the tune of fifteen thousand pounds.

That escapade had banished Baird from the ranks of the gentry. Gentlemen looked through him when they passed, ladies sniffed in-audibly, and no one of consequence was ever seen in his company. His transgressions had made him a pariah.

Then, suddenly, he was being seen everywhere with Lillie Langtry, whose obvious fascination was inexplicable. She, who had always shown taste in her choice of clothes, decor and men, had dipped down to the dregs of the barrel.

The good ladies of London were secretly delighted. Lillie's critical success in *As You Like It* and *Antony and Cleopatra* had restored a measure of her respectability, and her continuing friendship with the Prince of Wales, combined with the kindness of Princess Alexandra, had made it difficult for anyone to snub her openly. Now the situation was changed, suddenly. Any woman who allowed herself to be seen with the despicable Baird was worthy only of contempt. Ladies who no longer invited the Jersey Lily to their homes but nevertheless bowed to her in passing were seen to walk or ride past her with their noses held at an elevated angle. Lillie lost, overnight, whatever standing she still possessed.

She didn't care what anyone thought of her, and she made no secret of her relationship with the Squire. Apparently they plunged into an affair almost immediately, and Lillie did not bother to conceal the fact that she was sleeping with Baird. Casting aside all conventions, she even allowed him to kiss and caress her in public.

What she saw in him was and is a mystery. She made it clear to Coghlan, Whistler and a number of others that she was not in love with him, and that under no circumstances would she think of marrying him. She may have been attracted by his enormous wealth, but she had rejected other rich men, and, in any event, she herself was now a millionairess in her own right.

Perhaps she had hitherto unsuspected and unrevealed self-destructive tendencies. Perhaps she chose the Squire as an instrument of her own unrequited rebellion. He may have fulfilled sex needs of whose existence she herself had been unaware. Whatever the reason, she behaved like a woman who had been mesmerized.

Her friends found him repulsive, her colleagues avoided him, and her business associates refused to have anything to do with him. Her butler departed, and so did one of her maids. She knew better than to take him to Jersey to meet her mother and daughter, and it is unlikely that he would have gone. In fact, nothing that had been important in her life mattered to Baird. He rarely went to the theatre, and admitted that plays bored him. Gracious living was lost on him, he had no taste for gourmet cooking, and he had been known to wipe grimy hands on petit-point chairs. Even Lillie's handsome clothes were lost on him. He was infatuated by the loveliest woman he had ever seen, but he rejected the setting which had become so much a part of her life.

Lillie and her new lover had two interests in common, fine horses and fine jewelry. During the racing season they could be seen daily, cheering the Squire's winners and visiting the paddock. And Lillie blazed with new bracelets, brooches, rings and earrings of diamonds, rubies and sapphires. According to an unsubstantiated rumor, Baird gave her an emerald ring allegedly worth a vast sum. She did own such a ring, it is true, and kept it for the rest of her long life, but whether the Squire gave it to her is unknown.

No matter how lavish his gifts, he did her career no good. He demanded so much of her time, insisting they spend every moment together, that it was impossible for her to prepare a play for the 1891-92 season. He even objected when she went to Jersey for visits of one to two weeks at a time with her mother and daughter.

A crisis occurred in the strange relationship early in 1892, when the Squire went off to Scotland for a hunting and drinking trip of uncertain duration. Lillie went to Jersey to see Jeanne Marie, and then traveled to Paris so she could add to her already overflowing wardrobe. While there she discovered that Robert Peel, a handsome and personable young man, grandson of the great statesman and soon to inherit his father's baronetcy, was a guest at the same hotel. He was an old friend, and they dined together one evening. A few days later they lunched together, then came back to Lillie's suite for a chat.

While they were talking, George Baird burst into the sitting room. He had found Lillie absent when he had returned to London, and had followed her to Paris. He had been drinking, and lost all self-control when he saw her chatting with another man. First he accused Lillie of cheating, and when Peel tried to intervene, turned on him.

A courageous member of a family noted for its fortitude, Robert Peel was no physical match for a drunken madman. The Squire knocked him down repeatedly, then threw him bodily out of the suite.

Lillie had no chance to call for help. The furious Baird assaulted her, blackening both her eyes and inflicting an ugly bruise on her cheekbone. It was a miracle that none of her bones were broken. When she screamed and tried to call for help, he choked her until she lost consciousness.

His rage unabated, the Squire made a shambles of her apartment. Paintings and tapestries were ripped from the walls, furniture was overturned and smashed. Several new gowns had just been delivered by Worth, and he ripped them to shreds, also scattering the contents of her dresser drawers.

Lillie spent ten days in a hospital, and swore out a warrant for Baird's arrest. It took four policemen to subdue him, and the whole story made screaming headlines throughout the world. Lillie, the ha'penny press was quick to claim, had been so disfigured that she could never again appear on a stage. The actual facts were lurid enough, but the newspapers made them worse. Some of the less responsible hinted that Baird had found Lillie and Peel in bed. The vicious beating was exaggerated. Lillie would die in the hospital, and Baird was certain to face the guillotine.

Britain was embarrassed, and her government quietly took steps. Young Peel refused to press his own charges against Baird. The British Consul General visited Lillie at the hospital the day before she was released, and an hour later it was announced that she, too, had dropped charges. Baird, who had been held in jail without bail, was freed.

Lillie returned to her hotel suite, which had been completely refurbished at the Squire's expense, and found a diamond bracelet from Cartier's, worth a king's ransom, waiting for her. She kept the jewelry, but refused to see the donor.

She remained in Paris for two weeks, convalescing, and each day new gifts arrived. One afternoon she received fifty gowns from Worth. The following day a ruby pendant arrived. She was sent certificates making her the owner of three magnificent racehorses, all of them future champions. But her door remained closed to George Baird.

When she went to Cherbourg to take the Channel steamer to Dover, a steward in a tailored white uniform was on hand to tell her that "her" yacht awaited her. She was conducted to a magnificent steamship of 750 tons, 220 feet long, that was riding at anchor in the harbor. Her name, *The White Lady*, was new to Lillie.

She went on board, and there an abject George Baird awaited her. He handed her documents giving her ownership of the yacht, for which he had paid twenty thousand pounds, second-hand. He also gave her a check for fifty thousand pounds for the vessel's maintenance and crew salaries. Casually, with no strings attached, he was making her a gift worth one-half million dollars.

Lillie undoubtedly remembered the publicity benefits she had reaped from the *Lalee*. Ownership of *The White Lady* should prove even more beneficial, so she accepted conditionally. Baird could not drink in her presence, nor would she see him when he had been drinking. He could no longer interfere with her career or personal life, and she was free to go where she pleased and see anyone she pleased. He would visit her only at her invitation, and if, in her opinion, he misbehaved in her presence or mistreated any of her friends or associates, she would never see him again.

The penitent Squire accepted the conditions without question, and Lillie forgave him. They spent several days at sea before *The White Lady* put into port.

The story of her ownership made new headlines. Newspapers and magazines ran countless pictures of the ship's interior and exterior, and disapproving publications indicated that Lillie deserved her association with a man of Baird's caliber. American newspapers called the vessel *The Black Eye*, and the name was picked up around the world. Society was aghast, and some of Lillie's friends privately believed she had gone too far.

When she finally returned to London she found that the biggest theatrical hit in town was *Lady Windermere's Fan*, with Marion Terry playing the role that had been written for her. She was eager to return to work, and after renting the intimate Criterion Theatre, immediately went into rehearsals in a light comedy with a title that couldn't have been accidental, *The Fringe of Society*.

Her role, that of a bad woman with the proverbial heart of gold, was not taxing, and when she opened in early May, 1892, the critics were kind to her, but could not treat her vehicle seriously. They were unanimous in praising her appearance, however, and said she had never looked lovelier or more radiant. At thirty-nine she had discovered the fountain of youth, and in it was a pot of gold: there were lines at the box office, and the play was sold out for the next eight weeks. Lillie had never appeared in a real failure, a record that few members of her profession could equal.

Early in June, with the still penitent Squire accompanying her, Lillie went to the Kempton Park track to see the first race run by one of her own horses. Milford, one of Baird's gifts, was believed to be among the best two-year-old colts in England, and Lillie bet heavily on him. The jockey wore her new colors, turquoise and fawn, and she only half-concealed her own identity, listing the owner as "Mr. Jersey." She took the precaution because women were not listed as the owners of racing horses.

Milford won, and the newspapers reported that Lillie was one thousand pounds wealthier. The Squire happily admitted to the press that he had won ten thousand pounds.

Lily's play closed in August. The yacht had been redecorated in accordance with her wishes, Baird picking up the tab; according to some accounts he paid twenty thousand pounds, but the figure probably was exaggerated. Mrs. Le Breton and Jeanne Marie came on board, and Lillie, with Baird in attendance, went cruising. She spent some of her time at Cowes, and the press made much of the fact that *The White Lady* was not only larger than J. P. Morgan's famous *Corsair*, but dwarfed the yachts of Queen Victoria and the Prince of Wales.

Lillie's presence on the ship started a whole new school of rumors. She intended to make a trip around the world. She planned to sail to the United States for the new theatrical season. She was going to give up her homes on land and spend all of her time at sea.

The Jersey Lily made no attempt to stem the ceaseless flow of gossip. She could have silenced the press by announcing her actual plans, but she knew that talk increased sales, so she said nothing that might pinch off her priceless publicity. She told Griffith, who spent a week on the yacht, that she intended to double her fortune, and that she would have to work hard in order to achieve her goal. The world thought of her as a fortune-hunting glamour girl, and she had no intention of destroying that image as long as it remained profitable.

X

NEW PLAYS SUITABLE FOR A STAR OF LILLIE LANGTRY'S stature were not easy to locate, and the best she could find in the autumn of 1892 was a comedy-melodrama by Outram Tristram and Haddon Chambers called *The Queen of Manoa*. It opened at the Haymarket in late September, and Lillie had the satisfaction of knowing she had rented the first theatre in which she had ever played as a professional.

The critics praised her beauty, her clothes and her performance, in that order, but attacked the play without mercy, saying it was an inadequate vehicle. It sold out, nevertheless, and Herbert Beerbohm Tree, now a star in his own right, remarked one night when he came backstage, "It doesn't matter what you play, Lillie. You hold all London in the palm of your white steel hand."

The season was made more tolerable for Lillie because George Baird went off to the United States to see the British heavyweight, Charlie Mitchell, fight Gentleman Jim Corbett. On occasion she admitted to Griffith and wrote to Sir George Lewis, who was living in Kent, that she had grown tired of the Squire's constant presence. He had kept his promise not to drink when with her or come to her after he had been drinking, but he was still a boor and still associated with disreputable people. In all probability Lillie was afraid of him. His generosity was overwhelming, to be sure, but she could not have forgotten the physical beating she had suffered at his hands, and must have known he had not conquered his quick, terrible temper. She must have feared that he would lose control of himself if she dismissed him from her life. And it was likely, too, in spite of his promises, that his behavior would be unbearable if she became interested in some other man.

But Lillie was spared further embarrassment. Late in March, 1893, she was informed that Baird had died in a New Orleans hotel room. He had caught pneumonia after going on a three-day drinking spree, and was in such a weakened condition that he could not combat the ailment.

Lillie's grief was restrained, and Griffith said, years later, that he thought she seemed somewhat relieved. But she was forced to rearrange some of her own interests. Her horses had been housed in the Squire's stables under the direction of his own trainers, so she had to hire a trainer of her own. She also bought a three-story house called Regal Lodge in the tiny town of Kentford. The place had its own stable, and was known as a racing box.

The yacht was an even bigger expense, and with Baird no longer on hand to take care of the bills, Lillie had no intention of dipping into her own capital. So she put the ship up for rent, and the shrewd maneuver paid handsome dividends. There were so many people who wanted to say they had spent time on the Jersey Lily's yacht, among them a number of wealthy Americans, that she actually made a profit on the series of transactions. Edward Michael, Frank Griffith's assistant and the man who managed most of her personal financial affairs, was the authority for the statement that Lillie was congenitally incapable of losing money. After her death he told interviewers she would have been successful in any vocation.

By the summer of 1893 Lillie believed that her daughter was old enough to tolerate any London whispers that might reach her ears, so the child and Mrs. Le Breton took up permanent residence in the house on Pont Street. Their presence made life easier for Lillie, too, since she was no longer forced to shuttle back and forth between London and the Isle of Jersey. But she kept the house there, using it as a holiday home, just as she did her Kentford racing box.

Michael was in part responsible for taking *The White Lady* off Lillie's hands. He leased the ship to an American, Ogden Goelet, for twenty-five thousand dollars per year, and Goelet was obliged to pay all of the vessel's expenses, so the sum paid to Lillie was clear profit.

Rather than appear in another inferior play, Lillie preferred to wait until she found one that was suitable. Besides, after devoting herself almost exclusively to Baird, she was anxious to get back into the social swim. And she wanted to enjoy the experience of living permanently under the same roof with her daughter. So she took a year's sabbatical, and when London became boring she went to Kentford and bought more horses for her growing stable.

Many of the ladies of London continued to snub her, but the gentlemen felt no desire or need to avoid her, and it was inevitable that her name should be romantically linked with those of a number of prominent men. In fact, the rumor mills began to grind the first time a man escorted her anywhere in public, and if she was seen with him a second time, the newspapers speculated on the possibility of a forthcoming marriage.

Two of her more frequent escorts were members of the diplomatic corps. The Portuguese ambassador, the Marquis Luis de Soveral, was a bachelor with a full beard and a sharp sense of humor. The Austrian chargé d'affaires, Prince Paul Esterhazy, was a dashing member of Hungary's most prominent noble family, and he, too, was a highly eligible bachelor. One or the other escorted Lillie to some of the more important and glittering social events of the season, and it was impossible for the good ladies to avoid her.

Whenever the Prince of Wales was present he danced with her, or chatted with her at length, and on two occasions he escorted her to supper. So it was difficult for those who believed she had broken society's codes to turn their backs to her. Lillie was too proud to seek their unwanted friendships, but she deliberately made life more difficult for them, and spoke to them when in the company of the future Edward VII or a diplomat who could not be ignored without the creation of international complications. Had Lillie cared what society thought of her she might have been unhappy, but her senses of balance and humor saved her. She had created a fantastically successful life of her own, and she was content.

Mark Twain, who met her on a number of occasions, was impressed, and wrote at length about her clarity of judgment. He said:

Contrary to what one would expect of a woman whose fame was based on her beauty, Mrs. Langtry is an exceptionally intelligent person. She must read constantly because she is able to discuss in detail any book, classical or modern, English or American or French, that is mentioned to her. I know she isn't shamming, because I questioned her in some detail, and she KNEW the books. She also reads the newspapers, and doesn't bother with the trivia. She can talk about world affairs or financial matters or whatever with the good sense one would expect of a man who keeps up to date. She meets a stranger as an equal, and although she's so pretty her beauty is blinding, and she doesn't rely on feminine charm. She's what she is, and she expects one to take her or leave her. She is good company with her friends, but it would be hell to be married to her. She's too damn bright.

She was also too wise to bear grudges against old friends, and by the autumn of 1894 she and Oscar Wilde had resumed their friendship. Success had made changes in Wilde, who had grown even fatter. He lost his temper quickly and resented criticism, and Lillie disapproved of the handsome young men who followed him everywhere and laughed at his witticisms. But his wit was sharper than ever, and he put on none of his insufferable airs with old friends.

He had written a new play, *A Woman of No Importance*, but did not offer it to Lillie in spite of the burial of their hatchet. He could not have forgotten her rejection of his previous effort, and undoubtedly wanted to avoid another rebuff. Lillie was conducting a search for a new play, but did not blame him for not approaching her. She was one of the few in show business who refused to engage in long feuds, and she demonstrated to Wilde that she held him in affection and esteem by attending the opening night performance of his play.

He returned the compliment on March 19, 1894, when he went to the Comedy Theatre, where Lillie was opening in *The Social Butterfly*, an inferior play which, nevertheless, offered her a long, emotional role. Before the curtain rose the playwright, Robert Buchanan, broke every theatrical precedent by appearing on the stage and, in a vehement speech, denouncing the critics. They were trying to crush him, he said, but he defied them.

The audience was embarrassed, making it far more difficult for the cast to elicit a response, and the critical failure of the play was certified. Lillie's reviews were good, however; the critics said she succeeded in spite of her material, and they welcomed her back to the stage after her absence. They praised her beauty, her costumes by Worth and her ability to milk her part for its maximum effect.

Theatre-goers loyal to the Jersey Lily didn't care what kind of play she used as a vehicle, and trooped to see her, as usual. The play kept her busy through the spring, and far more important, it earned a profit, so she had no complaint.

The clamor in the United States for a return of the actress whose presence guaranteed box office was rising, so Lillie agreed to a new tour under the management of E. B. Norman. She would spend sixteen weeks on the road and would end the tour by playing for a month in New York. She hired James Pygott-Smyth as her leading man, and carried forty trunks of Worth clothes with her. Jeanne Marie traveled with her, but Mrs. Le Breton, who was ailing, remained behind in London.

New York was growing so rapidly that Lillie hardly recognized the city when she reached it in late summer, 1894. The theatrical district was no longer centered on Twenty-third Street, but was inching uptown; there were many theatres on Thirty-fourth Street now, and others were being built as far uptown as Forty-second Street. But some things were unchanged, and the usual army of reporters met her on her arrival. The American press never failed to pay homage to the Jersey Lily.

The house on Twenty-third Street that the now-married Fred Gebhard had bought for her was unrented and run-down, and at Abe Hummel's suggestion she put it on the market. She also learned that many of her investments were paying big dividends. At her direction Hummel sold some property in Salt Lake City that brought her a net profit of more than forty thousand dollars, and the sale of some lots in rapidly-growing Chicago realized another eighteen thousand. Hummel promptly reinvested the money for her, and Lillie wrote to her brother, Clement, that the theatre was no longer her principal source of income.

She and Jeanne Marie traveled in the *Lalee*, which had been repainted and redecorated, and the staple of her repertory was *Esther Sandraz*, which was advertised as a "new" play. She alternated it with the reliable *Peril*, and everywhere she did capacity business. She also received excellent reviews, it being taken for granted now that Lillie Langtry was a first-rate actress.

A dinner was given for her at Rector's, now the smartest restaurant in New York, when she returned to the city. *Esther Sandraz* proved to be a strong draw there, too, so Lillie extended her tour for four weeks, then another five.

She also was involved, briefly, in another scandal, and this time was completely blameless. On several occasions she was escorted by a wealthy Cuban, Antonio Terry, and the press played up these supper engagements so much that the young opera star with whom Terry had been having a highly publicized affair, Sibyl Sanderson, cut short her own tour and returned to New York.

Then Terry's wife sued him for divorce, and named Lillie as correspondent. The newspapers engaged in their customary circus, but Lillie followed her custom and refused to discuss the subject. She told Diamond Jim Brady and other friends, however, that the charges were absurd. Terry was only a casual acquaintance, and she had literally spent no time alone with him.

Apparently Senora Terry discovered the truth, because the charges against Lillie were dropped and Sibyl Sanderson was named in her stead. But the damage to Lillie's reputation was done, on both sides of the Atlantic, and there were millions who believed she had engaged in another unsavory affair.

But her romances, real or imagined, did no harm to her professional standing. The clamor from theatre managers all over the United States was so great that Lillie decided to remain in the country for the next season. She was anxious to appear in a play by an American author, however, and wanted Americans in the cast. The time had come for a complete change of pace, she decided, and didn't want to be typed as an English actress.

This time she had no difficulty in finding the right vehicle. Clyde Fitch, who would become the most successful dramatist in the history of the American stage, had just enjoyed his first great hit, *Beau Brummel*, in which Richard Mansfield was starred. He came to Lillie with his new play, a comedy called *Gossip*, and even the title was provocative.

Lillie's role was unlike anything she had ever done, and was that of a meddler who helped the lesser characters achieve their goals. There was a part for a younger, attractive woman in the play, too, so Lillie accepted both the challenge and *Gossip*, hiring the attractive Effie Shannon for the second lead.

The play opened at Palmer's Theatre in New York on March 11, 1895, and Lillie was subjected to an experience she hadn't suffered for a long time. With the exception of the always loyal William Winter, the critics attacked her. The play was good, they said, but Mrs. Langtry paid far more attention to her clothes and dazzling jewelry than she did her role.

Her Worth gowns made the audience forget the play, they said, and her gems were ostentatious to the point of suffocation. The assault centered on a diamond tiara she wore in the play's climactic scene, and they commented on the phenomenon that occurred when she appeared in it. Every woman in the audience gasped, and the onstage action halted.

The usual line at the box office assuaged Lillie's feelings, but Fitch was upset. He wrote at length about the incident some years later, saying he agreed that the jewels detracted from the play. But Lillie told him the climax was weak, and needed the diamonds to bolster if. Fitch insisted the drama would stand on its own.

So Lillie agreed to an experiment. For two performances she would wear nothing on her head, and if the playwright was satisfied with the reaction of the audience, she would put away her diamond headpiece. Fitch stood at the back of the theatre on the second night, and watched the audience sit in a dull, semi-stupor when Lillie made her appearance in the big scene. He hurried backstage to her dressing room.

"Don't ever play that scene without your tiara!" he said.

Gossip sold out, and seats were unavailable at any price. Audiences came to see Lillie in the clothes and jewels that had drawn so much critical fire, and Fitch, hauling in his royalties, was happy.

The incident called attention to Lillie's collection of gems, and the *Sun* became sarcastic. "Mrs. Langtry's brilliant company of diamonds, sapphires and the largest ruby in captivity is ably supported by Mrs. Langtry and several other living actors."

It was true that Lillie owned the largest ruby in the world. It was set in a brooch she seldom wore, but occasionally she pinned it to a gown just before going onstage. The audience buzzed, and thousands of women bought seats in the hope that they would attend a performance when she wore her fabulous gems.

The jewels were publicized by the press, which speculated at length on their worth, and the estimates ran as high as two million dollars. Only Lillie, who knew that many of her jewels were made of paste, realized the net worth of her collection in the vault was less than one hundred thousand pounds. Jewelry insurance was virtually unknown in the latter days of the nineteenth century.

Michael, the assistant manager, was responsible for carrying the box containing the jewels to and from the theatre every night. According to an account he wrote many years later, that duty cost him part of his longevity. "I was always afraid," he said, "that I would be attacked by robbers. But Mrs. Langtry didn't care. She thought of her jewels as stage props, and always said she could get more if they were lost or stolen."

At least a few people learned the true worth of the jewels later that same year, after Lillie had returned to England. When she went off to Paris on her customary clothes-buying jaunt, she put the box containing her collection in a prominent London bank for storage. On the day of her return a messenger went to the bank and presented a note bearing her signature, asking that the box be given into his custody for delivery to her.

The clever trick became known the following day, when Lillie went to the bank to pick up her jewelry. The officials presented her with the note, which she immediately recognized as a forgery. The gems had vanished.

Lillie sued the bank for negligence, and its officials, afraid the story would leak into print, asked for a conference. She was represented by her brother, and when the bank offered a settlement of forty-five thousand pounds, half the sum Lillie had demanded, Clement accepted it. His subsequent correspondence with her indicates he was pleased because she hadn't suffered a financial loss. Thereafter, until she rebuilt her jewelry collection, she wore only a thick rope of pearls, and as a consequence pearls became fashionable.

Her principal concern, while still in the United States, was the business she did in *Gossip*. The play did so well that she extended her engagement until the end of the summer, but refused to go on tour in the United States, in spite of the fervent pleas of theatre owners and managers. Her last London appearance had done nothing to enhance her reputation there, the competition was becoming keener for a woman who had passed her fortieth birthday, and she knew she needed a major success in England.

So, late in the summer, she departed from American shores, leaving Abe Hummel an additional twenty thousand dollars to invest in real estate and securities. She thought of leaving Jeanne behind to attend an American boarding school, but rejected the idea, even though the move would have solved many problems. They had been separated too often in Jeanne's earlier childhood, and Lillie wanted them to be together now.

Little is known about their personal relationship, but it could not have been a simple one. Jeanne was in her teens, an exceptionally pretty girl who more and more resembled her mother. In public she always called Lillie "Aunt," and virtually everyone, including Lillie's close friends, believed the girl was the daughter of Maurice Le Breton, who had died in India. A miracle had prevented gossip about her, and almost no one, including members of the press, knew she was Lillie's daughter.

Since Edward Langtry was still living, and still presumably didn't even know of the child's existence, Lillie could not claim Jeanne as her daughter. Edward would have been certain to insist, publicly, that he could not have been her father. So it was necessary, for the present, to make no changes in a situation that must have been uncomfortable for everyone concerned.

Lillie returned to her Pont Street house in London, hurried to Paris for a new wardrobe, and, in the autumn of 1895, opened at the Comedy Theatre in *Gossip*. The critics, taking their cue from their American colleagues, mauled the play and attacked her as a clotheshorse and jewelry dummy. Nothing had appeared in print about the loss of Lillie's gems, and she had new ones made of paste. The deception, including her new diamond tiara, remained undiscovered.

But the London theatre-going public reacted precisely as New Yorkers had, and *Gossip* became one of the Jersey Lily's most solid successes. She played in it through the autumn and winter, and did not close until May, 1896. It was the longest single run she had ever enjoyed in London. Then she went on tour for eight weeks in the provinces and there wasn't an empty seat anywhere.

A story Michael told about her in Manchester is typical of her hard-headed business sense. The proprietor of the theatre there, an industrialist, died while Lillie was playing in his house, and the manager wanted to close for twenty-four hours as a mark of respect. This would have necessitated refunding the money paid by twelve hundred ticket holders. Michael argued in vain, so Lillie herself took charge.

She had no objection, she told the manager, if he wanted to close the theatre and repay the ticket holders. But she insisted that he also compensate her for her share of the proceeds. The theatre remained open.

When *Gossip* closed Lillie went with her mother and daughter to the racing box in Kentford to put her stables in order. She owned six horses, four of them the winners of various minor races that made the operation solvent, but she was dissatisfied. Lillie Langtry had two constant demands: any project with which she was associated had to be the best, and had to earn substantial sums of money.

Her first step was to discharge her trainer and hire another, a man who had a long record of steady successes. She imported two young horses from Australia, Merman and Chesney, and told the trainer to sell any animal in the present stable that failed to win consistently. She was building for the following year, and, making her preparations far in advance, signed a contract with the leading American jockey, Tod Sloan, to ride exclusively under her banner.

Lillie wanted to buy a stud farm and raise her own champions, but she needed money for the purpose, and decided to sell her yacht. It was her own idea to dispose of the furnishings and fixtures separately, as she believed she could make more that way. She was right. She picked up twenty thousand pounds, and the yacht itself was then sold at auction. It went for a whopping quarter of a million pounds. These sums were clear profit for Lillie, as she had not spent a penny of her own money on either the ship or its interior.

She immediately put fifty thousand pounds into a stable, which she hoped to expand to a stud farm, and invested the rest. As nearly as can be estimated, she was now worth approximately two million dollars, and was becoming wealthier every year.

Her plans to return to the stage in the autumn of 1896 were dealt a sudden, severe blow when a San Francisco newspaperman unearthed the hitherto hidden story of her divorce. It became headline news all over the world, and Lillie decided to remain in seclusion at Kentford for a time.

The fact that Jeanne Marie was Lillie's child was included in the divorce proceedings, as she was given custody of her daughter. And almost immediately her worst fears were realized. An enterprising reporter for William Randolph Hearst's New York *Journal* went to Southampton and obtained an interview with Edward Langtry, who said, "However cruel it may be, I affirm that I never heard that my wife gave birth to a child of which I am reputed to be the father, until I learned of our divorce. That should dispose of the question of desertion."

The London press maintained a thunderous silence on the subject, but the public drew its own conclusions. The press elsewhere was less restrained, and there was considerable speculation in print regarding Jeanne Marie's paternity. The more responsible newspapers in the United States, France and elsewhere gallantly declared that Edward Langtry was being spiteful. The yellow journals gleefully played guessing games, but stayed within the limits of their national libel laws.

Lillie stayed in seclusion at the racing box, and would see no representative of the press. Eventually, she knew, the furor would die down. This was not the time to call herself to the attention of the public, so she could not appear on the stage during the coming season. If she returned to the United States, she knew, the freewheeling American press would go wild, and if she went to France she would be similarly treated. British reticence, combined with British libel laws, made England the best place to ride out the storm. Since Kentford was remote, it was preferable to stay there rather than brave the whispers of London. So she stayed at the racing box, and built up her stable until she owned thirty-six horses.

Her neighbors minded their own business, and paid no attention when Lillie and Jeanne went riding for several hours each day. Both mother and daughter were superb horsewomen, and appeared in high spirits. Lillie must have enjoyed one consolation: it was no longer necessary to hide Jeanne's true identity. Hereafter the girl could appear openly as her daughter.

Edward Langtry was not yet out of print. One day in the spring of 1897 he was found by several workmen wandering on the railroad tracks near Chester. His clothes were badly torn and filthy, he hadn't shaved for several days and he spoke incoherently. He was emaciated, and it appeared that he hadn't eaten recently, but he smelled strongly of whiskey.

He was taken to the Chester jail, but even after he became sober his talk was rambling and made no sense. By now the story was splashed in headlines, and Lillie paid the fees of three prominent physicians to examine her former husband. They certified him as insane.

He was taken to court, and was committed to a county asylum for the feebleminded. The news remained on the front pages for a full week, and several of Lillie's associates, among them Griffith and Michael, came to Kentford in order to hold reporters at bay.

Lillie did not appear in public again until the racing season began. Knowing she could not remain permanently in seclusion, she courageously decided to show herself, even though she undoubtedly realized she would be subjecting herself to fresh barrages of criticism. Every time one of "Mr. Jersey's" horses won a race — and they were winning consistently — the news was duly reported.

The prize horse of her stable, Merman, was entered in the Cesarewitch at Newmarket, the most important race in the entire English season. But he showed badly in his trials and in a number of lesser races, and Lillie was concerned about him. Then a friend told her that in Australia horses ran shoeless, so she tried an experiment, and Merman's shoes were removed. His speed improved, and he beat every other horse in the stable during his trials, never exerting himself.

Lillie kept the information to herself, and when the day of the Cesarewitch arrived, she bet the staggering sum of ten thousand pounds on her horse. The Prince of Wales also owned a horse running in the big race, and bowed to her from a distance. Members of society who were present presumably believed he was snubbing her.

Merman won the Cesarewitch easily, beating the Prince's horse and nine others. Lillie not only won the purse of thirty-nine thousand pounds, but the betting odds had been eight to one, and she collected an additional eighty thousand pounds.

The Prince of Wales conducted her to the paddock for the ceremonies that followed the race, and allowed himself to be photographed at her side. Those pictures appeared in newspapers throughout the civilized world. Then he escorted her to the Jockey Club, which no woman had ever entered, and could be seen by the press as he toasted her in champagne.

That night Lillie gave a small party at her racing box. She was the first woman whose horse had ever won the Cesarewitch, and her earnings that day had been phenomenal. For the moment, at least, her troubles of the past year were forgotten.

Late that night she received the final blow from Edward Langtry. An hour before the Cesarewitch had been run, he had died, insane and penniless, in the County Asylum of Upton, near Chester.

A torrent of press abuse was heaped on Lillie. The coincidence of her victory at the track and Edward Langtry's death as a pauper was too great for the newspapers to overlook, and they made the most of the story. It would have been useless for her to protest that she had supported him for many years, and had stopped only the previous year, when news of their divorce had been made public. In any event, it was against her principles to comment on personal matters.

But Clement Le Breton and Sir George Lewis felt that the attacks could not be allowed to pass unchallenged. So, without consulting Lillie, they issued a statement telling in detail of the financial arrangement Lillie had made with Edward Langtry. Lillie wrote both men furious letters, but they managed, to some extent, to counter the unfair and thoroughly unsavory publicity she had received.

XI

A SHORT TIME AFTER THE DEATH OF EDWARD Langtry, Lillie announced what had been a fact for a year, her retirement from the stage. The brief statement, issued by Clement Le Breton, offered no details, but merely said, "Mrs. Langtry is fulfilling a desire to return to private life."

Lillie was forty-five years old in 1898, and her private fortune was worth over two million dollars. She had no need to work, no need to subject herself to the publicity a public figure drew, and it was incumbent upon her to provide her growing daughter with a dignified home atmosphere.

Besides, her horses were winning her far more than she had ever earned as an actress. Merman was raking in one huge purse after another, and by the turn of the century he became the biggest money winner of the previous decade on the English turf. Six or seven of Lillie's other horses were also consistent winners, and it must be presumed that she bet consistently on all of them. Many years later she told friends in New York that her total profit in the years she owned her stable amounted to a great deal more than $500,000. The Jersey Lily had a knack for making money.

It has been said that the Prince of Wales met Jeanne at a very small, very private dinner party which Lillie gave at her racing box. According to this story, there were no more than a half-dozen guests present, the girl was presented to Prince Albert Edward, curtsied to him and then sat opposite him at the dinner table.

This story has never been either confirmed or denied. No guest list was ever revealed, and, if the party actually took place, none of those who were present saw fit to discuss the dinner. Lillie herself made no mention of the alleged affair, nor did any of the other principals, so the reader is free to decide for himself whether it actually took place.

When Lillie returned to London in 1898, she and Jeanne Marie began to be seen in public together for the first time. Sometimes they dined or lunched in fashionable restaurants, and frequently they attended the theatre together. Their resemblance was marked, and *Punch*, which published a sketch of them standing together, remarked that they looked more like sisters than mother and daughter. But Lillie refused to grant any interviews on the subject, and Jeanne made no statements to the press, either.

It quickly developed, however, that a woman who had been in the public eye for so long could not withdraw into comfortable anonymity. All of her movements — real, alleged and imagined — were duly reported by the world press. If she dined with a man, or went to the theatre with someone, or even engaged in casual conversation with an acquaintance at the races, it was reported that she was immersed in a new romance. Crowds gathered outside her front door at all hours in the hope of catching a glimpse of her entering or leaving, and her house was included on sight-seeing tours. In fact, it was said that as many colonials and foreigners wanted to see where Mrs. Langtry lived as were anxious to peer at Buckingham Palace.

According to the newspapers, if not in fact, Prince Paul Esterhazy was Lillie's favorite beau of the moment. Certainly she was seen with him more often than with anyone else. A widower in his late fifties, enormously wealthy and socially impeccable, Prince Paul was a polished diplomat, a brilliant conversationalist and shared one of Lillie's greatest interests.

He, too, was a horse fancier, and frequently bought racehorses in England for the Emperor Franz Josef. He was also a superb rider, and it was he, more than anyone else, who joined Lillie on her daily canter.

He made no secret of his own affection for her: he was quoted as saying that no man could resist her charms, and that anyone who knew her couldn't help falling in love with her. He also let it be known that he had asked her to marry him and that she was considering his proposal.

Lillie wasn't in love with Prince Paul, but must have been tempted to accept. As a princess and member of Hungary's most prominent noble family, she would instantly regain the social standing that had eroded through the years. And some of the ladies who took delight in snubbing her would be forced to curtsy to her at formal gatherings. Prince Paul's fortune was much larger than her own, so she had no fears that he was interested in her money.

But she put him off, and continued to see others, including the Marquis de Soveral, with whom she dined on a number of occasions when she went to Paris on one of her clothes-buying expeditions. She also had a number of engagements with various Englishmen, one of whom completely escaped the attention of the press. It is probable that no one thought of Hugo de Bathe as a serious suitor, since he was only twenty-seven years old.

Hugo was tall, slender and elegant, one of the more eligible young bachelors in England. His father, a retired general who had played a prominent role in the Crimean War, was a baronet, and when he died Hugo would inherit his title. Like so many aristocrats, Hugo did no work, but lived on a fairly small income. He was charming, but he had no intellectual or other achievements, and what Lillie saw in him was something of a mystery. That mystery would deepen.

Meanwhile there were other things to occupy Lillie's time and mind. Her horses continued to win, and her earnings from her stable grew larger. She bought a new cottage in Jersey, outside Saint Helier, overlooking the sea, and spent a great deal of her time there with her mother and daughter. Hugo de Bathe, who resigned his commission as an officer in the Royal Infantry, went there for a quiet, unannounced visit, and the islanders who saw him with Lillie raised their eyebrows. The two seemed inseparable.

Going to great pains to avoid publicity, Lillie married Hugo at her father's old church, St. Saviour's, in the summer of 1899. No word of the wedding leaked into print, and the Jersey Lily continued to be known privately, as well as publicly, as Mrs. Langtry.

By the late summer Lillie was bored by her retirement and decided to return to the stage. Marriage, like racing, could not occupy all of the furious energies she had generated over a period of so many years. She was forty-six years of age, nineteen years older than her husband.

Lillie's contemporaries could not understand why she married Hugo, and her motives remain incomprehensible three-quarters of a century later. She must have known he had no estate of any importance, and that he was barely able to support himself on his income, which meant that, for all practical purposes, she would be forced to contribute to his support. Granted that most of her affairs had been with younger men, but the difference in her age and Hugo's was rather startling. He had achieved nothing in the world, had no accomplishments and it seemed unlikely that he would achieve prominence on his own initiative.

If, as was suggested, Lillie knew he would inherit a baronetcy and that she would then become Lady de Bathe, the argument that this was her motive seems flimsy. She could have been a princess had she elected to marry Paul Esterhazy, or a baroness had she become the wife of Luis de Soveral.

Oscar Wilde was widely quoted as remarking on "a famous actress, who, after a tragic domestic life, has married a fool. She thought that because he was stupid, he would be kindly, when, of course, kindliness requires both intellect and imagination."

Wilde had been having his own troubles. Convicted on a morals charge after a spectacular trial in 1895, he had been condemned to a term of imprisonment at hard labor. He had been released in 1897, and had gone to France, where he was living under the name of Sebastian Melmoth. Most of his old friends had cut him, although his literary reputation was enhanced, in 1898, by the publication of what many consider his best work, the "Ballad of Reading Gaol."

Lillie, who understood prejudice and was never one to avoid an issue, made a point of coming publicly to Wilde's defense. His morals, she. told the press, were his business and that of his partners in intimacy. He and they were adults, and she saw no reason for the furor that had been created. Her attitude was the better part of a century ahead of its time.

Not content with words, Lillie gave Wilde concrete support. She met him in Paris on her trip there in 1898, and, as his funds were pitifully low, gave him a substantial sum of money. This fact was not revealed until late in her life, and even then, although Wilde died in 1900, she refused to discuss the matter or let anyone know how much she had given him.

She could be very secretive about her own private life. Attending the races in both England and France in the late summer of 1899, she continued to call herself Mrs. Langtry, although Hugo now accompanied her everywhere.

She ended her supposed retirement that autumn, renting the Haymarket Theatre and going into rehearsals in a new play that Sidney Grundy, the author of *Esther Sandraz,* had written for her. It was called *The Degenerates,* and, according to the standards of the day, was far advanced. Lillie undoubtedly knew it would create a critical storm, and that many of the critics would consider it lewd.

She returned to London, Hugo at her elbow, and he accompanied her to rehearsals every day. Before the play opened the news of her marriage leaked out, and made headlines all over the world.

Lillie refused to receive the press, so Hugo made a brief announcement, revealing the place of the marriage. The reporters had so little to write about that the representatives of the ha'penny press invented their own news, and Hugo was called a millionaire.

This was far from the truth, as Lillie undoubtedly knew. All three of his sisters had married well, but General Sir Henry de Bathe lived on his government pension, and owned nothing but his small house in the English countryside.

Hugo's family promptly made major contributions to the circuslike atmosphere. Sir Henry disinherited his son, and refused to receive Lillie under his roof. The bridegroom's three sisters, Mrs. Henry Lawson, Lady Crossley and Mrs. Harry McCalmont, declined to be interviewed, but made their own opinions very clear. They did not expect to entertain Hugo and his wife, or to be entertained by them.

American newspapers added to the uproar. Lady de Bathe, Hugo's mother, was said to have been her husband's mistress for years before their marriage, had given birth to several illegitimate children and had never been recognized by society. That was why she and Sir Henry lived in virtual seclusion. The New York *Journal*, describing Hugo for its avid readers, called him "an empty-headed young noodle." The Chicago *Inter-Ocean* referred to him as "a typical English saphead."

Regardless of what appeared in the news columns, however, most American newspapers wished Lillie the best of good fortune in their editorials. She was more in the news than ever before.

The demand for seats was so great that the entire run of *The Degenerates* sold out prior to the opening, making the reviews academic. Nevertheless the critics were duly outraged. Lily played the part of a courtesan who was not accepted by London society, and it was the consensus of the reviews that the play was degrading, that Lillie's performance was in keeping with the tone of the work itself, and that she had lowered herself by even consenting to appear in such trash.

The American press printed a series of juicy rumors that sparked the desire of audiences in the United States to see the play. *The Degenerates* was said to be the "true, authentic" story of Lillie's own life, and the set, supposedly furnished with her own chairs, divans, lamps and tables, was purported to be an exact replica of the furniture in her own drawing room. Gossip-hungry theatre-goers found it difficult to contain their desire to purchase seats.

The success of the play in London was so great that Lillie extended the run, then did it again. She also celebrated by selling her house in Pont Street, and buying a larger, even more elegant establishment at 2 Cadogan Place, in the same neighborhood, a house previously owned by Charles Dickens. Lillie always kept up with the latest in comforts, and over the years installed a telephone, electric lights and other modern conveniences.

The house itself was a showplace. Sitting rooms were done in Regency, Georgian and Louis XV styles. The trophy room was filled, and included a stuffed bear, the gift of a group of Denver admirers. On the mantel were several large silver nuggets. Lillie's bathroom was done in mosaic tiles of three different colors, and she had a special wardrobe room, with walls of double-damask silk, to house her many hundreds of dresses. She could entertain sixty guests in the dining room, and adjoining it was a ballroom, with a platform for an orchestra. Her bedchamber was lined in satin, and the walls of Hugo's room were done in tweed, an expensive innovation that duly shocked the gentry when reported in the press.

Life must have been dull for Hugo, who dutifully accompanied his bride to the theatre every night, then went on to dine with her daughter. Jeanne was now eighteen years of age, a striking beauty who closely resembled her mother, and many who saw her in restaurants and other public places with Hugo assumed that the handsome young couple were romantically inclined. Inasmuch as Hugo loved his wife and Jeanne Marie was loyal to her mother, those who indulged in guessing games were mistaken.

Mrs. Le Breton also made her home with the newlyweds, but took no active part in their lives. Her memory was failing, she was suffering from a number of the infirmities of old age, and Lillie had to hire a nurse to take care of her.

Late in the autumn of 1899 war erupted in South Africa between Great Britain and the Boers, and the Crown asked for volunteers. Hugo, who may have grown tired of living as an appendage to the world's most beautiful, glamorous woman, offered his services. The most immediate result was a change in his family's attitude. Sir Henry and Lady de Bathe invited him to bring his wife to their house, and his sisters, along with their husbands, joined in the family celebration. Hugo was going off to fight for Queen and country, so his notorious wife became socially acceptable.

Lillie could not have been surprised when her father-in-law found her lovely and charming. They became close friends, and the relationship was maintained until the end of his days. She also managed to placate his sisters, and established firm, lasting friendships with them. Like all the others who came to know her, they found her fascinating.

The twentieth century arrived, and Lillie went off to Paris for her new wardrobe at the house of Worth, Hugo accompanied her, and then left from France for South Africa. His commission had not yet been restored, but apparently he expected the oversight to be rectified when he joined a volunteer regiment.

Meanwhile Lillie prepared for a new campaign of her own. She intended to reconquer the land that had earned her so much money, and was planning a new tour in the United States. She would travel alone. Her mother, who now required the daily attentions of a physician, would remain in the new house, and Jeanne, a young lady in her own right, would stay in London with Mary Cornwallis-West, who would introduce her, informally, to society.

Jeanne's position was unlike that of her mother, and no doors were closed to her. By now a great many people were conscious of the question of her paternity, and not even the highest-placed aristocrat wanted to incur the possible wrath of the man who had spent a lifetime in preparation for the day when he would succeed his now aged, ailing mother on the throne. Jeanne was a beautiful, self-effacing young lady, and was welcome everywhere.

The welcome her mother received when she reached New York in early April, 1900, was riotous. Fireboats steamed out to quarantine, and threw sprays of water high in the air. A band made up of members of the Policeman's Benevolent Association played martial airs from the deck of a rented ship. So many reporters came out to the liner that they filled two boats.

Lillie, wearing a suit trimmed in ermine, greeted the press in the salon, ordered champagne for all and chatted with practiced ease. Her husband shared her disappointment that he had not been able to accompany her, but was engaged in fighting for the Crown. She had no idea how much her horses had earned in the past year, but one owned racehorses for sport, not for income. She was still an American citizen, and was delighted to return to her true home. She had gained only two pounds in the past decade, and attributed her trim figure to exercise and careful diet. And she was returning to the stage from her retirement because she could not bear to disappoint the many friends who had written to her, begging her to do another play.

The reception accorded *The Degenerates*, which opened a week after Lillie's arrival, with the original English cast intact, was similar to London's. Audiences were deliciously scandalized, and the star took more curtain calls than anyone cared to count. The critics were shocked, and hinted that the actress playing the leading role might be as degenerate as the play in which she was appearing. The drama was unworthy of the name, and it was a criminal shame that one who had delighted audiences as Cleopatra and Rosalind should consent to bathe in mud.

But theatre-goers responded as they had always done, and the Garden Theatre was sold out for every performance. Lillie's record remained intact, and was unique in her time: she had never suffered a financial failure.

A battle of a different sort remained to be won, however. Lillie agreed to act as the patroness of a luncheon at Sherry's, the proceeds of which were to be used for medical supplies to be sent to South Africa. A subtle boycott was formed, and the ladies of the Four Hundred, New York's social elite, quietly refused to purchase tickets.

The war, which had been conducted secretly, suddenly burst into print. The *Post* wanted to know whether the boycott was justified, the *Sun* called the cause noble, regardless of what society thought of Mrs. Langtry, and the *Journal* asked the rhetorical question in an editorial, "Should good, pure women associate with Mrs. Langtry, even for the sake of charity?"

The question was answered in the affirmative. Mrs. William B. Astor, one of the acknowledged leaders of society, unexpectedly agreed to become a co-sponsor of the luncheon. So did Mrs. O. H. P. Belmont. The rush was on, and Mrs. George Gould, Mrs. Ogden Mills, Mrs. Stuyvesant Fish and many others leaped onto the Jersey Lily's bandwagon.

No one knew what had caused society's sudden change of heart, but the New York press, echoed by newspapers throughout the United States, came to a juicy, speculative conclusion. The Prince of Wales had allowed it to become known that he would look with social disfavor on anyone who snubbed the Jersey Lily. A cartoon showing Lillie and the future Edward VII driving a team of horses called the Four Hundred was reprinted in hundreds of newspapers.

This was the era when scores of American heiresses had married or were marrying into the British nobility, when an

American debutante's success or failure was determined on the basis of whether she had been received at a Buckingham Palace audience. So New World society, totally Anglophile in its orientation, was sensitive to any nuances emanating from London.

No known factual basis has existed, down to the present day, for the allegation that Prince Albert Edward frowned on those who wanted to boycott Lillie Langtry. The truth of the matter well may be that he knew nothing whatever about the snubbing game taking place on the far side of the Atlantic. If his name was actually used to bring pressure on the recalcitrant ladies, he took good care to stand apart, saying and writing nothing himself.

The mere hint of his displeasure would have been just as effective as a real threat, of course, and Lillie would not have been reluctant to use any weapon at her disposal. Her prestige was at stake, and she would have become something of a laughingstock had she lost the campaign. So it is possible that she herself created the rumor that resulted in the total capitulation of the good ladies.

The best her foes could achieve was a minor, hollow victory. Always publicity conscious, Lillie had announced that a number of New York debutantes and attractive young actresses would act as barmaids at the luncheon. But the Women's Christian Temperance Union, prodded by unnamed ladies, made a formal complaint to the New York police, so the pretty young women remained untainted, confined their activities to the serving of food and left the handling of liquor to professional barmaids.

The luncheon was an overwhelming success. Lillie acted as an entertainer, appearing in a sketch with Maxine Elliott and Cissie Loftus, two of the great actresses of the American stage.

Antonio Scotti, the gifted tenor of the Metropolitan Opera, sang several selections, and the mistress of ceremonies was Edna May, another American actress of the first rank. Everybody who was anybody in New York society was present, and the *World* reported that the chief bartender was the Earl of Yarmouth, who happened to be an old friend of Lillie's. The affair netted almost ten thousand dollars for Boer War medical relief, and Lillie emerged the victor.

Other campaigns remained to be fought after she completed a successful run of eighteen weeks in New York. *The Degenerates* went on the road, opening in Philadelphia, and one of the city's leading newspapers, the *North American*, attacked her as she had never before been assaulted. Three pages were devoted to articles written by members of the clergy, housewives and others of high repute, all of them condemning not only her play, but her own life. The lead article, written by a reporter named Arthur McEwen, was the worst, and said in part:

> Mrs. Langtry is ophidian in the temperature of her blood, and her heart is a cash register. She has always been her collected, selfish, cynical self in society, the theatre, and her own pleasures, resolved to get out of life whatever money could bring her in the way of luxury and freedom.
>
> Anybody who has a fortune to spend has been welcome to do it — raw boy, dissipated rounder, dissolute old sport, prince, commoner, gentleman, blackguard, anybody.

The attack was far too serious to be ignored, for very good reason. The police in Washington, D.C., and Cleveland had already notified the theatre owners in those cities that *The Degenerates* would not be allowed to play there. Detroit, Cincinnati and St. Louis were questionable. If the savage assault went unanswered, it might be necessary to close the play.

Abe Hummel was summoned to Philadelphia, and Lillie held a council of war with him. The attorney wanted to sue the *North American*, but Lillie demurred. A suit would take months before the outcome became known, and a newspaper always had the last word. More immediate measures were required.

Either Lillie or Hummel conceived the idea of getting in touch with James Gordon Bennett, publisher of the New York *Herald*, long an admirer and friend of the Jersey Lily, and a man who was not afraid to do battle with anyone. A telephone call was made to Bennett in New York, and the next day's *Herald* featured a long defense of Lillie by Clement Scott, the British critic who was spending a year in the United States as a guest critic for the newspaper.

The irony of the situation was that Scott, who had seen *The Degenerates* in London, had attacked the play without mercy there. But he made a sharp distinction between Lillie Langtry, his friend of many years, and the character she portrayed on stage. Many great artists, he said, had led scandalous lives, and among them he named Charles Dickens, Thomas Carlyle, Edmund Kean and Sarah Bernhardt. Were the works of Dickens to be boycotted because of alleged immorality in his private life? Should pianists refuse to play the works of Chopin because he had lived openly with George Sand? It was necessary to make a distinction between the artist and his private life; besides, Scott declared, he could not share the opinion that Mrs. Langtry was herself degenerate in any way. She was one of the loveliest ladies it had ever been his privilege to know.

Copies of Scott's article were sent ahead to every city on the itinerary. The police in Pittsburgh and Detroit responded by banning the play there, too, but elsewhere the results were favorable. Other American cities were prepared to demonstrate their sophisticated hospitality by welcoming the Jersey Lily and *The Degenerates*. The play sold out in Boston, Buffalo, Louisville, St. Louis, Memphis and Nashville before going on to Chicago for a run.

There Lillie faced a different sort of crisis. One night, moments before going onstage, she received a cablegram informing her that Hugo de Bathe was seriously ill in a South African hospital. The message contained no details, and she didn't know whether he had been wounded in battle or otherwise incapacitated.

When taking her curtain calls at the end of the performance Lillie's iron-willed composure suddenly broke, and she startled the audience by weeping. But her instinct saved her, she took the entire group of sixteen hundred people into her confidence, and was awarded a standing ovation.

The following day she made a rare public statement, saying, "I confess that I have felt wounded at some of the attacks on the play and upon myself, but at nothing so much as the accusation made in some places that mine is a vulgar performance. Whatever people may say about me and my affairs, nobody who knows me could believe I would appear in a performance that was unrefined in spirit and tone. *The Degenerates* is critical and harsh, perhaps, but is in no sense vulgar."

The statement was memorable because it was the only time in a quarter of a century that Lillie stooped to answer those who pilloried her. Presumably her feelings were assuaged somewhat by the unprecedented box-office success of the play in every city.

While Lillie was creating a sensation in the United States, her daughter was enjoying a success of her own in London. Jeanne Marie was invited everywhere, and was the guest of duchesses and marchionesses. Whenever the Prince of Wales saw her at a social function, he invariably singled her out for a chat, as did Princess Alexandra. Late in the spring of 1900 she was presented to Queen Victoria at a formal Buckingham Palace audience, which put the ultimate seal of approval on her respectability.

The name of Miss Jeanne Marie Langtry appeared regularly in the society columns of London newspapers. She was seen everywhere, at dinners, at balls, at receptions and attending the races, where she loyally placed bets on her mother's horses. Then a rumor appeared in the ha'penny press that was echoed by the American newspapers. It was said that Arthur Hill, nephew of the Marquess of Downshire, a wealthy playboy in his late twenties, was enamored of the girl and had presented her with a valuable gift of jewelry.

Lillie, still touring in the United States, learned via an exchange of cablegrams that the rumor was false. Jeanne had been escorted on a number of occasions by Hill, but had no personal interest in him and had accepted no jewelry from him. But Lillie decided the time had come to return to England.

She had enjoyed a long, highly profitable tour in *The Degenerates*, and she wanted to play the provinces before the play lost its notorious luster. Above all, she wanted to keep a closer watch on her daughter. So, by late summer, 1900, she was back in London, and soon thereafter she took her mother and Jeanne off to Jersey for a holiday.

While there she participated in an extraordinary event, and gave a special performance of *The Degenerates* to open Saint Helier's new theatre, the only one on the island. She delivered her curtain speech in Jersey French, and, of course, brought down the house.

After an interval devoted to watching her horses race, Lillie toured the provinces for ten weeks, and her gross receipts were the largest she had ever earned. Everything she touched still turned to gold, and the newspapers speculated that her personal fortune was now worth more than three million dollars.

Then Hugo de Bathe returned from South Africa with a medical discharge. He had spent several months in a Capetown hospital, suffering from a fever, and was being returned to civilian life. His military service had changed him, and a new experience confronted Lillie, a humiliation unlike anything she had ever before known.

XII

THE ROMANCE OF LILLIE LANGTRY AND HUGO DE Bathe, if it can be called that, was short-lived. A bride and groom who had been married only a short time before being forced to undergo a military separation might be expected, under normal circumstances, to enjoy an ecstatic reunion. But Lillie and her husband had as little regard for precedent as, it appeared, they had for each other.

Within a week of Hugo's return to London in December, 1900, he was being seen in public escorting other women. One, a generation younger than Lillie, was a chorus girl, currently appearing in a musical comedy, who had achieved a measure of fleeting and questionable fame by painting butterflies on her bare shoulders when she wore an evening gown. Her admirers said she was the only chorus girl in London who had wit and intelligence as well as a flashy beauty.

Friends who reported to Lillie that they had seen Hugo with the girl also told her that he had been the girl's frequent escort prior to his marriage. But Lillie, according to Mary Cornwallis-West, showed a complete lack of concern, then went on to express her philosophy. She approved, in both principle and practice, she declared, of husbands spending time with women other than their wives. All men liked to roam, and there were fewer strains on a marriage when a man strayed with the knowledge and consent of his wife. And if a wife was sure of herself, as well as of her hold over him, he would be more attentive than ever when he finally returned to her.

These advanced theories were put to a sudden, embarrassing test one evening when Lillie was dining with a party of friends at one of London's most fashionable restaurants. Hugo and the chorus girl with the butterfly shoulders were seated opposite the party on the far side of the room. Lillie's friends froze, and the girl looked very uncomfortable. But Lillie was equal to the occasion, and not only waved to her husband, but smiled at the girl. Hugo, who didn't seem in the least ill at ease, returned his wife's wave.

Whether Lillie suffered privately, and to what extent, is not known. But it is a matter of record that Hugo did not accompany her when she went off to Paris for the Christmas holidays. Her only companion was Jeanne, and her husband remained at their London town house, which he was able to use as his headquarters for his evening forays with a variety of handsome young women.

If Lillie was upset, she had no chance to grieve in Paris. The usual dinners and other parties were given for her by her many friends there, who recognized Jeanne as a beauty in her own right. The girl came into her own, and it was said that three young French gallants proposed marriage to her. If the rumors were false, neither Jeanne nor her mother denied them.

Lillie's rift with Hugo ended abruptly after her return to London, and within a few days she departed again, this time taking him with her on a holiday journey to the Riviera. Apparently reconciled, they spent much of their time at the Monte Carlo casino, and newspaper reporters who had nothing better to do regularly wrote stories to the effect that the Jersey Lily had broken the bank there. Nothing of the sort was true. Lillie lacked the sure hand in card games and at roulette that marked her as a horse player, and she lost small sums almost daily. But she enjoyed the climate, and the excitement of the casino appealed to her so much that she wrote to friends in London saying she hoped, some day, to retire to Monaco.

On her return to London she plunged into the biggest gambling venture of her life. She had long wanted a London theatre of her own, where she could book other attractions when she herself wasn't playing, and on several occasions had engaged in abortive negotiations with a number of owners. Now the proprietors of the Imperial Theatre came to her with an offer.

They would give her the house on a long-term lease for the trivial rent of only twenty-five pounds per week. But she would be required to install electricity and make a number of other repairs, which would cost approximately four thousand pounds.

Edward Michael, who was now Lillie's manager, didn't like the deal. The Imperial, which had twenty-five hundred seats, was one of the world's largest legitimate theatres, and was so barnlike that audiences complained. Michael believed that not even the Jersey Lily was a strong enough draw to fill it regularly.

Lillie not only accepted the challenge, but decided to have the entire theatre redecorated. New dressing rooms and a Green Room would be installed for the actors. Complete new lighting equipment would be built on stage. The royal box would be decorated in purple silk, the other boxes in yellow satin, and new seats of red plush would fill the auditorium, which would also be painted. And the unattractive lobby would be torn out and replaced with one that she herself helped design.

The proprietors gave her an option, granting her the right to buy the theatre outright at any time she wished during the next five years. Edward Michael protested vigorously, both verbally and in writing, but Lillie paid no attention. Her restless energies had found a new outlet, and she was on hand every day to watch the interior of the most beautiful theatre in London taking shape.

She paid dearly for the privilege of repairing and redecorating the Imperial. Michael later estimated that she spent $150,000 on the project, and he admitted that the estimate was conservative. Even under the best of circumstances Lillie could not recoup her investment for many years, and the house was so large that producers and stars were reluctant to play there, wanting the intimate atmosphere of a smaller theatre.

This venture marked the only time in Lillie's long career that she showed poor judgment; never before and never again did she lose money. In all, over a period of several years, the Imperial cost her more than a quarter of a million dollars, and the return to her in prestige was not worth the cost. But, as she herself eventually wrote to Michael, she did not regret her efforts. Her stable paid for the investment, and she had the satisfaction of knowing she had created a showcase worthy of the Jersey Lily.

Somewhat to the surprise of others in show business, she did not rename the theatre the Lillie Langtry. "I have been criticized for my refusal to name the theatre after myself," she wrote to Abe Hummel. "I have no yearning for a memorial of that nature, and if future generations wish to remember me, I trust they will look at my photographs. I console myself with the realization that the criticism would have been worse had I given the theatre my name."

While Lillie occupied herself at the theatre, Jeanne was busy in the London social swim, and her name was linked with that of one or another prominent young nobleman. She went to Paris again with her mother for the 1901 Christmas holidays, and soon after her return to London, Lillie announced her engagement.

Jeanne's betrothed was Sir Ian Malcolm, a prominent member of a wealthy Scottish family and the heir to a title. Thirty-three years old, he was a Member of Parliament, and had seen service in the diplomatic corps and as a secretary to Lord Salisbury, one of the leaders of the Tory party. He was considered one of the more important of the younger men in the Commons, and his political prestige, combined with his social standing and money, made him one of the marital catches of the decade.

The reaction of the Malcolm clan was emphatic. Jeanne was accepted, but her notorious mother was not. None of the usual premarital festivities were held, Jeanne loyally refusing to attend any function to which her mother was not invited.

The Prince of Wales had succeeded to the throne as Edward VII on January 22, 1901, when Queen Victoria had died, and there was considerable speculation regarding his attitude toward the forthcoming marriage. Queen Alexandra solved the problem in her own way at a ball given by the Duchess of Devonshire, given a year after Victoria's death. It was the first social event of significance after a year of mourning, and the always gracious Alexandra ended the gossip by pointedly seeking out Jeanne, chatting with her for some minutes and then leading her to King Edward VII to make her curtsy. If the universally respected Queen Alexandra openly approved of Jeanne and of the marriage, society was in no position to criticize either the bride or groom.

The wedding took place at St. Margaret's of Westminster on June 30, 1902, and was attended by several hundred persons, among them representatives of many of the great families of England and Scotland. The bride was given away by her mother, who casually broke precedent because she did not want the function performed by her own, much younger husband or by some friend of the family.

Immediately following the ceremony Lillie gave a bridal luncheon for two hundred at her house. It was a formal affair, complete with a string orchestra playing on the dais in the ballroom, and the champagne flowing freely.

On exhibition in one of the drawing rooms, guarded by several private detectives, were some of the bride's gifts. Among them were a diamond horseshoe pin sent by members of the Rothschild banking family, a diamond necklace from the groom's parents and an even larger diamond necklace from the groom. Lillie gave her daughter a large diamond brooch, and privately presented her with a handsome check, her linen and other gifts. She also settled the sum of five thousand pounds per year on her in order to make the new Lady Malcolm financially independent for life. No matter what the future might hold, Jeanne would never be forced to work for a living, as her mother had done.

Conspicuous by its absence was any recognition of the occasion by King Edward VII, but the press later reported that he had given Jeanne "a splendid jewel," and had written a letter in his own hand to the girl "in whom he had been strongly interested since her birth."

The party ended soon after the departure of the bride and groom on their honeymoon, and Lillie spent the rest of the afternoon with friends at the races. One of her own horses was running, and she was observed placing larger bets than was her custom. It was also said that she was unsmiling and quiet. Her horse came in first, and she won six thousand pounds on him, which paid for the wedding and many of her gifts to the bride.

One of the curious features of the proceedings was the absence of Hugo de Bathe. Lillie remained true to her tradition, and offered no excuses to anyone, but it was generally believed that Hugo had been requested by his wife to take himself elsewhere. He was younger than the groom, and his presence could have been an embarrassment to all of the principals. The American press reported that he was seen on the Riviera, but he eluded reporters, and a subsequent search indicated that he was not a guest at any of the hotels in the area. He reappeared a week later in London, and refused to discuss his journey.

Hugo may not have been a model husband, but he was remarkably accommodating. Presumably that was all Lillie asked of him.

With the wedding out of the way, the Jersey Lily turned her thoughts to business. A young playwright with a popular appeal, J. Hartley Manners, came to her with a new comedy-drama, *Crossways*, which she saw as a possible vehicle. It needed a great many changes, however, and she was so wise in the ways of the theatre by now that she was able to make suggestions herself. Manners incorporated them into the play, and, with an eye on the box office, agreed to include Lillie's name as co-author.

Lillie had wanted to try out the play in the provinces and then bring it into London, but she knew the Imperial was too large a theatre. Besides, America was beckoning again, and she could earn more there. Michael had a hand in making the decision; he had booked the Imperial solidly for the coming season, and there was a chance it might earn back some portion of Lillie's substantial investment, so he wanted no changes made.

Rehearsals were scheduled to start in September, but were postponed when Lillie received word that her mother had died in Jersey. Mrs. Le Breton had been in failing health for two years, and had been in such poor condition that she had been unable to attend the wedding of her granddaughter. She died peacefully in her sleep.

Lillie and Clement, her only surviving children, went to Jersey immediately. Most of Mrs. Le Breton's old friends had preceded her in death, so the services were private, and she was buried in St. Saviour's churchyard beside her husband.

Lillie went into rehearsal in *Crossways* early in October, opening the play in the provinces the following month. She was forced to curtail her tour by five weeks in order to meet her American commitments.

Just before she left England she received a mark of royal favor signifying to the world that her association with Edward VII had not come to an end. On the night of December 9, a special command performance of *Crossways* was held at the Imperial, and only those who received invitations, presumably with the approval of the royal household, were permitted to purchase tickets. Lillie announced that the night's proceeds would be given to Queen Alexandra for distribution to charities as she saw fit.

The presence of King Edward and Queen Alexandra in the royal box was an extraordinary event. This was the first time since he had reached the throne that the King had consented to the giving of a command performance, and his assent signaled to the world that he still held Lillie in high esteem. Those who understood the subtleties of royal etiquette suffered no false illusions regarding their relationship, however. The presence of Queen Alexandra at the performance meant they were good friends, and signified that the sixty-two-year-old monarch and the forty-nine-year-old Jersey Lily were not engaging in an affair.

Most Americans were not aware of such intricacies, however, and the command performance aroused great interest on the western shores of the Atlantic. It was no accident that Lillie's American press agents and the managers of the theatres at which she was booked saw to it that the public knew a special performance had been given for the King, who had applauded heartily.

No publicity of any kind attended the command performance in London, but the whole city seemed to know about it. A number of seats found their way into the hands of ticket speculators, who were demanding the unprecedented price of one hundred pounds, or approximately five hundred dollars, for a pair of seats. There were no empty seats on the night of the performance.

Crowds began to gather in front of the Imperial shortly after noon, and by sundown were so large that the special detail of police assigned to maintain order and keep traffic moving was twice augmented. The throng continued to grow, however, and by theatre time it was estimated that more than ten thousand persons had gathered, clogging many streets and making it almost impossible for vehicles to move. The curtain had to be delayed almost a half hour because the King and Queen were delayed in the streets as they rode to the theatre from Buckingham Palace.

Lillie and the members of her cast gave their usual performance, in no way indicating their awareness of the royal couple's presence. Then, during the second intermission, the King and Queen retired to the large, private anteroom adjoining their box, accompanied by an equerry and a lady-in-waiting. At the King's request Lillie was summoned.

There is no record of what was said. Michael, who was present, later was questioned closely by the American press, and said only that His Majesty had congratulated Mrs. Langtry on her performance, and asked her to convey his thanks to the rest of the company. Her Majesty also expressed great pleasure. They asked Mrs. Langtry to share the special refreshments that had been provided for them, but graciously consented to her refusal, realizing that she never ate or drank during a performance.

Nothing else was revealed, but the press agents saw to it that the American public knew the meeting had taken place. Rarely had any command performance been given greater publicity.

Lillie and her supporting company sailed on the White Star liner *Celtic* on December 10, immediately following the special performance. The American public began to buy seats, and the American press whetted its knives. Mrs. Langtry, said the New York *Sun*, soon would be fifty years of age. If she tried to rely on her beauty, much less the glamour of her relationship with King Edward, she was very foolish. She would be judged exclusively on her acting ability, if any.

The New York *World* was even more severe. It was time for Mrs. Langtry to grow up. She was no longer the radiant creature who had dazzled all of America, and the public wanted to see a real actress, not a fading beauty who played at acting.

The *Celtic* reached New York on December 19, 1902, and the seventy-five reporters and photographers who came out to meet the ship were stunned. Lillie Langtry greeted the press on the open deck, attired in an ermine-trimmed coat of sable, and never had she been lovelier. With it she wore a matching fur hat, and doffed both in the first-class smoking room, where the interview was conducted. Her figure was as slender, trim and supple as it had ever been, and her dress of soft, green wool showed off every famous line to superb advantage. What astonished the photographers was her youthful face, which had not changed in twenty years, and they took pictures for a half hour while she obligingly posed.

The *Sun* ate a large helping of crow. "Mrs. Langtry," wrote the bemused reporter, "should be renamed Ponce de Leon, but on second thought he should have been called Lillie Langtry. He searched for the Fountain of Youth, but it was obvious to all who greeted her on board her ship, as it soon will be obvious to all New York, that she has found it. One would be lacking in gallantry to beauty if one revealed her true age, so let it suffice that she looks half her years."

The *World*'s portion of crow was even larger: "Mrs. Langtry's age is of no importance. She is still the most beautiful woman in the world."

On the surface the interview was the most candid Lillie had ever granted. No questions were out of bounds, and she answered all of them. But experience had made her nimble, and she fielded line drives and deceptive dribbles with the deft poise of the true veteran:

Why had she allowed anyone to command her to give a performance?

"We gave it before such a marvelously distinguished audience. It was given by request of the King, and a king's request is the same as a command, isn't it?"

Why was she doing the play in the United States before playing it in London?

"We didn't want to be subjected to English criticism. Americans are so clever that if they like a play it is sure to be well received in London. So we'll go there with all the laurel wreaths I'm sure our marvelous play is going to win here. You might say we're using good American common sense."

Was it true that she was intending to obtain a divorce while in the United States?

"I am very well satisfied with my present domestic state, thank you."

Then why was it her husband had not accompanied her on her present trip?

"My husband objects to extensive traveling. Moreover, he is afraid of coming to America because the newspapers here are so much freer than those in England. He dislikes being interviewed."

Didn't he like America?

"Since he's never been here, he's in no position to judge this country."

Didn't he want to become acquainted with it?

"I dare say he'd have joined me if he had been curious. I assume he's content to stay in England."

Was it possible for a marriage to be successful when the partners were separated for long periods?

"I can only speak for Mr. de Bathe and myself, and would not presume to offer advice to others. Our marriage is a very happy one."

Did she know that a letter sent to her by King Edward and bearing his signature was on sale in a New York shop?

"How extraordinary."

How did she account for this?

"The servants, I dare say. I received twenty-five or thirty letters from the King when he was Prince of Wales, so I suppose one of them escaped."

Might she buy it back herself?

"Certainly not! It was nothing more than a note from a friend. It couldn't have been anything more. But I suppose someone will want to buy it. There are souvenir collectors who will buy anything."

Would she explain her beauty secrets?

"Gladly, although I wouldn't call them secrets. I've read all sorts of rubbish about a skin-peeling process I supposedly use, and about electrical massages I'm believed to take. My secret is work, plenty of sunshine, soap and water. I eat plain food, I drink very little, I inhale fresh air and I have a happy spirit."

Did she still engage in physical exercise?

"Daily. I start my day with a cold bath after getting plenty of sleep, and I do exercises for an hour. When I'm in the country I go out for long walks, but I find it too difficult in the city, where people follow me. So I make up the difference with more exercise. Any woman can do what I do!"

Having duly dispensed with the inevitable advice, Lillie brought the interview to a merciful close. The story appeared on the front page of every New York newspaper the next day, and hundreds of others throughout the United States printed their own versions of it.

The critics were equally flattering to her, and she confided to Michael that the reviews of *Crossways*, which were only faintly scornful, were better treatment than the London critics would have accorded it. As always, however, the public paid no attention to her reviews, and long lines formed at the box office.

The extraordinary publicity Lillie received was partly responsible. In addition to the reviews, special articles were written about her wardrobe, the furnishings of her suite at the aptly named Imperial Hotel, the identities of her visitors and the dishes on her breakfast tray. The *Journal* went farther than all the rest of the newspapers, and printed a rhyme on its front page:

Sing a song of Lily
Who never seems to fade,
In four and twenty gorgeous gowns
Alternately arrayed.
All hats and fans and feathers,
That cost like anything:
Isn't that a blossom fair
To set before the King?
The King was in his royal box
"Plugging" the applause,
The Queen was there beside him
Applauding, too, because.
When came the dainty Lily
To learn the drama's fate
The good King beamed a beamy beam
And shouted out, "It's great!"

A number of magazine, book and newspaper publishers came to Lillie with offers for her life story, written by herself, ghostwritten or told to a writer. The bidding became intense, and William Randolph Hearst believed he would win the prize, but Lillie announced she was not interested in selling at any price. Not until late in her life did she finally write — herself — the most innocuous of bland autobiographies, *The Days I Knew*, which the George H. Doran Company of New York published in 1925. In it she made no mention of her daughter, the name of the Prince of Wales appeared casually two or three times, and she discussed nothing of substance in her life. In fact, the book was devoted almost exclusively to harmless anecdotes about fellow actors and various friends in high society. Few women in public life have ever been more discreet.

Lillie's behavior was impeccable during her New York run, too. She was duly recorded paying a visit to her former house on Twenty-third Street, which Abe Hummel had sold to the Pasteur Institute. She made the front page of the *Herald* when a reporter following her wrote that she had purchased eleven dozen handkerchiefs the previous afternoon, and still another article revealed that she was sending the handkerchiefs as gifts to various friends in England.

There were subtle changes in her habits. Although she dined on occasion with Diamond Jim Brady at such popular establishments as the Gilsey House, she was seen less frequently in public places. Friends entertained her in their homes, and Harriet Hubbard Ayer gave several small supper parties for her. Lillie returned their hospitality in her hotel suite. Perhaps she was growing a trifle weary of reading about her social life every time she opened a newspaper.

When she went on tour, however, late in the spring of 1903, she continued to travel in the style that left Americans open-mouthed. The *Lalee* had been destroyed by a railroad-yard fire, so the American manager of her tour, Harry S. Alward, rented another private car for her. She was served by a butler and two maids, and in every city her railroad car was worth a front-page story. One of her less publicized activities was that of visiting the box office of each theatre on the day of the opening to check the advance sale.

When *Crossways* played for a week in Washington, D.C., the Jersey Lily received a dinner invitation from the White House, and President Theodore Roosevelt arranged the dinner hour so she could reach the theatre in time for her evening's performance. T.R., who brought authors and artists, athletes and aesthetes to the White House, and who found people of many types interesting, was as charmed by Lillie as she was fascinated by him. She sat on his right, and they chatted with great animation through the meal. As had happened in her relations with Gladstone and many others, Lillie always rose to the challenge of prominent, powerful men.

Asked her impression of the President, she replied, "I never discuss a host or a friend, and I consider the wonderful Mr. Roosevelt to be my good friend."

Henry Adams, a lifelong intimate of Theodore Roosevelt, who was present at the dinner, commented on the evening in his own unique way. "I've never envied Theodore's successes," he said, "because I've attributed so many of them to luck. But I was so jealous of him during his animated talk with that radiant creature that my appetite would have been ruined if the food hadn't been delicious."

Not until T.R. ended his second term as President did Lillie reveal to friends what had made the greatest impression on her at the White House dinner. Her host, she said, had astonished her by revealing that he thought of himself as a professional author who happened to be spending "a few years" in public service. Asked what they had discussed, she replied, "Why, Mr. Roosevelt's books, of course. I made it my business to read several of them before I went to the White House."

One of the highlights of Lillie's tour was her appearance in Providence, Rhode Island, although she had no advance notion of what was in store for her there. The previous year she had commissioned an English author, Percy Fendall, to write a play for her, and had paid him the sum of two hundred pounds, which was considered an outrageously high fee.

Fendall had done a comedy, *Mrs. Deering's Divorce*, which Lillie had considered too frivolous. Her contract with Fendall had made it mandatory for her to produce it within twelve months, but she had delayed the presentation, intending to sit down with him first to discuss rewrites. Now she received a cablegram from her brother, Clement, informing her that

Fendall was demanding she live up to the contract. If she refused, all rights would revert to the playwright.

So the Jersey Lily and several members of her company made hasty preparations for a single performance of the play in Providence. She would fulfill the letter of her contract, and her reputation wouldn't be harmed by the production in the New England industrial city that was removed from the mainstream of international theatre.

She and her actors enjoyed themselves thoroughly, playing the comedy so broadly it became a farce. To her amazement the audience loved the play, and called her back for repeated curtain calls. The next day an even bigger surprise was in store. Not only did the Providence press rave about the evening, but the Boston critics had come to see her, too, and gave her the best reviews she had ever received from them.

Mrs. Deering's Divorce, they said, provided one of the most amusing evenings in the theatre that Americans had seen in years. And Mrs. Langtry had found her true home in light comedy. She had a sure touch, an instinct for farce, and gave her best performance.

The play was polished in hastily scheduled additional performances during the remainder of the tour, and Lillie made immediate plans to present it in London when she returned there in the autumn of 1903. It was destined to become one of her greatest box-office successes, and may have been her most outstanding critical triumph. She included it in her permanent repertory, and over the period of the next decade it earned her a fortune, and also contributed materially to Fendall's comfort.

She returned to London in August, 1903, intending to take a holiday of eight weeks before returning to work, but unexpected complications caused her distress. The Imperial Theatre had been sold to a religious sect that disapproved of the stage, and the building would be razed before the end of the year. A study of Lillie's contracts with the previous proprietors offered her no safeguards, and she was powerless to prevent the destruction of the place into which she had poured so much money.

But the Jersey Lily never surrendered easily, particularly when money was at stake, and waged a bitter fight. On several occasions she accompanied Clement to meetings with the business managers and solicitors of the sect, and earned their grudging respect, even though they disapproved of actresses in general and of the notorious Mrs. Langtry in particular.

Negotiations dragged on, but Lillie and Clement finally persuaded the new owners of the property to make a cash settlement. The sum Lillie received was only a fraction of what she had spent, and she suffered the only major financial reversal of her entire career.

What bothered her even more was the lack of availability of another theatre. London was enjoying its best season in many years, and there were no theatres open for bookings until the following spring. She had no intention of waiting, and told Michael her one desire was to recoup her losses as rapidly as possible. She could spend money lavishly when she chose, but under no circumstances could she live with the knowledge that her current operations were in the red.

A few cablegrams were dispatched, and that solved one immediate problem. The Jersey Lily would return to the United States later in the autumn of 1903, and would present *Mrs. Deering's Divorce* in New York, following the engagement with an ambitious coast-to-coast tour.

In order to ensure the success of the tour, Lillie conferred with Fendall, and at her suggestion the playwright added a brief new scene to the play. In it Lillie removed her dress, and would be exposed to the audience for a few moments in her underwear before donning a dressing gown. She well knew the effect she would create and the publicity she would receive.

Not that disrobing on stage was particularly new, but it was still considered daring. Ada Isaacs Menken, who had achieved a certain standing in the artistic world because of her poetry and her literary lovers, had created a sensation on both sides of the Atlantic a half century earlier when she had appeared on stage wearing pink tights in a play called *Mazeppa*.

Ever since Ada had broken the ice, others had followed her example. The beautiful Anna Held, also an American favorite, had achieved renown of a sort by appearing on the stage immersed in a bathtub filled with milk, whose cosmetic properties she praised, via her press agents.

But no actress of stature ever appeared in a state of undress before turn-of-the-century audiences, and it was shocking that a lady would dare to remove her gown in full view of the paying customers. Lillie well knew she would appear on the front pages again, and told Michael she was looking forward to the furor she would create. As to the question of decency, or the lack of it, she intended to wear a full-length slip, and the audience would see less of her body than was revealed in an evening gown. Nevertheless the cunning maneuver was certain to guarantee sold-out houses in every city on the new tour.

She didn't wait for the tour to start bringing in money, however. One of the best three-year old horses in her stable, Smilax, was running in four races over a six-week period, and she bet heavily on him in the first three races, allegedly winning fifteen thousand pounds. In the last and most important of the races, however, she refused to wager a penny on him. He was first-rate, she said, but two of the other horses running against him were equally good, and she had no intention of placing a substantial bet when the odds were against her. Her hunch proved accurate: Smilax came in second.

"Horse racing is like the theatre, which is a reflection of life," she said. "And in life I place bets, including those on myself, only when I believe I'm going to win. One never knows what will happen, but one always weighs the odds before plunging."

London, Lillie was discovering, had become a dreary place. Oscar Wilde had died in France, and in the summer of 1903 James Whistler had died. Other good friends had scattered; some were on the Continent, a few were making extended visits to South America, which had become fashionable, and still others were in the United States.

Virtually nothing is known of Lillie's relations with her daughter during this period. It has been said that Sir Ian believed it would be wise if Jeanne was not seen with a woman who was so notorious, but there is no evidence available that substantiates this claim, which has been made by two or three of Lillie's biographers. She and her daughter had been close for many years, Sir Ian had known the family background of the girl he married, and nothing untoward happened that caused a rift between mother and daughter.

What seems more likely is that Lady Malcolm behaved discreetly for the sake of helping her husband's career, and that she and Lillie visited each other in private. Both had large town houses in London, and it was a simple matter for them to dine together, spend afternoons in each other's company or manage visits in other ways without exposing themselves to the public gaze.

Whatever the reasons, Lillie's sojourn in England was made without fanfare of any kind. She was seen on a number of occasions at the races, but otherwise spent all of her time living quietly, out of the limelight. She was still newsworthy, but no one saw her in restaurants or supper clubs, and she attended no dinners or other functions. Perhaps she wanted to enjoy a brief period out of the public eye, and it may be that she was accommodating Hugo, who detested publicity.

He did agree, however, to spend a portion of the coming year in the United States with her. Her tour would be a particularly long one, so it must be presumed that neither wanted a separation that might last for a full year.

In any event, the brief stay in London was the lull before the greatest publicity storm the Jersey Lily had ever created. As she well knew, her disrobing scene in *Mrs. Deering's Divorce* would cause the heavens to open, and would saturate the front pages of every newspaper in the United States.

XIII

MRS. LANGTRY HAS MADE A CAREER OF SHOCKING the American theatre-going public, and this time she goes too far beyond the bounds of good taste by unnecessarily removing her clothes on stage. She cannot be faulted for wanting to demonstrate that her figure would be the envy of a woman of thirty, but one expects a greater sense of propriety when an actress of Mrs. Langtry's stature steps on stage.

The review of *Mrs. Deering's Divorce* that appeared in the *New York Times* was austere in its disapproval, but other newspapers were less circumspect. Lillie was accused of being cheap, flamboyant and immoral, but she ignored the criticism and undoubtedly felt content when she paid her daily visits to the box office. Her entire run of sixteen weeks was sold out, but she had booked such a long tour that she was unable to extend the engagement.

As always, she traveled in a private railroad car, and as always, she gladdened the hearts and enriched the bank accounts of theatre owners in every city she visited. The critics said the play was thin and that her performance utilized only a fraction of her talents. But women came to see the glamorous actress wearing another of her dazzling wardrobes, and their husbands came to see her undress. Lillie traveled to California by the northern route, returned by the southern, and nowhere was there a single vacant seat.

Hugo de Bathe arrived in New York shortly after his wife's departure, early in 1904, timing his arrival so he would escape publicity. The ruse was successful, and he joined Lillie in Cleveland, met her again in Chicago and St. Louis, and spent two weeks with her in New Orleans. Nowhere was his presence announced, and he remained anonymous when he returned to New York to buy himself a small racing sloop.

When Lillie reached San Francisco she followed Abe Hummel's advice and sold the ranch she had owned near the city for so many years. The property brought her no income, which annoyed her, and she disposed of it for forty-five thousand dollars. She lost several thousand on the investment, one of the few times she wound up in the red on a transaction, but she promptly put the money to good use by buying a number of lots in Los Angeles and Santa Barbara. Hummel thought she was wasting her money, and wrote to her that San Francisco was the only city of the future on the Pacific, but Lillie disagreed with him. The climate of southern California would attract many settlers, she believed, and she predicted that she would triple her money. It might be noted, for the sake of the record, that she kept the lots until several years after the end of the First World War, and more than tripled her investment when she finally disposed of them.

On her return across the continent Lillie finally paid a visit to the town that bore her name. The Sunset Limited passed through Langtry, Texas, and officials of the Southern Pacific Railroad were sufficiently publicity-conscious to be delighted to honor her request that a halt be made there.

Langtry was a typical turn-of-the-century cow town located in the heart of the cattle flatlands of Texas. There were no trees anywhere, and the grasslands and tumbleweed stretched to the horizon in every direction. Shacks were made of sandy, caked mud, or of wood that had been imported from distances of two hundred miles or more. The station was a dilapidated shed, but a newly painted sign was nailed to a pole, announcing to the world that this was LANGTRY. The unofficial population at the time of the Sunset Limited's unprecedented stop was one hundred and fifty-seven persons, not counting the "young ladies" who made their headquarters in the two saloons that stood opposite each other on the rutted main street.

When the train came to a halt, Lillie wrote later, she thought a mistake had been made. She could see nothing but grazing lands, and not until she left her private car at the rear end of the train did she realize that the front portion of the train had halted in front of the station, leaving her car far behind in the open country. The entire town had gathered to greet her, and a delegation appeared to act as her escort.

Lillie was disturbed to discover that "Judge" Roy Bean, the town's founding father who had renamed it in her honor, had died several months previously. The delegation was headed by the new justice of the peace, a man named Dodd, and the new postmaster, whose name was Fielding. The owner of the general store, the blacksmith and other local dignitaries were presented to her, and were followed by the cowhands, one of whom outraged his colleagues by throwing his arms around the guest of honor and planting a grubby kiss on her mouth.

A serious fight was barely averted. The citizens of Langtry rushed to Lillie's defense, and pistols were drawn, forcing the amorous cowhand to reach for his own gun in self-defense. Fascinated passengers on board the Sunset Limited, who had been watching the ceremonies, hastily drew back from the windows.

The guest of honor herself saved the day and prevented a pyrotechnical display by laughing, patting her enthusiastic admirer on the cheek and kissing the most belligerent of her defenders. Peace was restored.

The ceremonies continued, and the married men brought their wives and children forward to be presented. Lillie gravely shook hands with each woman and child to whom she was introduced. Then someone remembered the fancy ladies of Langtry, who were clustered together at one end of the little platform, and presented them en masse.

Lillie proved equal to the occasion, and again she shook hands, carefully asking each girl her name. The prostitutes were in awe of the woman whose reputation indicated that she was the world's most successful practitioner of their own profession, and they carefully studied her makeup and attire. Lillie returned the compliment by treating the girls graciously, chatting with them and, above all, refusing to condescend to them.

Then she was taken on a tour of the town. The largest and most impressive building in town was the late Judge Bean's saloon, which he had also used as his office and courtroom. It was called the Jersey Lilly, and the guest of honor commented on the spelling. A bar ran the entire length of the ground floor, and behind it were tacked twenty to thirty posters of the woman Roy Bean had idolized. Most were advertisements for some of her earlier plays, and were yellowed, faded and torn. A member of her entourage immediately went back to the train for a set of new posters.

The working headquarters of the daughters of joy affiliated with the Jersey Lilly saloon were located on the spacious second floor, but the guest of honor diplomatically regretted her inability to inspect these rooms, due to a lack of time. Justice Dodd, now the proprietor, broke out whiskey for everyone present, and Lillie was handed a shot, too. She forced herself to emulate her hosts, and downed her raw frontier liquor in a single gulp. Nearly everyone in the admiring throng noted that she didn't cough, gasp for breath or shudder, although she later wrote that she had been forced to exercise all of her considerable will power to prevent herself from retching.

A tour of the town didn't take much time. Lillie inspected the newest of the wooden buildings, the schoolhouse, and gave the schoolmaster one hundred dollars to buy textbooks. She was taken to the cemetery, and stood for a few moments at the grave of Roy Bean, who, she was informed, was one of only fifteen persons buried there who had died a natural death.

Several housewives wanted the guest to sit in their kitchens for a few moments over a cup of coffee, and Lillie solved the dilemma by proposing that everyone have coffee together in the post office. This was the first occasion in the history of Langtry that the respectable ladies and trollops sat down together under the same roof, and the matter was the subject of considerable controversy in the town for many months thereafter.

Lillie was reminded that her hour had passed when the engineer of the Sunset Limited blew the train's whistle. The entire population of Langtry accompanied her to her car, and there, standing on the steps, she made a brief address, not one word of which was transcribed for future generations. A small boy made her a gift of two "natural born Texas horned toads," and a youth in his teens presented her with a caged mountain lion cub.

Then she was given an official gift, a pistol bearing an engraved plate, which read, "Presented by W. D. Dodd of Langtry, Texas, to Mrs. Lillie Langtry in honor of her visit to our town. This pistol was formerly the property of Judge Roy

Bean. It aided in finding some of his famous decisions and keeping order west of the Pecos. It also kept order in the Jersey Lilly saloon. Kindly accept this as a small token of our regards."

The cowhands fired their pistols and rifles in salute as the train pulled away. Lillie was so touched by the visit that she wept, retired to her stateroom and was not seen again by other members of her company that day.

The tour took *Mrs. Deering's Divorce* to Canada, and in Toronto Lillie did a good deed that she refused to publicize. An exceptionally pretty young English actress named May Hallett, who was stranded there when the play in which she had been appearing closed abruptly, came to her seeking employment. Lillie had no openings, but hired the girl as an understudy, and kept her on tour with the company until they returned to New York. There she introduced May to the producer, Charles Frohman, who hired her for the ingenue lead in a new play, *The Silver Slipper*, starring Edna Wallace Hopper.

The girl created a minor sensation, and went on to a limited stardom of her own. Not until many years later did she reveal the story about her benefactress, whom she called the kindest and most considerate of women. Lillie helped many struggling young actors and actresses, she said, but always insisted that these gestures remain unpublicized.

Hugo de Bathe awaited his wife in New York, and was anxious to escort her to the city's more fashionable restaurants and supper clubs. But Lillie had other matters on her mind. Her brother, Clement, had just arrived from England in response to her summons, and sat down with her and with Abe Hummel to review her entire financial situation. Hummel had been urging her to consolidate her holdings, and Clement agreed that her extravagances were costing her a fortune.

Her brother returned to England and immediately sold her London town house, complete with furnishings, for a staggering £75,000. He also placed some of her unmatched jewelry with Christie's, the antique, art and jewelry dealers. These pieces had been stored away in a safe-deposit box, and were never used, so Lillie realized a huge profit on them. They sold at auction for a sum in excess of £137,000, and the story made new headlines.

The Jersey Lily, the newspapers of North America and Europe declared, had gone bankrupt, and was forced to liquidate her holdings. She was alone in the world, ignored by her friends and deserted by her daughter. She was paying the price for her dissolute life, and respectable people pitied her.

Like so many tales told about Lillie through the years, the story was fabricated out of whole cloth. The truth of the matter was that her financial situation had never been more solid, and she invested the sum of more than $150,000, her profits from the American and Canadian engagement of *Mrs. Deering's Divorce*, in additional New York and Chicago real estate. Quietly, almost secretively, she had become a major property owner in both cities.

But the reporters, without knowing it, did tell the partial truth about one aspect of her situation. Lillie's relations with her daughter had been deteriorating for some time, and were still worsening. Had there been an active dispute, an altercation of some kind, Lillie might have found the break easier to bear. But there was no argument, no indication of hard feelings. What was happening was simple: the aristocratic Malcolm clan wanted nothing to do with England's most notorious theatrical star, no matter how great her wealth, and Jeanne was under constant pressure to keep her distance from her mother. The girl had allowed her correspondence to fall off, and no longer answered her mother's letters. Lillie, always sensitive to slights and rebuffs, appears to have realized what was happening, and made no attempt to force her daughter to remain close to her.

The outside world knew nothing of these events, and Lillie maintained a tight-lipped silence. It is significant that even in her autobiography she made no mention whatever of Jeanne's existence. A reader who depended exclusively on that book for the facts of the Jersey Lily's life would never know she had given birth to a daughter whom she had then reared.

But she seems to have been less reticent with a few people who were close to her. Soon after her death, a quarter of a century after her estrangement from Jeanne, David Belasco declared that the break with her daughter caused her the greatest suffering she had ever known, and that her grief remained unalleviated for many years.

If Mrs. Langtry and Lady Malcolm had any contact after the daughter drifted away from her mother in 1904, there is no record of it. Mary Cornwallis-West and some of Lillie's other friends, writing circumspectly, indicated they never saw each other, and said that Lillie, after writing several letters that went unanswered, made no further attempts to revive the relationship. Jeanne, busily building her own life, vanished from her mother's existence, and either by accident or design, their paths did not cross again until the very end of Lillie's life.

Lillie learned she had become a grandmother when New York reporters telephoned to ask how she felt on achieving the milestone. At the age of fifty-one she was the world's most glamorous grandmother — and a deeply hurt woman; she cabled her congratulations to Jeanne on the birth of a son, but received no known reply.

As always, the Jersey Lily sought solace and refuge in work, and accepted a new challenge. She received an offer to tour South Africa, to open a new theatre in Johannesburg, and to play as well in Capetown, Durban, Pretoria and a number of other cities. The lure proved irresistible, and when the news of the engagement became public, the New York *Herald* saluted her with an editorial, saying that work kept her young, that her new status as a grandmother was irrelevant to her standing as the most beautiful woman in the world.

De Bathe, remembering his own unpleasant experiences in South Africa during the Boer War, refused to accompany his wife there. Instead he returned to England, where his father was ill. Apparently Lillie made no strenuous attempt to persuade him to accompany her.

She had to go back to London, too, to prepare for the new tour, and moved into a suite at the rebuilt and renovated Savoy Hotel, where her presence and that of singer Nellie Melba made the place famous overnight. She decided to present a number of her most successful plays on the tour, among them *As You Like It*. Members of London's theatrical set raised their eyebrows at the thought of a fifty-one-year-old woman playing Rosalind, but Lillie had lost none of her business acumen. Her legs were still shapelier than those of most women half her age, and as new publicity photographs proved, she still looked spectacular in tights.

The guarantees she received from South African producers and theatre owners enabled the entire company of seventeen actors and actresses to sail in style on the *Walmer Castle*. Scenery and properties stored in the hold filled thirty-six large crates. Edward Michael made the trip as Lillie's business manager, and her personal entourage included two maids, a chef and her new secretary, Ina Goldsmith, an exceptionally bright young woman who also handled press relations.

There was no need for a publicity agent on the tour, however. The mere fact of the Jersey Lily's presence was news everywhere, and the entire tour was the greatest triumph Lillie had ever known. She intended to spend six months in South Africa, and instead stayed for a full year, leaving England in the early spring of 1905 and returning in May, 1906.

In city after city she was met by the mayors and reception committees made up of distinguished citizens. Bands escorted her to her hotel, and often were on hand to conduct her to and from the theatre. Everywhere her repertory was completely sold out in advance, and had to be extended. Never had the press gone overboard for her, and the critics raved about her performances, some calling her the greatest actress of the age.

Her personal success was equally great. A number of South Africa's wealthiest owners of diamond and gold mines presented her with gifts that would have cost a fortune elsewhere, and an apocryphal story insists that a Durban millionaire — unnamed — tried to commit suicide when Lillie refused to accompany him to his villa and stay there with him for a month.

Rudyard Kipling, twelve years Lillie's junior, and recognized as one of England's greatest authors, was paying one of several visits to South Africa, and his sojourn there coincided with Lillie's tour. He met her, was charmed, and insisted on acting as her guide on her many sight-seeing trips. She was an enthusiastic and indefatigable tourist, anxious to see everything in this land about which she had known nothing, and Kipling, making his fourth trip there, was anxious to show her all the sights.

Contrary to some of the rumors heard at the time, there is no evidence to indicate that Lillie and Kipling had an affair. In fact, the few letters they exchanged indicate they enjoyed a proper, almost prim friendship. Kipling was very much in love with his wife, Caroline, with whom he had collaborated in the writing of several works, and his reserve would have made it impossible for him to make love to another woman. As for Lillie, she had never interfered with a happy marriage. Kipling was her guide and her friend, nothing more.

Also, she developed a great admiration for his work. She had never read any of his writing, but he presented her with several volumes of his short stories, and she wrote to her brother that she had "discovered" an extraordinary talent. To be sure, she was not alone in making that discovery: in the following year, 1907, Kipling was awarded the Nobel Prize for Literature.

The younger actresses in Lillie's company also enjoyed unprecedented male attention in South Africa. They, too, were showered with expensive gifts, and Michael later said that a couple of them received an average of two proposals of marriage per day. Even if he exaggerated, they were popular.

When the company returned to England, Lillie was wealthier by more than $100,000, according to Michael, and this sum did not include the gifts of expensive jewelry she had received. She had earned a holiday before setting out on an even more extraordinary venture, and went to spend the better part of the summer at her racing lodge.

The season was the most successful Lillie had ever known. Two of her horses were champions, and the climax of the summer came at the Folkstone track, where both won major races on the same day. A crowd estimated at twenty thousand people cheered the Jersey Lily, and so many people milled around her, wanting her autograph, that the police had to rescue her. She was so wealthy now that money was no longer important to her, but the habits of a lifetime were hard to break, and she gained great satisfaction from the knowledge that she earned enough from the stable that summer to keep it in operation for the next two years without the need to put in outside funds.

Folkstone was a popular summer resort, located on the English Channel, and Lillie took advantage of her stay there to make concrete plans for the most unusual venture of her professional career. Before leaving the United States she had been approached by B. F. Keith, the vaudeville impresario, who had offered her a tour on his circuit.

Until the turn of the century vaudeville had been universally regarded as a low form of entertainment, ranking slightly — but only slightly — above burlesque. The staple fare consisted of acrobats, trained animal acts, third-rate comedians, inferior dancers and jugglers, with an occasional singer thrown in for good measure. Keith was making a conscientious, deliberate effort to change the medium's image, and was offering enormous fees to the greatest stars of the day, many of whom were now on tour for him.

Sarah Bernhardt had been the first to succumb to the lure of the fat weekly wages Keith paid, and had been followed by Lillian Russell. Between them they had given vaudeville a new dignity, a standing as a respectable theatrical medium. Now it was Lillie's turn.

Keith offered her the staggering sum of eight thousand dollars per week, and in return she would be expected to play two performances per day, six days a week, of a twenty-minute sketch. She would carry her own sets and props with her, of course, and would be expected to pay the salaries of her supporting cast out of the stipend she received.

Lillie shrewdly commissioned the writing of a skit called *Between the Daytime and the Night.* Its theme was infidelity, and the writing was period melodrama at its best — or worst. At the final curtain the unfaithful wife was shot and killed by her jealous husband, but she did not die before she made the last, tear-jerking speech. One of the most attractive features of the playlet was its small cast; Lillie was required to hire only two supporting players, and a simple, inexpensive set was built for her. She estimated that she would be able to keep about seven thousand per week of the eight thousand she would be paid.

Folkstone, like the other Channel resorts, boasted an amusement pier that jutted out into the water, and at the far end of it was a small but adequate theatre. The management was elated when Lillie decided to try out *Between the Daytime and the Night* there.

The sketch ran only seventeen minutes, so she meticulously insisted that three minutes of playing time be added to it so she would be able to play the full twenty minutes that her contract with Keith required. But that wasn't enough to satisfy her Folkstone audiences. Ticket buyers were under the misapprehension that they would be seeing a complete play, even though the billboards carefully spelled out the playing time, and during the week of the try-out there, Lillie suffered a new experience. Audiences booed her vociferously at every performance.

She was startled by the unexpected attacks, and thought of abandoning the vaudeville tour. But when she returned to London she attended the theatre on several occasions, and the audiences, recognizing her, stood and cheered her. The penny newspapers had been filled with accounts of her Folkstone reception, and the London audiences wanted her to know they were loyal to her.

Heartened by their reaction, she sailed for New York on board the *Philadelphia*, the newest ship in trans-Atlantic service, her personal entourage consisting of her secretary, two maids and a butler. As an added touch she traveled with two blooded wolfhounds, with whom she was always seen in public during the following months.

Her opening at the newly decorated Fifth Avenue Theatre on October 1, 1906, was the biggest event of the theatrical season. She might be appearing in vaudeville, but the mere fact that the Jersey Lily was playing in the medium enhanced the stature of vaudeville. The theatre was jammed with the customary crowds of first-nighters, many of whom had never in their lives seen vaudeville. The newspaper drama critics all treated the event as a regular theatrical opening, too, and were on hand in full force.

William Winter, still loyal, called the play and Lillie charming, and announced that he had been charmed. The other reviewers, even those who habitually attacked Lillie, treated her with kindness. They could find less to pick at in a brief sketch, of course, but most were struck by her courage in attempting a new medium twenty-four years after she had made her first appearance on the American stage. There was still another factor that accounted for the universal praise: Lillie was good in the role she played.

Richard Mansfield, one of the great actors of the day, discovered the reason. He was so struck by her performance that he reserved a box every night for a week so he could study her techniques, and later he confided to various friends that Lillie was superb because, in spite of her limited training for high drama, the brevity of her playlet enabled her to sustain an intense emotional level from start to finish.

Not only did Lillie's usual fans come to see her, but all New York decided it was chic to see the vaudeville show at the Fifth Avenue Theatre. Captains of industry, literary figures, society leaders and visiting United States Senators and Congressmen clamored for seats. The happy Keith saw lines at the box office every day, and told associates he had never before had such a successful bill. He offered his star an open-end contract, which would have enabled her to remain in vaudeville for as many years as she pleased. Lillie, however, was content to play the single season for which she had been engaged.

Reporters and photographers insisted that Lillie looked like a woman still in her twenties, and she was besieged anew for her beauty secrets. A statement she made to the New York *Sun* was more revealing. Asked if she was happy, she replied, "Of course I am happy, as happiness goes, for a woman who has so many memories and lives the lonely life of an actress. It is restricted, as all artistic life necessarily must be. I've often put in as many as forty weeks on the stage in a single year, so you might say I've had precious little opportunity to brood or feel sorry for myself. I've sometimes been accused of lacking sentimentality, a quality I haven't been able to afford, and I think that is all to the good. The sentimentalist ages far more quickly than the person who loves his work and enjoys new challenges."

Lillie's sojourn in vaudeville made her the reigning queen of the New York stage again, and she enjoyed more attention than she had received at any time since her initial appearance in the city almost a quarter of a century earlier. Her photographs were displayed everywhere, theatrical producers inundated her with offers of new plays, and Keen's Chop House, a restaurant that had never served a meal to a woman, opened its doors to her in an unprecedented gesture.

She was equally successful when she went on tour. She sold out everywhere, and was amused when critics who had invariably disliked her treated her with new respect. She had been forced to turn to a new medium to win their praise, and she told Edward Michael in a revealing letter that, as a result of her unorthodox booking, she would be able to do far better in the legitimate theatre when she returned to it.

There were inconveniences she had to suffer because of her vaudeville tour. She could not travel in a private railroad car, but she made the best of the situation, always engaging two drawing rooms for herself, another for her maids and a compartment for her butler. The wolfhounds always traveled with her, and the butler walked them on the platform whenever the train came to a halt for a few minutes.

While she was on tour a long-expected change altered Lillie's life, but she alone seemed unexcited by it, thoroughly bewildering everyone who knew her, and confusing the general public even more.

XIV

ON JANUARY 6, 1907, WHEN LILLIE WAS PLAYING A vaudeville engagement in Cincinnati, she received a cablegram informing her that General Sir Henry P. de Bathe had died. Her husband inherited his father's baronetcy, and became Sir Hugo. Lillie herself was now Lady de Bathe. The world's press, particularly in the United States and Canada, printed the news on page one under heavy black headlines.

Lillie's social position was enhanced, but her title meant nothing to her, at least on the surface. She didn't miss a performance, and she rejected the advice of Keith and his associates that she change her billing. She had made her fame as Mrs. Langtry, and refused to change her professional name. "Everything is precisely as it was," she told Richard Le Gallienne, the English poet, essayist and critic, who had taken up residence in the United States. "I'm still supporting my dear husband."

Her comment may have been cruel, but it was accurate. Sir Hugo's name may have been impressively resounding, but he had inherited little of value except his father's title. He was now the proprietor of several small, debt-ridden estates in Devonshire and Sussex, and when Lillie wrote to him, suggesting that he sell the lands, he refused. But debts of any kind were anathema to her, so she sent him the sum of ten thousand pounds to pay off his creditors. Her title was expensive.

By the end of June, 1907, Lillie was exhausted. She had been playing the vaudeville circuit for nine unrelieved months, and had traveled uncounted thousands of miles. She was also wealthier by a net that approached a quarter of a million dollars. She was in need of a rest, and stopped off in New York en route to England just long enough to be the guest of honor at a dinner given by David Belasco. Le Gallienne, the master of ceremonies, wrote a poem for the occasion, and dedicated it to her.

The racing season was under way by the time Lillie reached London, so she stayed in the city for no more than a few days before proceeding to her lodge at Regal Park. Sir Hugo, who had been waiting for her in the city, accompanied her. They stayed at the lodge for four months, and Lillie's horses were such consistent winners that King Edward, who owned a larger stable, paid her a half-dozen visits at teatime to discuss the buying and selling of mounts that wore his colors.

London's theatrical managers were clamoring for the Jersey Lily, but Lady de Bathe was tired, and decided to spend the late autumn and winter in Monaco. Hugo went with her, and they were accompanied by her secretary and two maids, his valet, two chauffeurs and a personal messenger.

Every day Lillie spent several hours at the Monte Carlo casino, where she became a familiar figure, and every day she lost heavily. It was estimated that, as the winter drew to a close, she had dropped approximately twenty thousand pounds. Then, at the end of February, on her last night on the Riviera, she plunged heavily. The following day's headlines blazoned the news:

JERSEY LILY BREAKS BANK AT MONTE CARLO

The newspapers exaggerated, but not by much. Lillie played roulette with abandon, and not only recouped her losses, but showed a profit of more than twenty-five thousand pounds. She knew enough to stop when she was ahead, and her bank account expanded accordingly. The fascinated public agreed with an editorial in the New York *World* to the effect that she was as lucky as she was beautiful.

But her luck failed to hold when she returned to London. She was anxious to go back to work after her long holiday, and went into rehearsals in a new play Sidney Grundy had written for her, *A Fearful Joy*.

It opened at the Haymarket early in April, 1908, and the critics damned it with faint praise. Mrs. Langtry, they said, skipped through a familiar role, that of a high society lady whose morals were dubious, and the play itself was weak. Most of the reviewers found little to commend other than the new Worth wardrobe Lillie had picked up in Paris.

A new generation of sophisticated theatre-goers had grown up in England, and the name of the Jersey Lily, as such, was no longer magical. Younger audiences had no desire to see the middle-aged Lillie on stage unless she appeared in a play worth their money and interest. *A Fearful Joy* sold out for three months, and then business dropped sharply. For two weeks Lillie played to half-filled houses, an unaccustomed experience, and when sales did not improve she closed the play abruptly and went off to Regal Park for the racing season.

Her stable provided her with the balm necessary to her wounded ego. Her new champion, Yentoi, won the Cesarewitch just eleven years after Merman had won the same race. The press said that the Jersey Lily collected more than fifty thousand pounds in bets on her mount, and although she refused to confirm the story, she would not deny it, either.

When the season ended Lillie looked for new fields to conquer, and sat down to write a novel. In a surprisingly short time she completed an effort of approximately seventy-five thousand words, which she called *All at Sea* and which was published under the name of Lillie de Bathe. Under no circumstances could it be called literature, but it was a light, amusing romance, tinged with just enough wickedness to titillate the early twentieth-century reader.

The story concerned a high-born married couple who, on a trans-Atlantic crossing, decided to travel separately, she posing as a widow and he as a bachelor. The book reviewers enjoyed themselves at the author's expense, but the book enjoyed a steady sale, although it was neither publicized nor advertised, and it earned Lillie the respectable sum of one thousand pounds. She was no genius, but she proved that her talents had many facets, and the *Telegraph*'s critic paid her the tribute of calling her "an extraordinary woman."

Absent from the stage for too long, Lillie commissioned the preparation of a short one-act play, a condensation of *The Degenerates*, which she called *The Right Sort*, and she played it in British vaudeville during the 1909-10 season. She duplicated her American vaudeville success, and in the autumn of 1910 she returned to the United States with the playlet for another tour of the Keith circuit.

She had been in a subdued mood through the late spring and summer. King Edward VII had died in May, 1910, and Lillie had immediately gone into seclusion, seeing no one and refusing all interviews. She made no public appearances that summer, and after her return to America, she turned a deaf ear to reporters' comments about her late friend and benefactor.

She was far less reticent, however, to discuss her age. When a Boston reporter told her she looked like a young girl, she made her feelings very clear to him. "What rubbish!" she declared. "I am fifty-seven years of age, and I don't care who knows it. I don't look in the least young, as you and I well know. There isn't a woman in this world who doesn't look every day and every minute of her age. We can't be younger than we are, and we can't look younger than we are. The most any woman of my age can do is hope she's well preserved."

For the next three years Lillie followed the new pattern, playing a vaudeville sketch in England, then taking it to the United States. She traveled uncounted thousands of miles, earned vast sums of money and enhanced her reputation as the hardest-working actress of her day. She spent her summers at her racing lodge, and each year made her usual trips to Paris for new clothes.

The truth of the matter was that the woman who had been the greatest beauty of her age had nothing but her work to keep her occupied. She and Sir Hugo were still married, and she continued to support him, but they were drifting even farther apart, and spent only a few token weeks together each year. Lillie enjoyed no known contacts with her daughter, who now had several children of her own. And most of her old friends were either dead or occupied in their own interests. She was still remarkably attractive, and was still one of the most independently wealthy women on earth, but she was lonely.

She adamantly refused to feel sorry for herself, however, and continued to rely on work as a cure-all. In 1913 she again pioneered in a new medium, and, following the recent example of Sarah Bernhardt, made a motion picture for Adolph Zukor's Famous Players Film Company. Produced and directed by her old friend Daniel Frohman, it was a comedy-drama called *His Neighbor's Wife*.

The entire motion picture was filmed in April, 1913, over a two-week period. It was shot in the New York studios of Famous Players, and unlike most of the other films made at that time, took no advantage of outdoor daylight. The entire movie was shot indoors.

His Neighbor's Wife opened in New York in the autumn of 1913, and the reviewers praised Lillie's performance, the photography and the screen play. Viewed almost six decades later, it seems no worse and no better than other films of the same period. The acting was stiff, the lighting poor and the photography often indistinct and jerky.

But Lillie was well satisfied with her efforts, and spent several incognito evenings watching herself on the screen. But she was too shrewd to wear out her motion-picture welcome. Films were still a novelty, she earned only modest sums from them, and she had no desire to repeat the experiment.

Returning to England late in 1913, Lillie contemplated retirement, telling Edward Michael that, like Alexander the Great, she had no more worlds to conquer. But the outbreak of World War I in 1914 revitalized her. Sir Hugo went off to war with a Royal Army commission, as did Lillie's brother, Clement, and Jeanne's husband. Lillie could not remain idle now, and opened at Drury Lane, London's largest theatre, in a new play by Sidney Grundy, *Mrs. Thompson.* Her own salary and the play's profits, she told the public in daily newspaper advertisements, were being donated to the Red Cross. Neither the inconveniences of wartime living nor the German zeppelin raids on London could deter her, and she played in *Mrs. Thompson* for an entire season.

In the autumn of 1915 she brought the play to New York, still giving the profits and her entire salary to the Red Cross. War or no war, she was impervious to the German U-boat threat that made trans-Atlantic travel hazardous, and arrived in New York accompanied by a secretary and two maids, and carried forty trunks of new clothes.

She traveled back and forth across the Atlantic throughout World War I, sometimes doing plays, sometimes vaudeville sketches. One of her leading men in the latter was Lionel Atwill, and when he left to take another engagement, she replaced him with a young actor of rare promise, Alfred Lunt. She took part in innumerable war relief drives, and gave scores of special benefit performances, acting as co-chairman with Will Rogers of a one thousand dollars per ticket affair at the Ritz-Carlton Hotel.

On one of her trans-Atlantic crossings, from Liverpool to New York, in 1916, a fellow passenger was Somerset Maugham, who had just achieved international renown as an author. Posterity is indebted to Maugham for his impressions of the Jersey Lily, which he recorded in his autobiographical *A Writer's Notebook*, published by Doubleday and Company in 1949. He wrote:

"She still had a fine figure and a noble carriage, and if you were walking behind her you might have taken her for a young woman."

At the time Lillie was sixty-three.

When Lillie, with whom Maugham struck up a shipboard acquaintance, mentioned the name of Fred Gebhard, the author had to confess he had never heard of the man.

Lillie appeared to be astounded, and said Gebhard had been "the most celebrated man in two hemispheres."

Maugham asked her why he had been famous.

"Because I loved him," Lillie said.

In 1917 Lillie wrote a form of her autobiography for the Hearst newspapers, and was paid the enormous sum of one thousand dollars for each of ten installments. No other author except the Nobel Prize-winning Rudyard Kipling had ever commanded such a fee. But, aside from the use of her name, Lillie did not give value received. The work was stilted, formal and so discreet it was bloodless. At best it was a collection of loosely strung anecdotes about famous people she had known, most of them in high society. Whenever she mentioned Edward VII, which was infrequently, she carefully coupled his name with that of Queen Alexandra.

By the autumn of 1917 the U-boat menace had become so great that trans-Atlantic passenger travel was difficult as well as hazardous. In order to return to England from the United States, Lillie had to take a small Spanish liner to Spain, a voyage of more than three weeks. Then she went to Madrid, managed to get a train ticket to Paris, and eventually, after almost six weeks of travel, finally reached England.

In the late autumn she did a vaudeville sketch at the Coliseum Theatre in London, and in early 1918 she played in yet another there. Zeppelins were dropping bombs on the city regularly, but she did not miss a performance, and refused to contemplate terminating the engagement prematurely.

By summer she was tired, however, far more tired than she cared to admit, and colleagues, who were urging her to rest, reminded her that she had not taken a holiday in more than four years. So she went off to her racing lodge that summer, and devoted most of her time to raising vegetables, acquiring a suntan and thinking. She had acquired great wealth, but looking back over her life, found few other satisfactions.

Jeanne was now the mother of three sons and a daughter, but Lillie had no contact with her, and had never seen any of her grandchildren. For all practical purposes she and her daughter were permanently estranged.

Under no circumstances could she consider her marriage satisfactory, although she harbored no hard feelings against Hugo. She decided to make her own plans and, when the war ended, he would either fit himself into them or would refuse, as he chose.

Above all else, Lillie was tired of working. At the age of sixty-five she had her fill of one-night stands, one-week stands, the disciplines of appearing night after night in the same play. She had enough money to live in style as long as she lived, and by the time World War I finally ended in November, 1918, her plans were solidified. She had made her last appearance on a stage, and would not act again. Younger beauties were appearing in the theatres of both America and England, and she had no desire to make herself look absurd. What was more, there were better actresses, and after enjoying rare triumphs, she didn't want to push her luck.

London was too cold for her, and so was New York. She could live anywhere she pleased, and it pleased her to contemplate a move to the French Riviera, where the climate was mild and the sun shone most of the year. Within a week of the war's end she sold her lodge and moved into the Savoy Hotel to await Sir Hugo's return.

Perhaps he didn't care for her scheme, but she used her own methods of persuasion. Lillie was buying a house for herself in Monaco, where she intended to live with a companion, and had already taken an option on a house in Nice, a half-hour's drive away, for her husband. She was as tired of scandalous headlines as she was of the grind of work, and preferred to avoid divorce.

Sir Hugo was content to let her continue to support him while he led his own life, without obligation to Lillie except to appear on formal occasions and escort her to dinners or other affairs. So he agreed to the arrangement.

Lillie's Monacan house was located on a steep mountainside overlooking the Riviera, and she had some alterations made in it before moving in. The kitchen was modernized, the living room was enlarged and two new bedrooms were added. She also had a smaller building erected behind the main villa to house the servants.

In the spring of 1919 she moved into her new home with her companion, Mrs. Mathilde Peat, a widow with whom she had been associated in the theatre. Lillie bought two automobiles, one a limousine and the other an open touring car, and hired a staff consisting of a cook, a personal maid, a housemaid, a butler and a chauffeur.

Her retirement, like her previous life, was hectic. She plunged into the social whirl of the Riviera's permanent residents, and a steady stream of famous persons she had known made their way to the Villa Le Lys for lunch, for tea, for cocktails, for dinner. Lillie became interested in growing flowers, but the hobby, as such, was not enough for her. Her competitive spirit could not be stifled, and she entered a series of contests, eventually winning a gold trophy which symbolized her status as the best amateur horticulturist on the Riviera.

One or two evenings a week she was driven to the Monte Carlo casino, and there played roulette and other games of chance for about two hours. She gambled modestly now, and her losses, like her winnings, were small.

The many friends who visited Villa Le Lys soon learned that their hostess had no intention of lapsing into old age, but continued to maintain a passionate interest in the world around her. She subscribed to a number of London and New York newspapers, and kept up with the news of the theatre in both countries. "Anyone who limits his vision to his memories of yesterday," she told one visitor, "is already dead."

Twice each year she and Mrs. Peat traveled to London for sojourns of one to three weeks. On these trips Lillie visited old friends, dined at some of her favorite restaurants and often attended the theatre. She was invariably recognized by audiences, and frequently was given an ovation, her loyal followers demonstrating that she was not forgotten.

On one of her trips to London the breach with her daughter was healed. No information is available regarding the date or the circumstances, so it is impossible to determine whether Lillie made the first move, whether Jeanne came to her or whether they were brought together by a third party.

It was during this period that Lillie became acquainted with her three grandsons and granddaughter, and quickly established a rapport with them. "I was in awe of her when I first met her," the eldest later said, "but I soon learned to admire her, and then to love her."

Subsequently the two eldest grandchildren paid a number of visits to the Villa Le Lys, and stayed for periods of a month or more. Photographs of all four children filled Lillie's bedroom, and the burden she had suffered for years in dignified silence was eased.

Always one to keep up with the times, Lillie bought modern wardrobes in Paris. The age of the flapper had arrived, so she shortened her skirts several inches, although she refused to bare her knees in the manner of younger generations. She was one of the first to follow the example of the dancer, Irene Castle, however, and bobbed her hair, abandoning the famous Langtry bun without regret. When she discovered that her hair was turning gray, she had it dyed an auburn shade, and wore it that way for the rest of her days. She had long smoked cigarettes in private, but now that mores were changing she adapted without effort, and did not hesitate to smoke in restaurants or at the theatre.

The escapades of Hugo de Bathe caused her occasional embarrassment. Now in his fifties, Hugo was one of the gallants of the Riviera, and continued to chase girls with the fervor he had shown in his youth. He appeared regularly at the spas, casinos and yacht clubs of the area, always with a chorus girl or debutante less than half his age on his arm. Occasionally one or another young woman expected him to marry her, and created a fuss when she learned he had no intention of obtaining a divorce from his famous, elderly wife. Some of his antics amused Lillie, and twice, when he was threatened with breach of promise lawsuits, she supported him by issuing statements that made it clear she intended to remain his wife, if only in name, for the rest of her life.

In 1925 Lillie's autobiography, *The Days I Knew*, was published in New York by the George H. Doran Company. Those who expected scandalous revelations and inside stories of hijinks in high places were disappointed. The book consisted of a collection of harmless anecdotes, social and theatrical reminiscences, and sheer trivia. The few mentions of Albert Edward, either as Prince of Wales or King, were impersonal. She barely mentioned her first husband, and there was not one word about her daughter. Her noted affairs were untouched, and she was austere, remote, when she happened to drop in the name of a former lover who had helped her make headlines. Lillie was observing, to the last, the code of a lady.

Echoes of the past came alive in 1927. One Peter Wright wrote and published a book in London called *Portraits and Memories*, and in it he claimed that Lillie had been the mistress of Prime Minister Gladstone. Viscount Herbert Gladstone, the son of the statesman, himself now in his seventies, branded Wright as a "liar and coward," and was promptly sued for libel.

Lillie came to the younger Gladstone's defense, and sent him a cable saying, "I strongly repudiate the slanderous accusation of Peter Wright."

Lord Gladstone won his case, but Lillie, remembering the old days, was afraid she might be made a social pariah again. Times had changed, however, her friends rallied to her, and she soon found that the furor in no way affected the regard in which she was held. There was a touch of bitterness in a newspaper interview she gave, however. "Sympathy is charming, but it does not make up for the pain," she told the reporter. "I have always been willing to take the blame for the things I have done, but it is hard to have blame fastened on me for things I never did."

In the autumn of 1928, when Lillie was seventy-five, she suffered a serious illness. She was visiting London, and while a photographer was taking her picture she had to interrupt the session to go to bed. Her ailment was diagnosed as bronchitis, complicated by pleurisy. At Lillie's insistence, a lawyer was summoned and she revised her will, which she had neglected to change in many years.

She recovered, but was still weak when she returned to the Riviera, and in the months that followed it became obvious that her mobility had lessened. The winter was unusually cold, so Lillie rarely left the house, preferring to entertain friends at home, usually at tea.

Then, in February, 1929, she fell ill again, this time with influenza, and early in the morning of February 12, Lillie Le Breton Langtry de Bathe breathed her last.

The bulk of her estate was left to her four grandchildren, each of whom received a trust fund. There were generous bequests to Mrs. Peat and various friends, and she left each of her servants a year's wages. Jeanne received her mother's silver and china. There was no mention of Sir Hugo de Bathe in the will, but it was presumed that Lillie had made a cash settlement a year or two earlier that would take care of his basic needs.

In accordance with a request in her will, Lillie was buried in the churchyard of St. Saviour's on the Isle of Jersey. Jeanne and her eldest son were present, but Hugo did not appear.

For the last time Lillie appeared on the front pages, and the New York *Tribune* published an editorial that said it all: "An era has come to an end."

Selective Bibliography

BOOKS

Bodley, John E. C., *Mr. Gladstone Prepares to Meet Mrs. Langtry*. New York, Brooks, 1925.

Booth, Horace H., *The Astonishing Mrs. Langtry*. New York, Geo. H. Doran, 1930.

Cornwallis-West, George, *Edwardian Hey-Days*. New York, G. P. Putnam's and Sons, 1931.

Cowles, Virginia, *Gay Monarch — The Life and Pleasures of Edward VII*. New York, Harper & Bros., 1956.

Dale, Alan, *Familiar Chats with Queens of the Stage*. New York, G.W. Dillingham, 1890.

Dunbar, Charles Fitzpatrick, *Mrs. Langtry, Heroine Extraordinary*. London, Ellis Cooper, 1930.

Frohman, Daniel, *Daniel Frohman Presents*. New York, Kendall & Sharp, 1935.

———, *Encore*. New York, Lee Furman, 1937.

Langtry, Lillie, *The Days I Knew*. New York, Geo. H. Doran, 1925.

Leslie, Amy, *Some Players: Personal Sketches*. Chicago, Herbert S. Stone, 1899.

———, *Mrs. Terry, Mrs. Langtry and Miss Russell*. Chicago, Herbert S. Stone, 1918.

Leslie, Shane, *Sketches in Sublime Failure*. London, Ernest Benn, 1932.

Leverton, W. H., *Through the Box-Office Window*. London, T. W. Laurie, 1932.

Maugham, W. Somerset, *A Writer's Notebook*. New York, Doubleday, 1949.

Maurois, Andre, *Edward VII and His Times*. London, Cassell, 1933.

Pearson, Hesketh, *Oscar Wilde*. New York, Harper & Bros., 1946.

——, *The Man Whistler*. New York, Harper & Bros., 1932.

Plimpton, Margaret, *The Life and Loves of Lillie Langtry*. London, Dumont, 1931.

Private Life of Edward VII, By a member of the Royal Household. New York, D. Appleton, 1901.

Rogers, Agnes and Allen, Frederick Lewis, *The American Procession*. New York, Harper & Bros., 1933.

Sichel, Pierre, *The Jersey Lily*. New York, Prentice-Hall, 1958.

Sonnichsen, C. L., *Roy Bean*. New York, Macmillan, 1943.

Stanley, Louis T., *The London Season*. Boston, Houghton Mifflin, 1956.

Taylor, Edna A., *Mrs. Langtry and Her Times*. New York, Macmillan, 1931.

Winter, William, *The Wallet of Time*. New York, Moffat, Yard, 1913.

Worth, Jean P., *A Century of Fashion*. Boston, Little, Brown, 1928.

PERIODICALS

Chicago *Inter-Ocean, Journal, News, Tribune*.

Golden, S. B., "The Romance of the Jersey Lily." *Theatre Magazine*, November & December, 1930.

Hughes, C., "Lillie Langtry: the Passion Flower," *Coronet*, January, 1950.

Kropotkin, Alexandra, "The Jersey Lily; the Life Story of the Lovely Langtry," *Liberty Magazine*, a 5-part serial, commencing December 14, 1929.

London *Post, Mirror, Telegraph, Times*.

Manchester *Guardian*.

New York *American, Herald, Post, Sun, Times, Tribune, World*.

O'Connor, T. P., "The London of Lily Langtry," *Living Age*, April 18, 1925.

"The Jersey Lily as a Later Helen of Troy," *The Literary Digest*, March 2, 1929.

A Note to the Reader

If you have enjoyed this book enough to leave a review on **Amazon** and **Goodreads**, then we would be truly grateful.

The Estate of Noel B. Gerson

Sapere Books is an exciting new publisher of brilliant fiction and popular history.

To find out more about our latest releases and our monthly bargain books visit our website:
saperebooks.com

www.ingramcontent.com/pod-product-compliance
Lightning Source LLC
LaVergne TN
LVHW021626100325
805603LV00009B/420